SEVEN SEAS ENTERTAIN...

D1229118

Toradora!

story by **YUYUKO TAKEMIYA** / art by **ZEKKYOU**   VOLUME 7

TRANSLATION
Adrienne Beck

ADAPTATION
Bambi Eloriaga-Amago

LETTERING
Roland Amago

LAYOUT
Mheeya Wok

COVER DESIGN
Nicky Lim

PROOFREADER
Shanti Whitesides

ASSISTANT EDITOR
Lissa Pattillo

MANAGING EDITOR
Adam Arnold

PUBLISHER
Jason DeAngelis

TORADORA! VOL. 7
©Yuyuko Takemiya / Zekkyou 2015
Edited by ASCII MEDIA WORKS.
First published in 2015 by KADOKAWA CORPORATION, Tokyo.
English translation rights arranged with KADOKAWA CORPORATION, Tokyo.

Seven Seas books may be purchased in bulk for educational, business, or
promotional use. For information on bulk purchases, please contact Macmillan
Corporate & Premium Sales Department at 1-800-221-7945 (ext 5442)
or write specialmarkets@macmillan.com.

Seven Seas and the Seven Seas logo are trademarks of
Seven Seas Entertainment, LLC. All rights reserved.

ISBN: 978-1-626920-96-5

Printed in Canada

First Printing: June 2015

10 9 8 7 6 5 4 3 2 1

FOLLOW US ONLINE: *www.gomanga.com*

READING DIRECTIONS

This book reads from *right to left*, Japanese style.
If this is your first time reading manga, you start
reading from the top right panel on each page and
take it from there. If you get lost, just follow the
numbered diagram here. It may seem backwards at
first, but you'll get the hang of it! Have fun!!

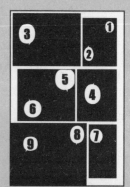

To ra do ra !

VOL. 7

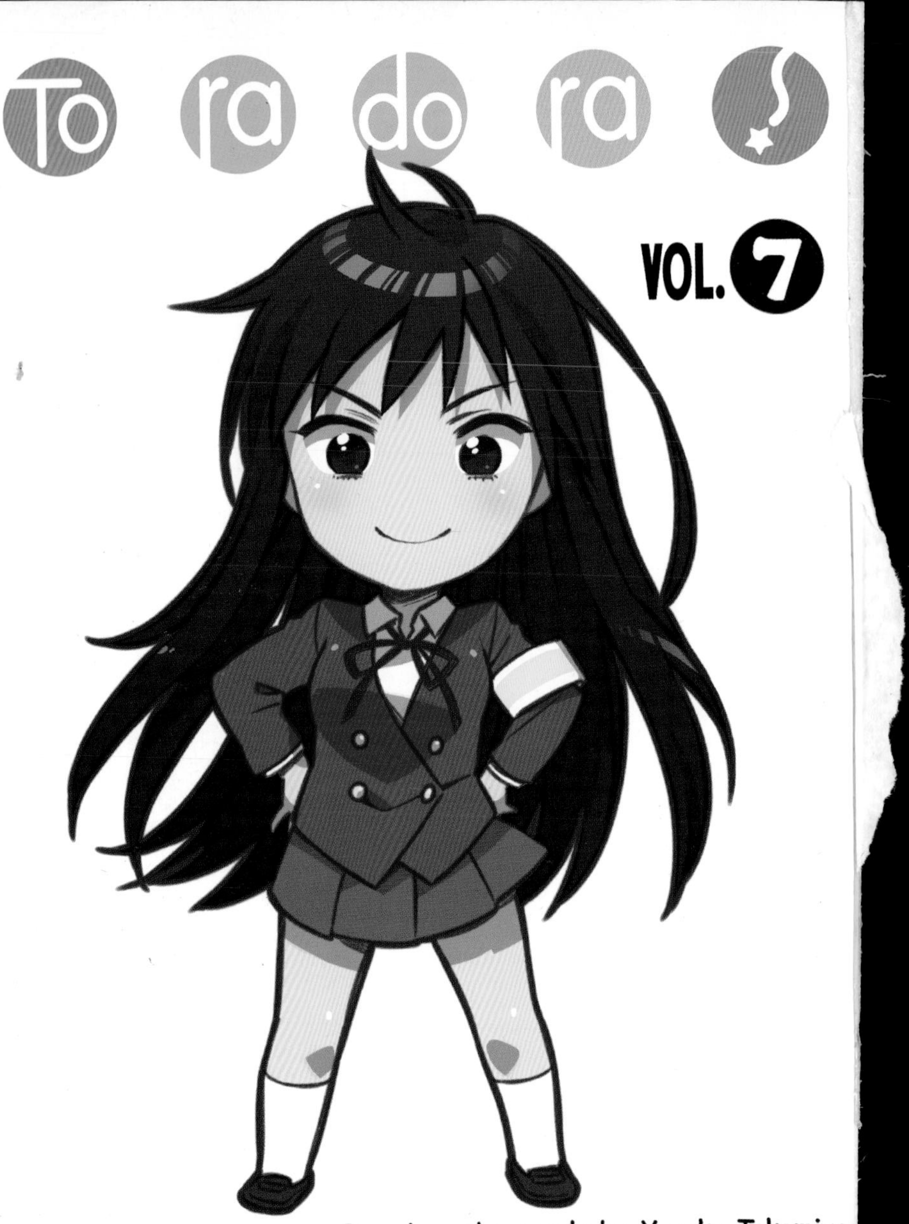

Based on the novels by Yuyuko Takemiya
Manga artwork by Zekkyou
Original character design by Yasu

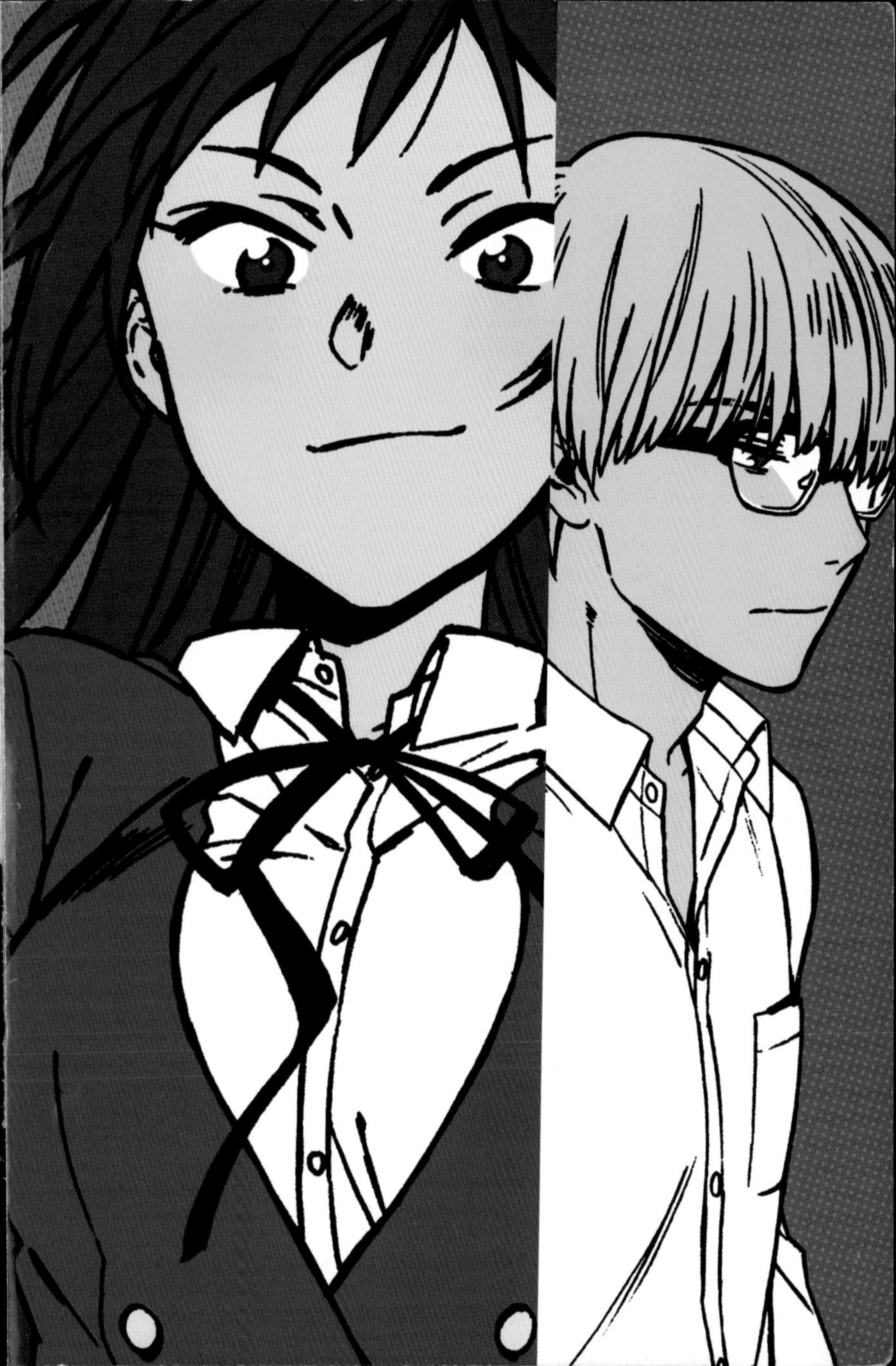

Chapter 56 ALONE

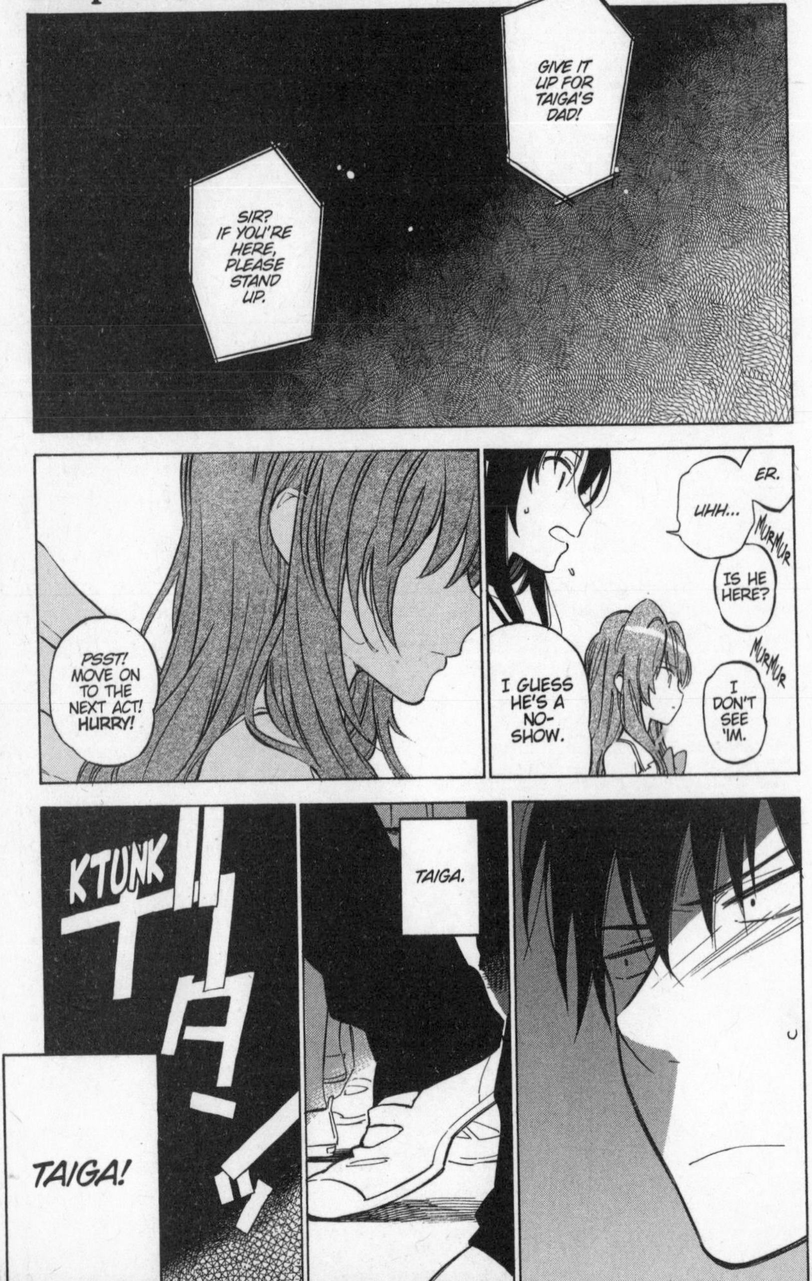

GIVE IT UP FOR TAIGA'S DAD!
SIR? IF YOU'RE HERE, PLEASE STAND UP.
ER.
UHH...
MURMUR
IS HE HERE?
MURMUR
I DON'T SEE 'IM.
I GUESS HE'S A NO-SHOW.
PSST! MOVE ON TO THE NEXT ACT! HURRY!
TAIGA.
KTUNK
TAIGA!

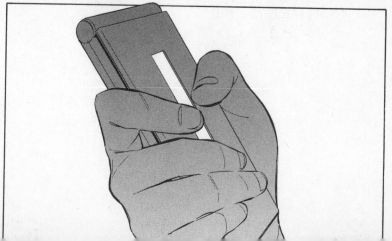

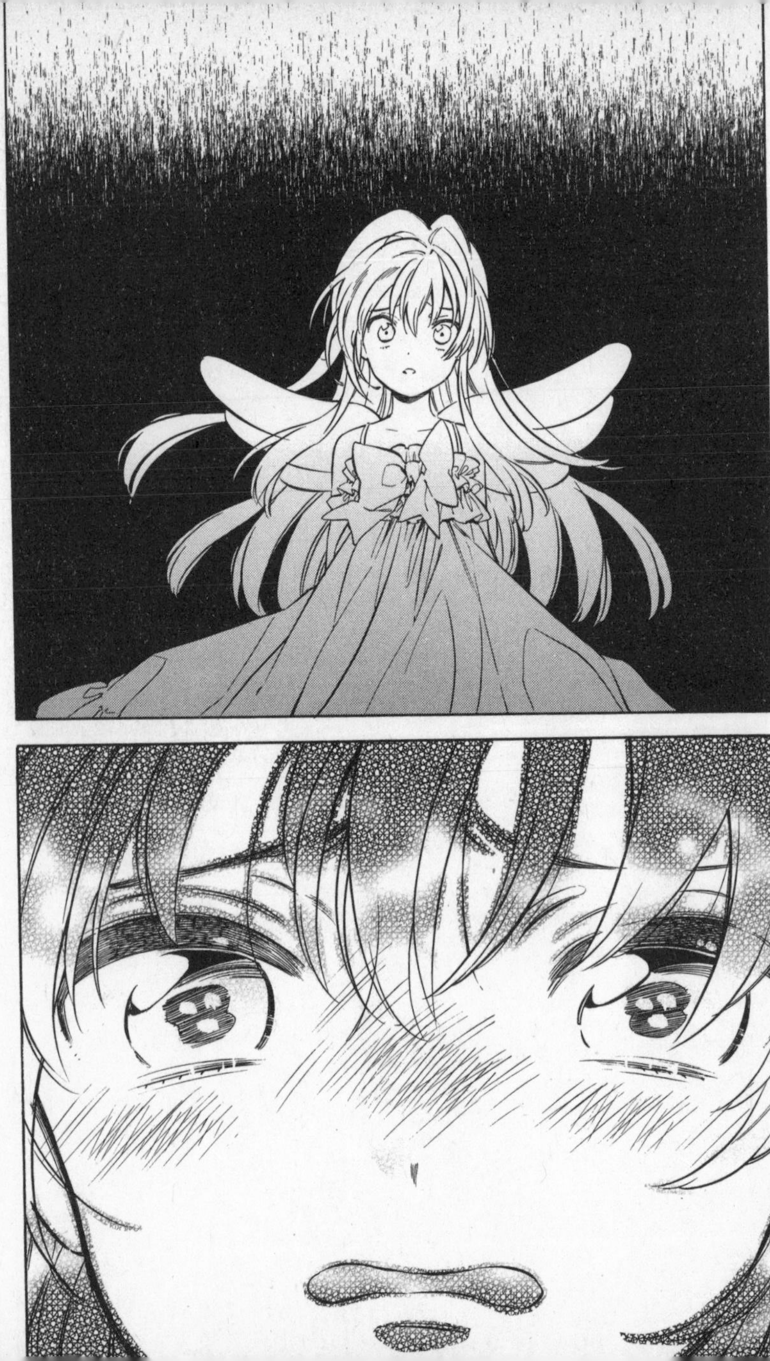

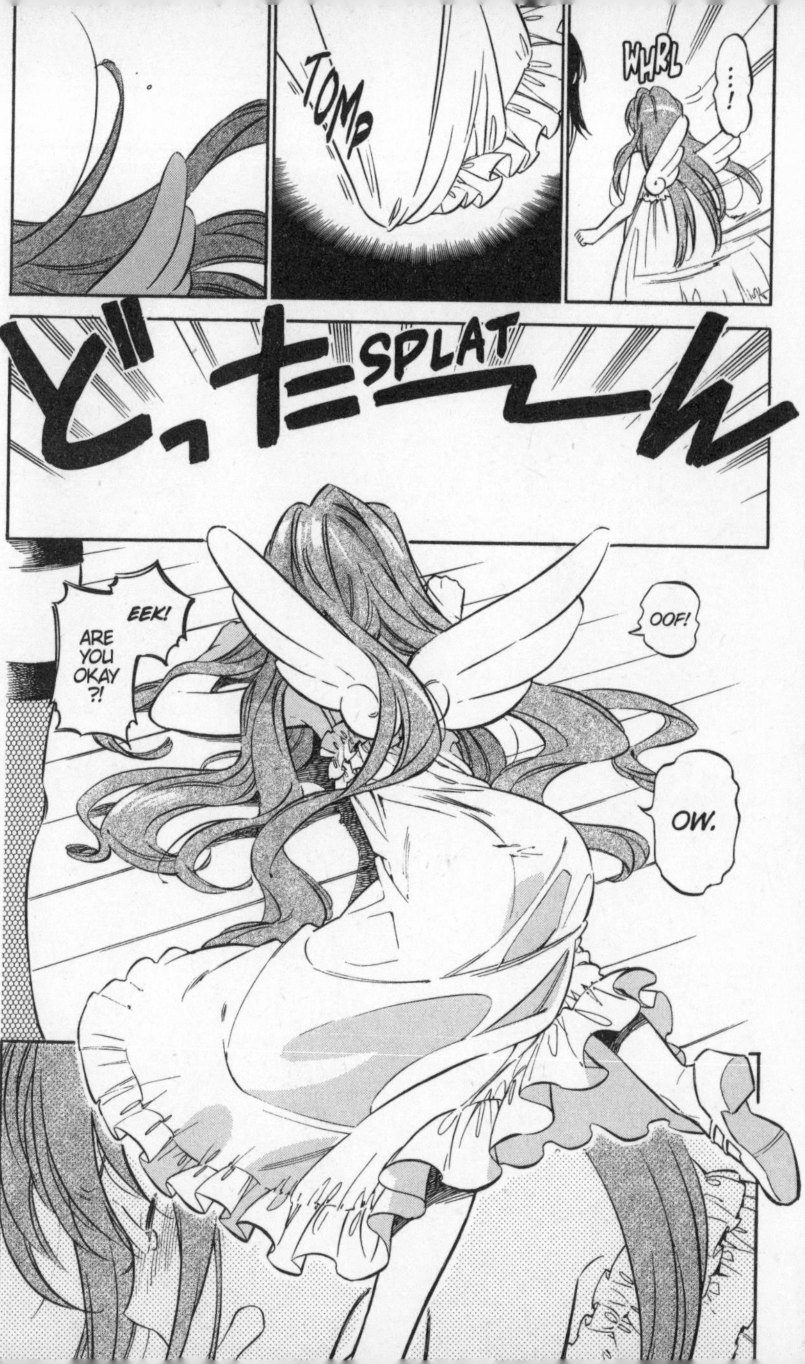
WHRL
...!
TOMP
どったーん
SPLAT
OOF!
OW.
EEK!
ARE YOU OKAY?!

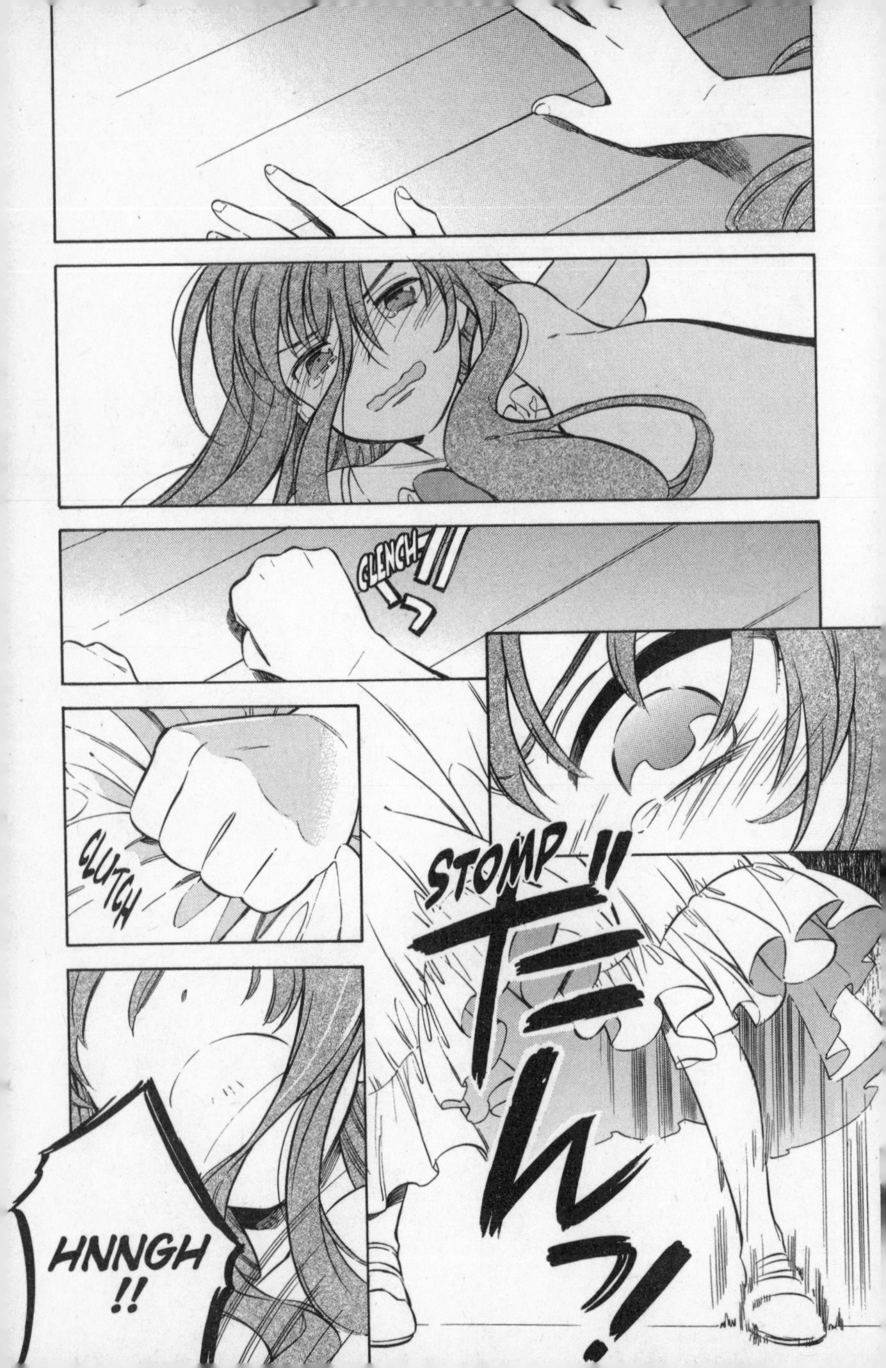
CLENCH
STOMP!!
CLUTCH
HNNGH!!

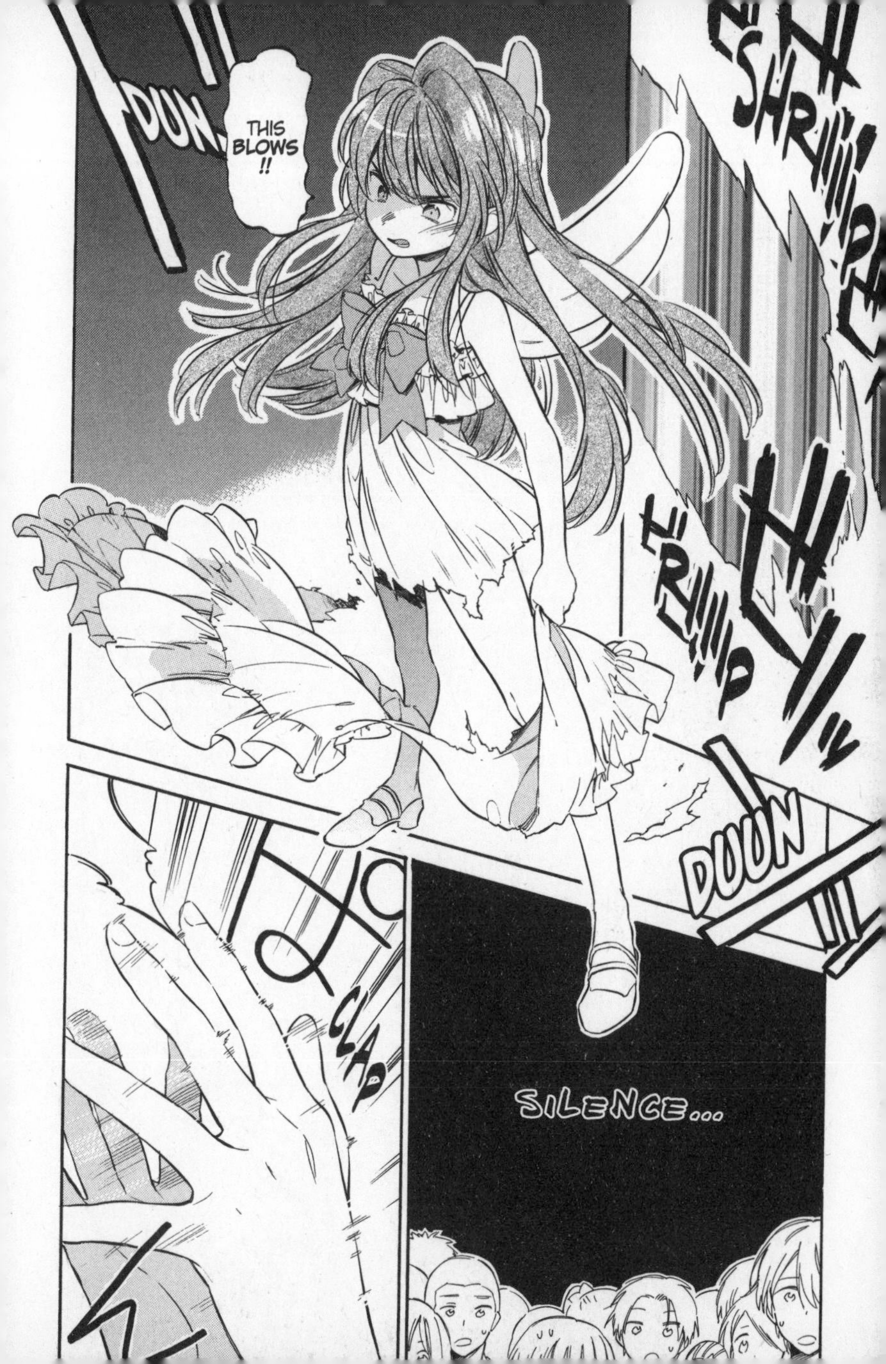

SHRIIIIIIPP
THIS BLOWS !!
DUN
RIIIIIIP
DUUN
SILENCE...
CLAP

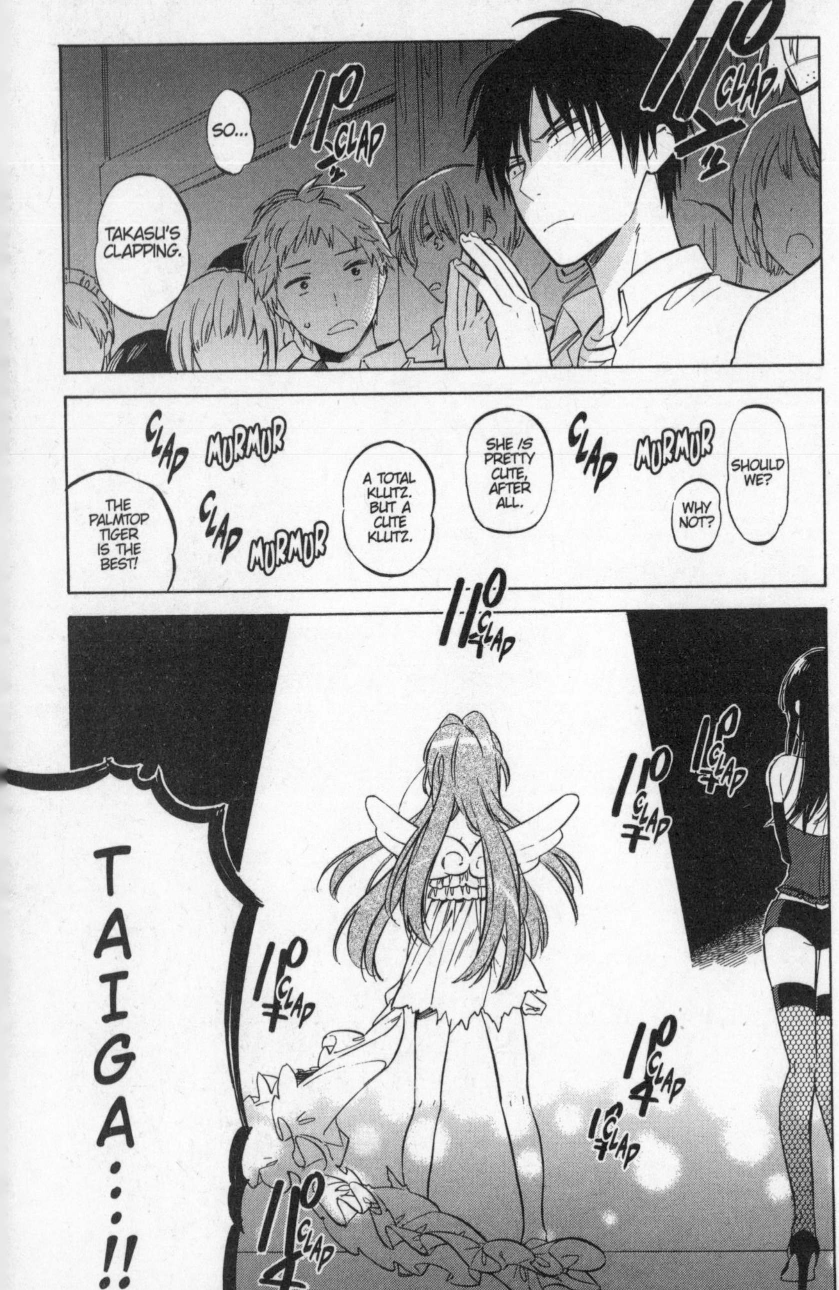
CLAP
CLAP
SO...
TAKASU'S CLAPPING.
SHOULD WE?
WHY NOT?
MURMUR
CLAP
SHE IS PRETTY CUTE, AFTER ALL.
A TOTAL KLUTZ. BUT A CUTE KLUTZ.
MURMUR
CLAP
MURMUR
CLAP
THE PALMTOP TIGER IS THE BEST!
CLAP
CLAP
CLAP
CLAP
CLAP
CLAP
CLAP
TAIGA...!!

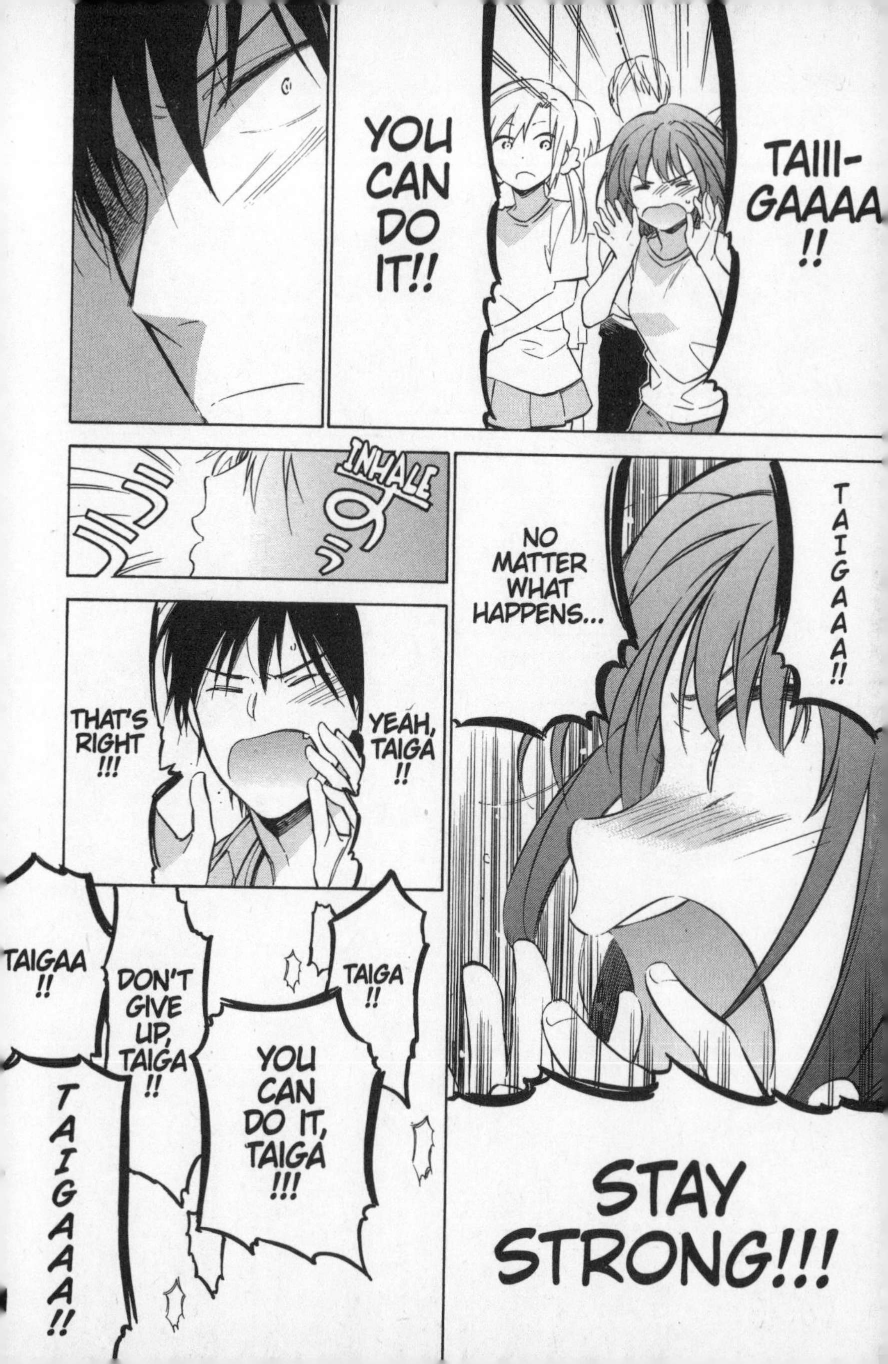
TAIII-GAAAAA!!
YOU CAN DO IT!!
TAIGAAAAA!!
NO MATTER WHAT HAPPENS...
STAY STRONG!!!
INHALE
YEAH, TAIGA!!
THAT'S RIGHT!!!
TAIGA!!
YOU CAN DO IT, TAIGA!!!
DON'T GIVE UP, TAIGA!!
TAIGAA!!
TAIGAAAAA!!

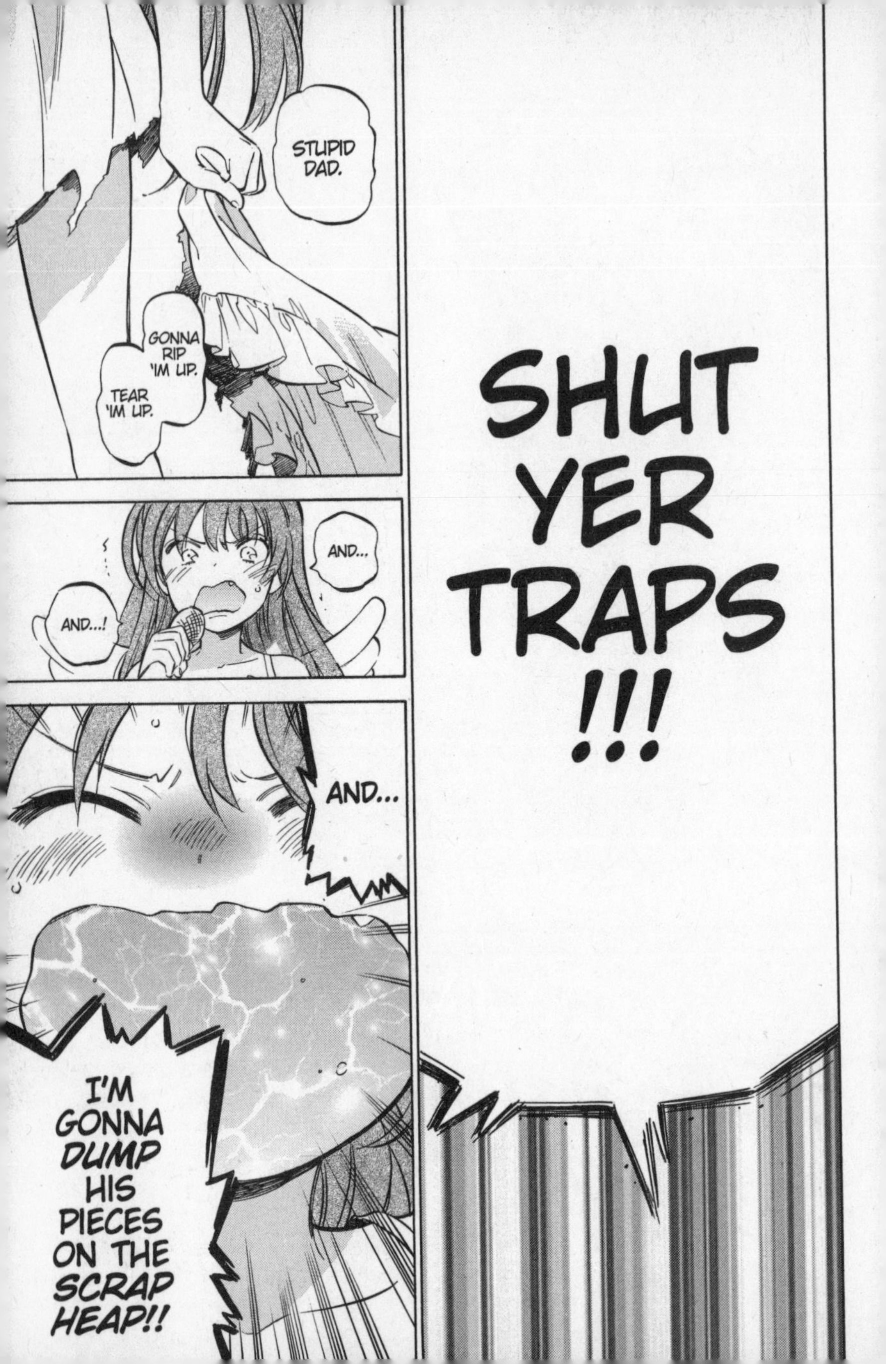
SHUT YER TRAPS!!!
STUPID DAD.
GONNA RIP 'IM UP.
TEAR 'IM UP.
AND...
AND...!
AND...
I'M GONNA DUMP HIS PIECES ON THE SCRAP HEAP!!

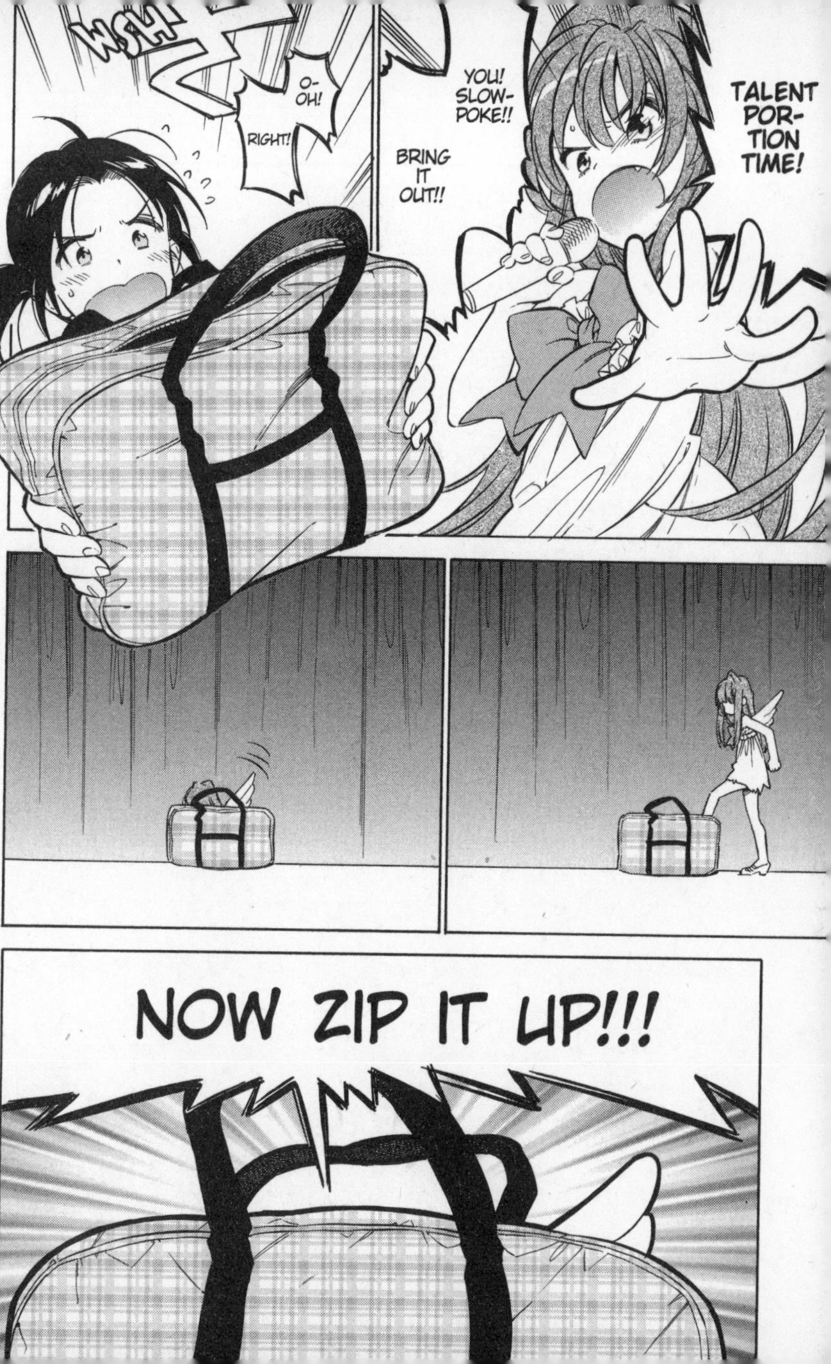
TALENT PORTION TIME!
YOU! SLOW-POKE!!
BRING IT OUT!!
O-OH!
RIGHT!
NOW ZIP IT UP!!!

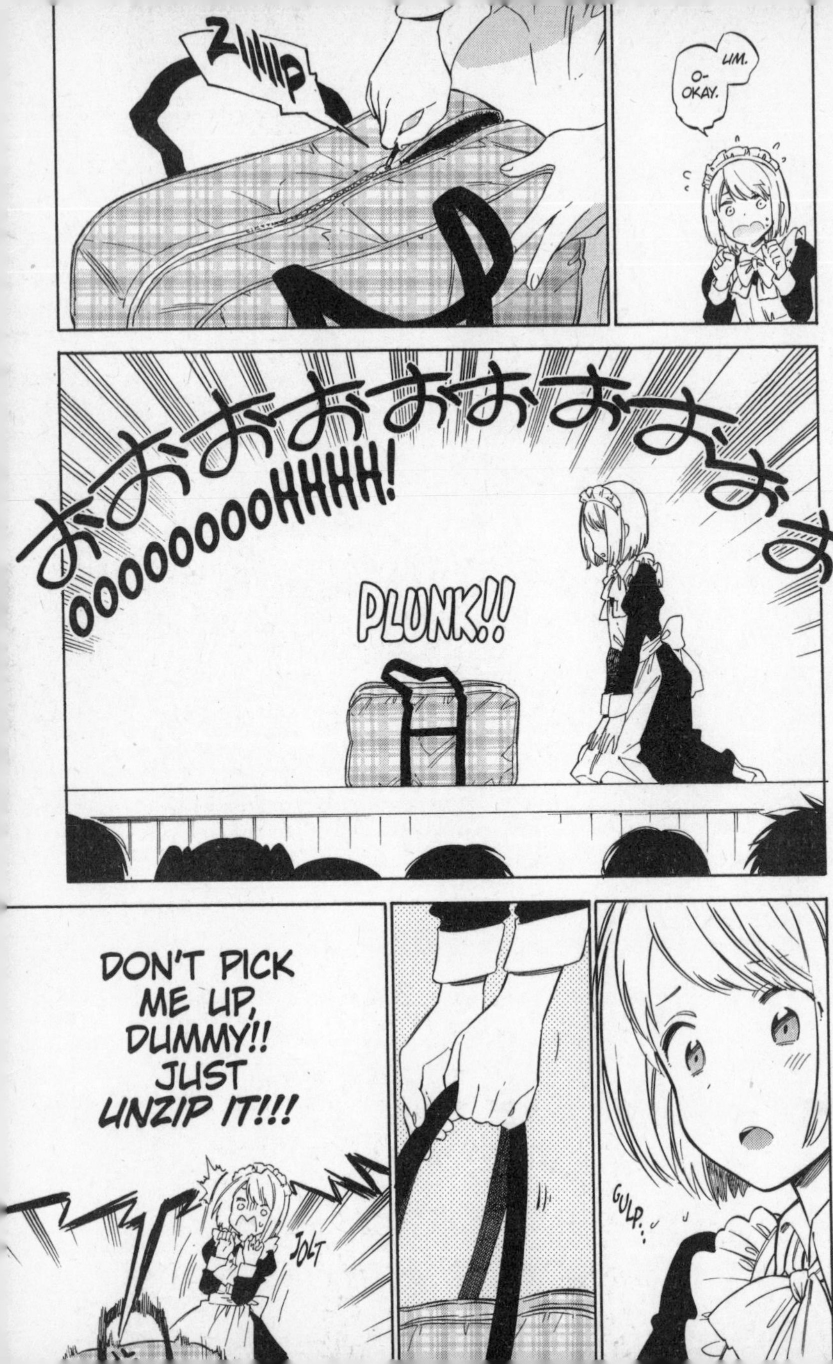
UM. O-OKAY.
ZIIIIIP
おおおおおおおおおお
OOOOOOOOHHHH!
PLUNK!!
GULP...
DON'T PICK ME UP, DUMMY!! JUST UNZIP IT!!!
JOLT

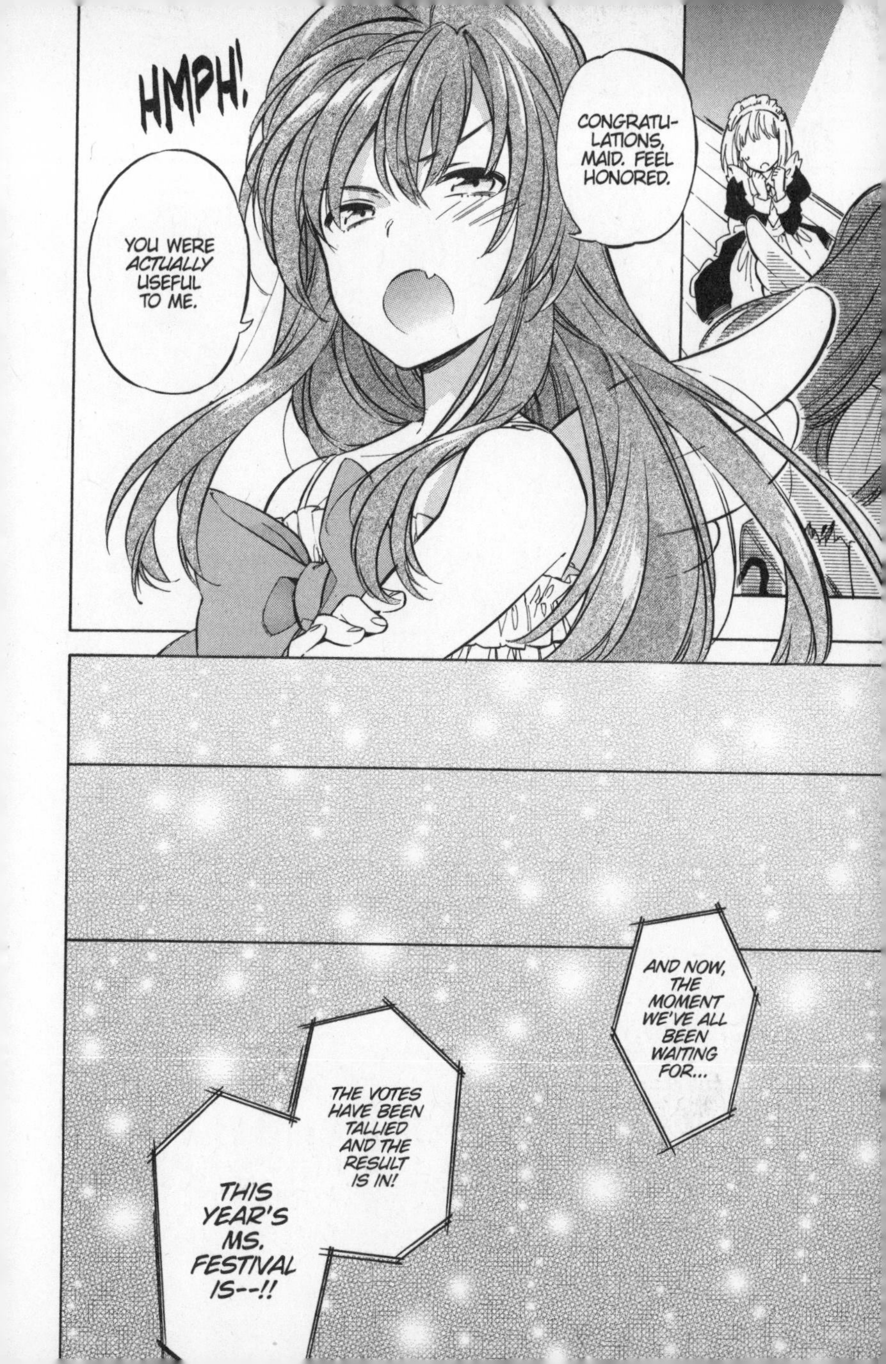
CONGRATULATIONS, MAID. FEEL HONORED.
HMPH!
YOU WERE ACTUALLY USEFUL TO ME.
AND NOW, THE MOMENT WE'VE ALL BEEN WAITING FOR...
THE VOTES HAVE BEEN TALLIED AND THE RESULT IS IN!
THIS YEAR'S MS. FESTIVAL IS--!!

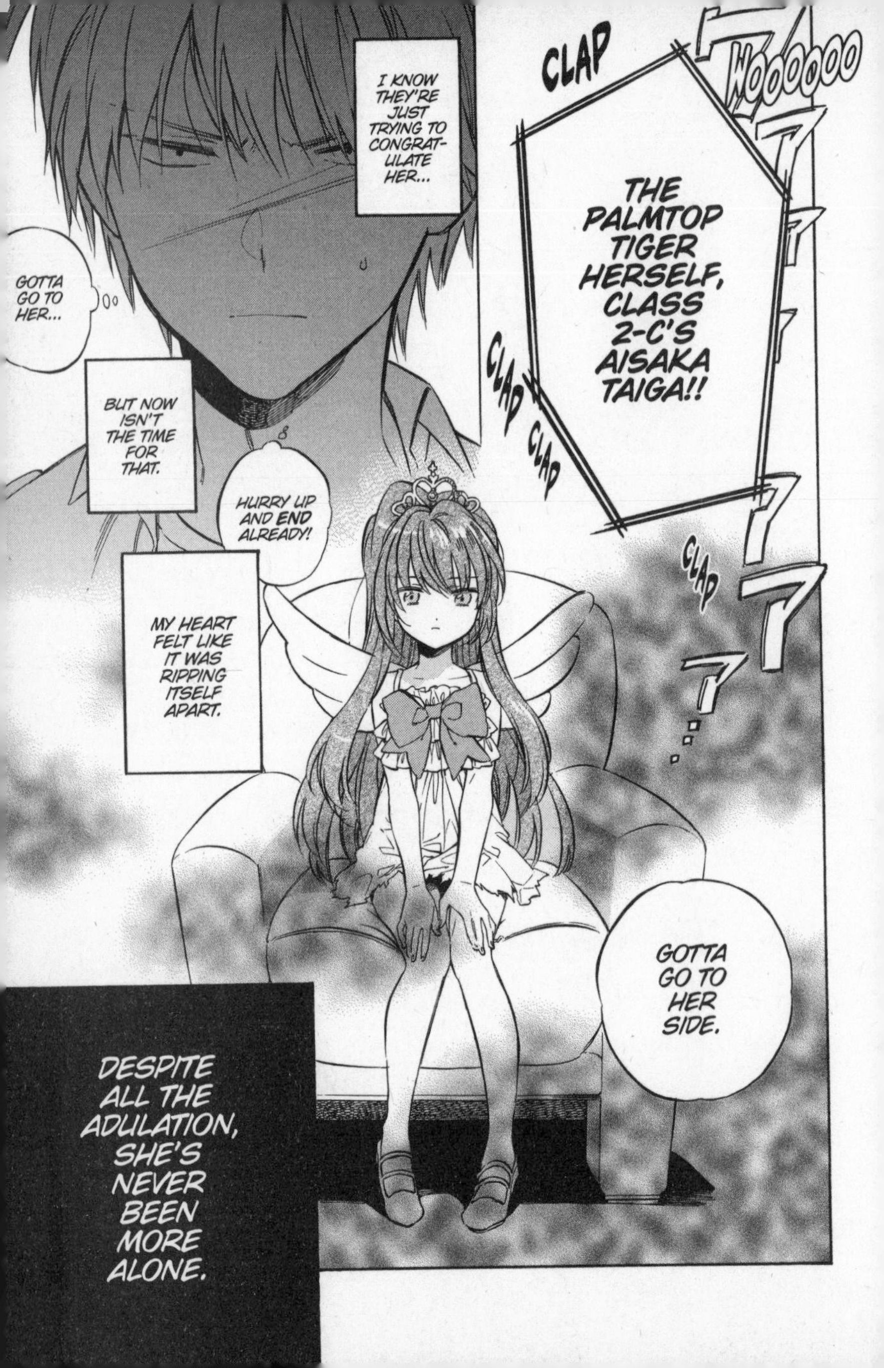
CLAP
WOOOOOO
THE PALMTOP TIGER HERSELF, CLASS 2-C'S AISAKA TAIGA!!
CLAP
CLAP
CLAP
I KNOW THEY'RE JUST TRYING TO CONGRAT-ULATE HER...
GOTTA GO TO HER...
BUT NOW ISN'T THE TIME FOR THAT.
HURRY UP AND END ALREADY!
MY HEART FELT LIKE IT WAS RIPPING ITSELF APART.
GOTTA GO TO HER SIDE.
DESPITE ALL THE ADULATION, SHE'S NEVER BEEN MORE ALONE.

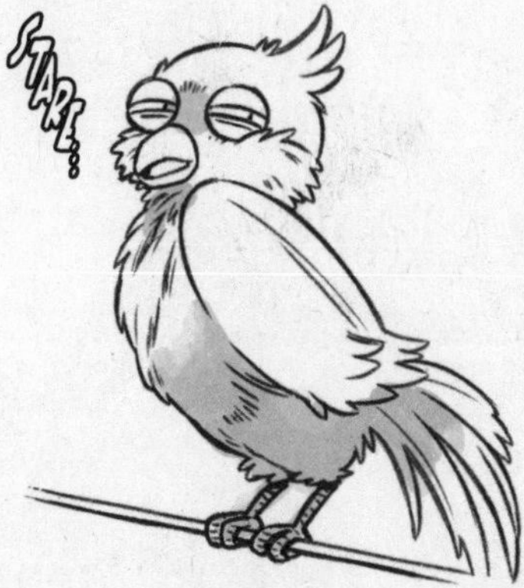
STARE...

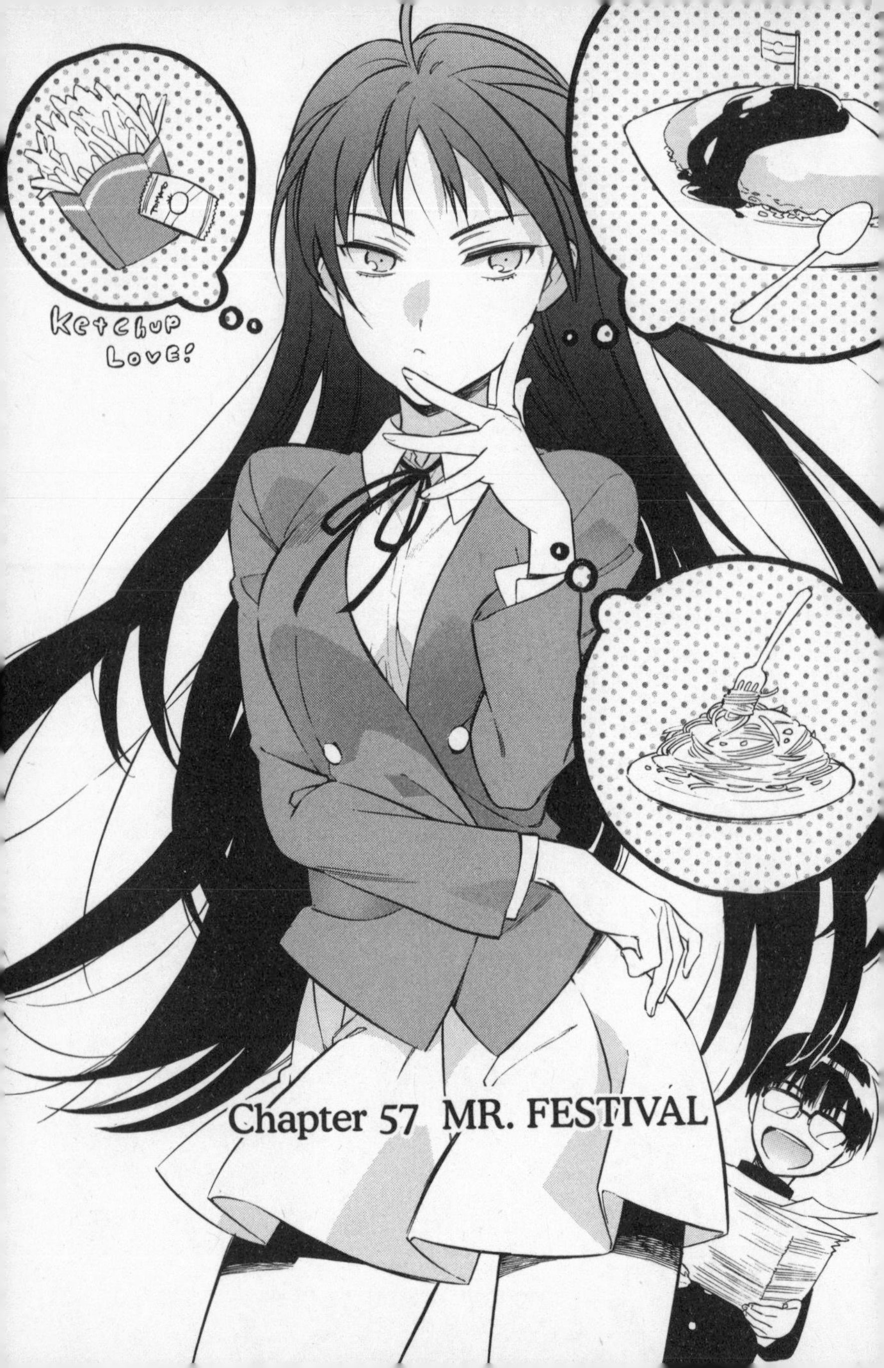
Ketchup Love!

Chapter 57 MR. FESTIVAL

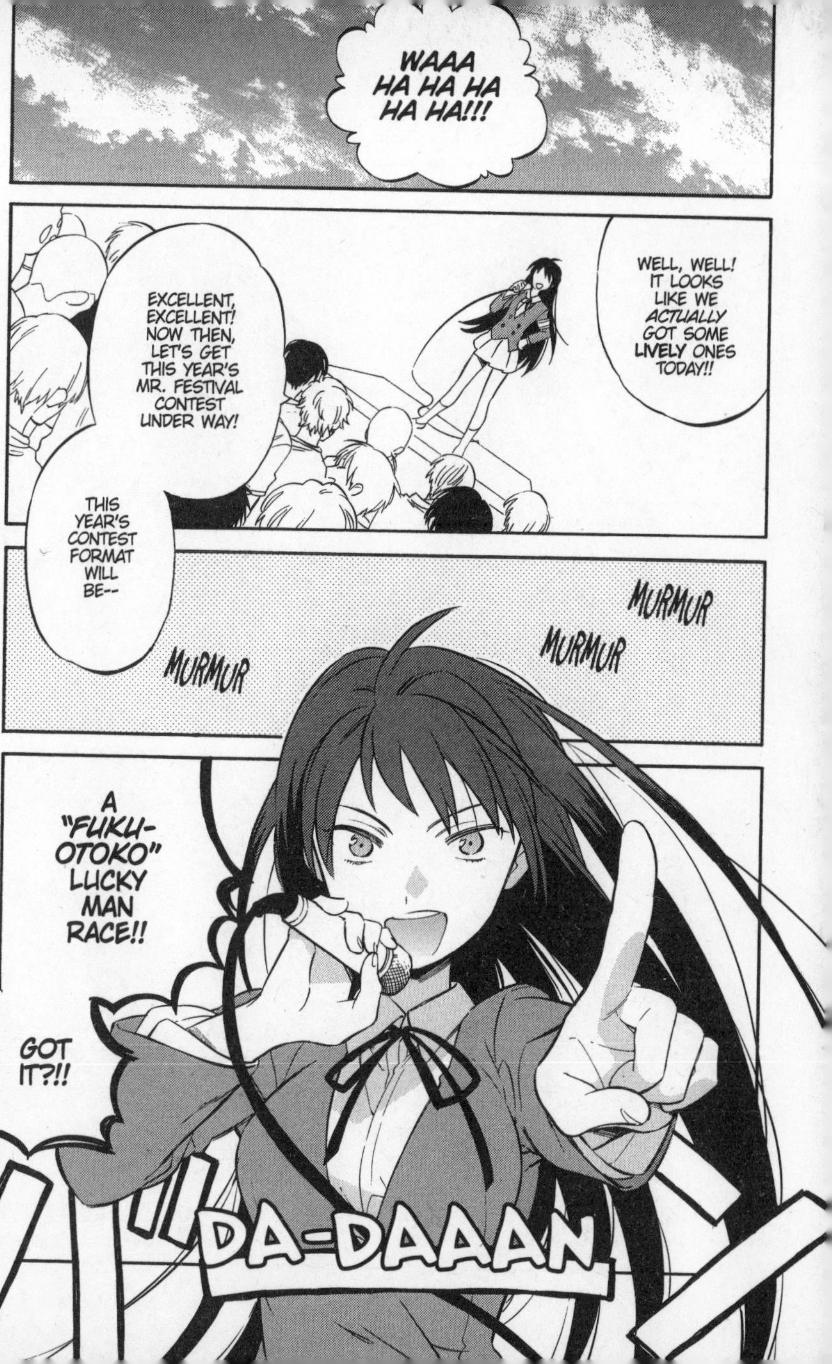
WAAA HA HA HA HA HA!!!
WELL, WELL! IT LOOKS LIKE WE ACTUALLY GOT SOME LIVELY ONES TODAY!!
EXCELLENT, EXCELLENT! NOW THEN, LET'S GET THIS YEAR'S MR. FESTIVAL CONTEST UNDER WAY!
THIS YEAR'S CONTEST FORMAT WILL BE--
MURMUR
MURMUR
MURMUR
A "FUKU-OTOKO" LUCKY MAN RACE!!
GOT IT?!!
DA-DAAAN

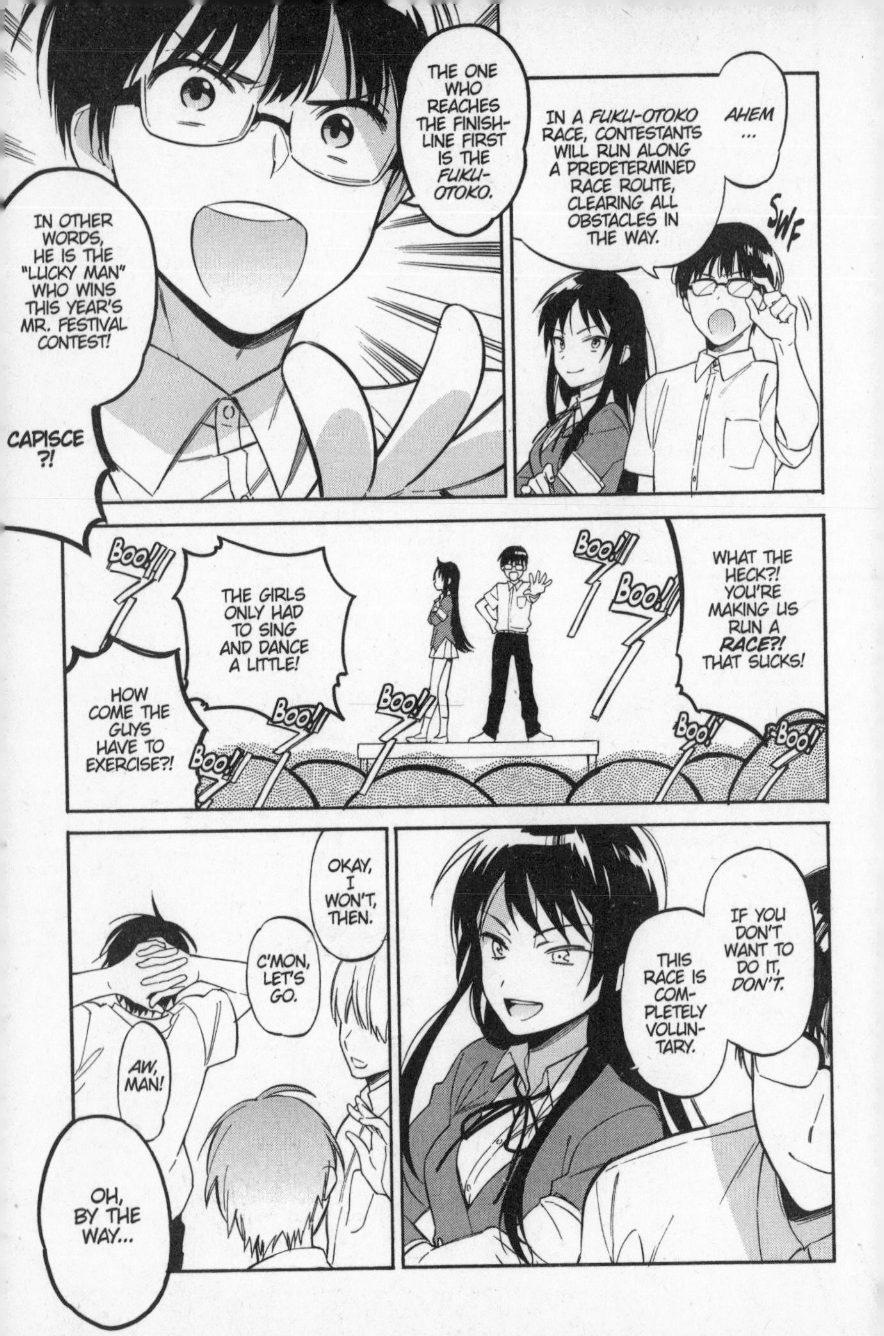
AHEM ...
SWF
IN A FUKU-OTOKO RACE, CONTESTANTS WILL RUN ALONG A PREDETERMINED RACE ROUTE, CLEARING ALL OBSTACLES IN THE WAY.
THE ONE WHO REACHES THE FINISH-LINE FIRST IS THE FUKU-OTOKO.
IN OTHER WORDS, HE IS THE "LUCKY MAN" WHO WINS THIS YEAR'S MR. FESTIVAL CONTEST!
CAPISCE ?!
WHAT THE HECK?! YOU'RE MAKING US RUN A RACE?! THAT SUCKS!
Boo!!
Boo!!
Boo!
Boo!
THE GIRLS ONLY HAD TO SING AND DANCE A LITTLE!
Boo!!
Boo!!
Boo!!
Boo!!
HOW COME THE GUYS HAVE TO EXERCISE?!
IF YOU DON'T WANT TO DO IT, DON'T.
THIS RACE IS COMPLETELY VOLUNTARY.
OKAY, I WON'T, THEN.
C'MON, LET'S GO.
AW, MAN!
OH, BY THE WAY...

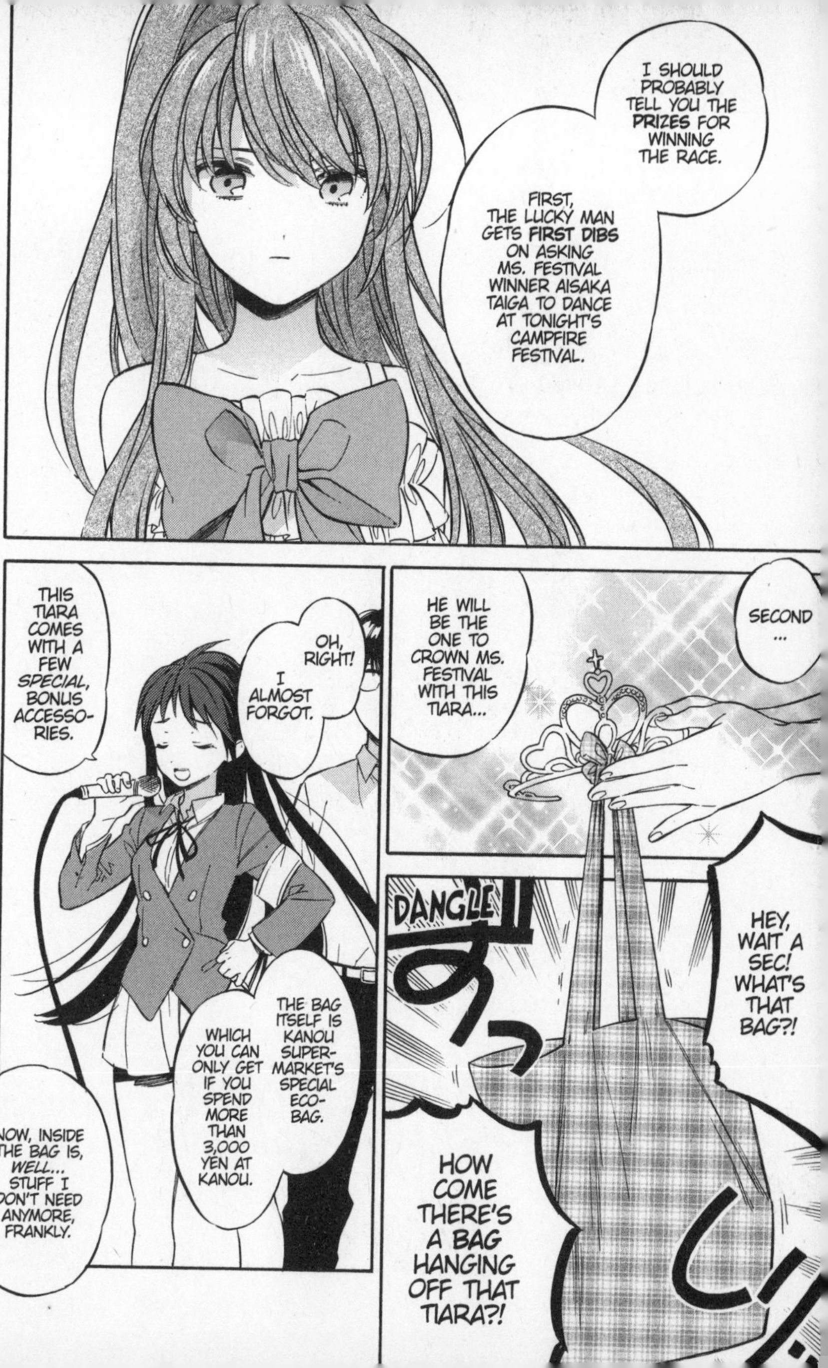
I SHOULD PROBABLY TELL YOU THE **PRIZES** FOR WINNING THE RACE.
FIRST, THE LUCKY MAN GETS **FIRST DIBS** ON ASKING MS. FESTIVAL WINNER AISAKA TAIGA TO DANCE AT TONIGHT'S CAMPFIRE FESTIVAL.
SECOND...
HE WILL BE THE ONE TO CROWN MS. FESTIVAL WITH THIS TIARA...
DANGLE
HEY, WAIT A SEC! WHAT'S THAT BAG?!
HOW COME THERE'S A BAG HANGING OFF THAT TIARA?!
OH, RIGHT! I ALMOST FORGOT.
THIS TIARA COMES WITH A FEW *SPECIAL*, BONUS ACCESSORIES.
THE BAG ITSELF IS KANOU SUPERMARKET'S SPECIAL ECO-BAG.
WHICH YOU CAN ONLY GET IF YOU SPEND MORE THAN 3,000 YEN AT KANOU.
NOW, INSIDE THE BAG IS, *WELL*... STUFF I DON'T NEED ANYMORE, FRANKLY.

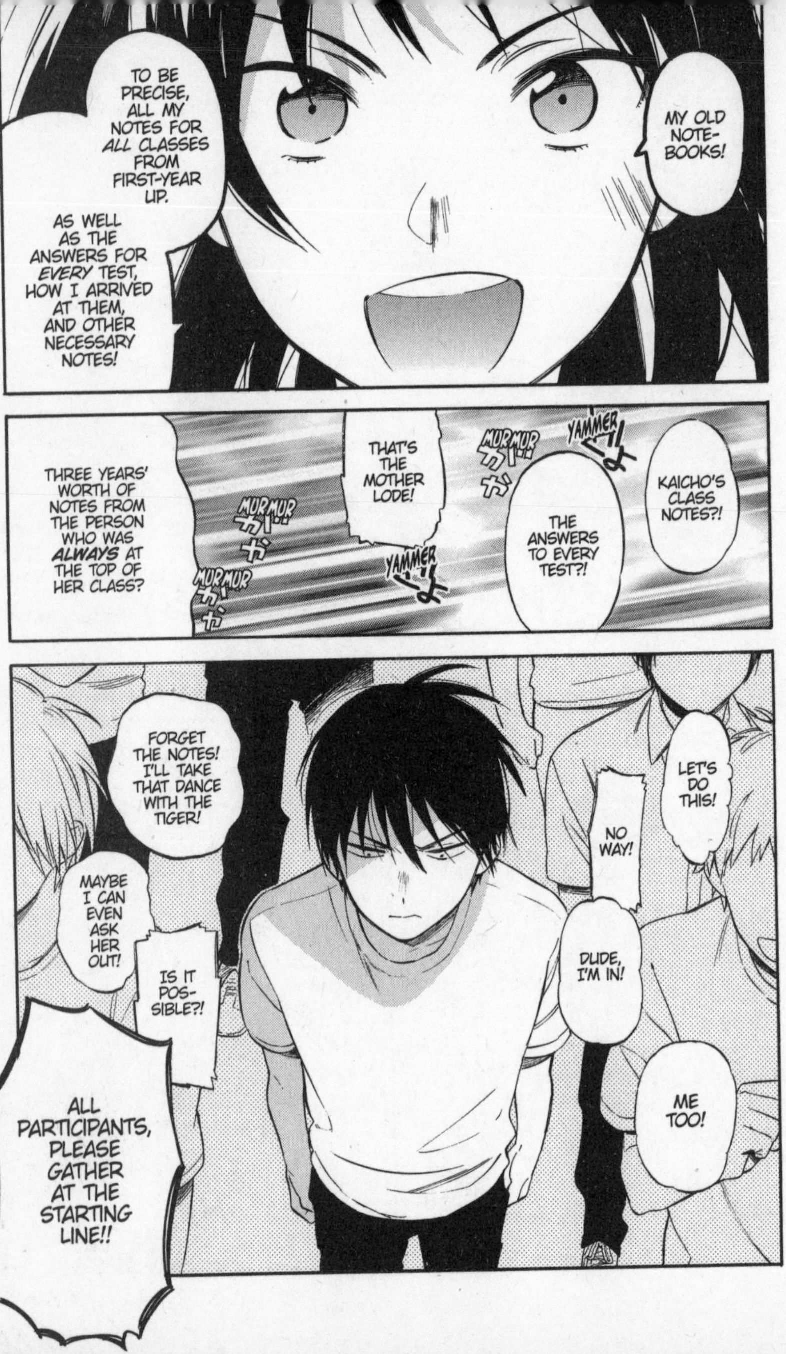

MY OLD NOTE-BOOKS!
TO BE PRECISE, ALL MY NOTES FOR *ALL* CLASSES FROM FIRST-YEAR UP.
AS WELL AS THE ANSWERS FOR *EVERY* TEST, HOW I ARRIVED AT THEM, AND OTHER NECESSARY NOTES!
KAICHO'S CLASS NOTES?!
YAMMER
MURMUR
THE ANSWERS TO EVERY TEST?!
THAT'S THE MOTHER LODE!
YAMMER
MURMUR
MURMUR
THREE YEARS' WORTH OF NOTES FROM THE PERSON WHO WAS **ALWAYS** AT THE TOP OF HER CLASS?
LET'S DO THIS!
NO WAY!
DUDE, I'M IN!
ME TOO!
FORGET THE NOTES! I'LL TAKE THAT DANCE WITH THE TIGER!
MAYBE I CAN EVEN ASK HER OUT!
IS IT POS-SIBLE?!
ALL PARTICIPANTS, PLEASE GATHER AT THE STARTING LINE!!

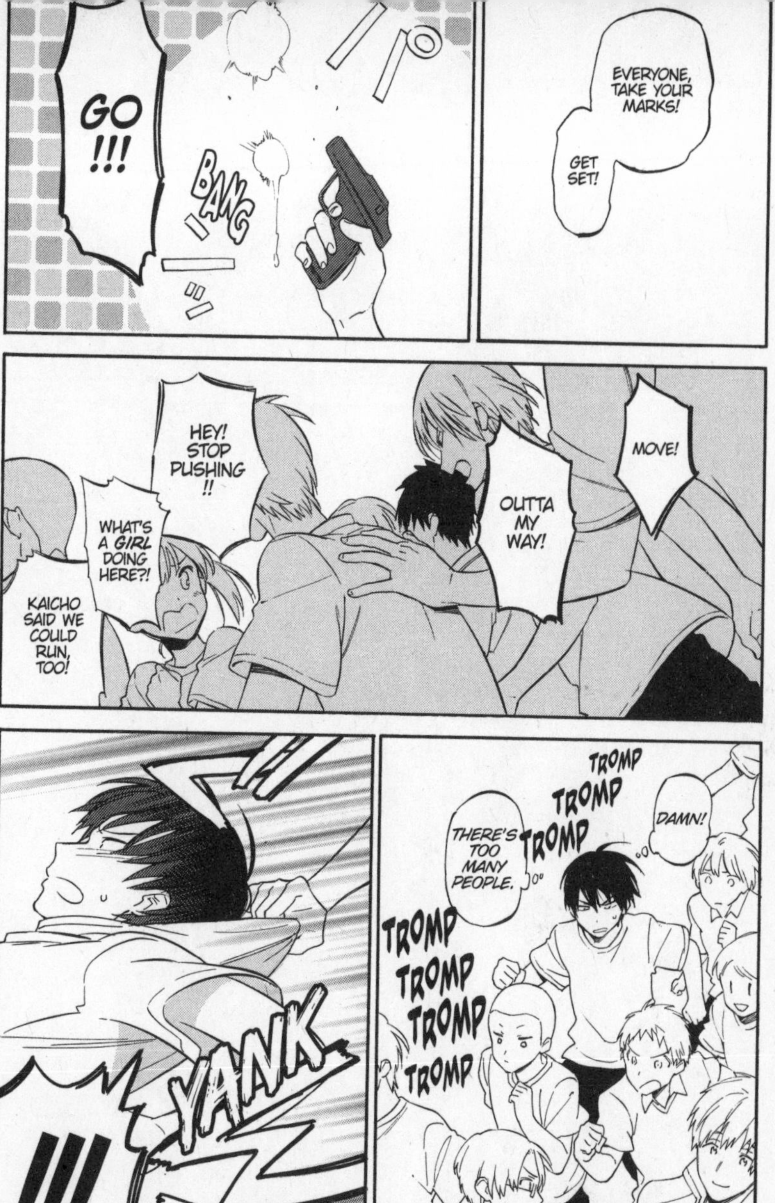
EVERYONE, TAKE YOUR MARKS!
GET SET!
BANG
GO!!!
MOVE!
OUTTA MY WAY!
HEY! STOP PUSHING!!
WHAT'S A *GIRL* DOING HERE?!
KAICHO SAID WE COULD RUN, TOO!
TROMP
TROMP
TROMP
DAMN!
THERE'S TOO MANY PEOPLE.
TROMP
TROMP
TROMP
TROMP
YANK
!!!

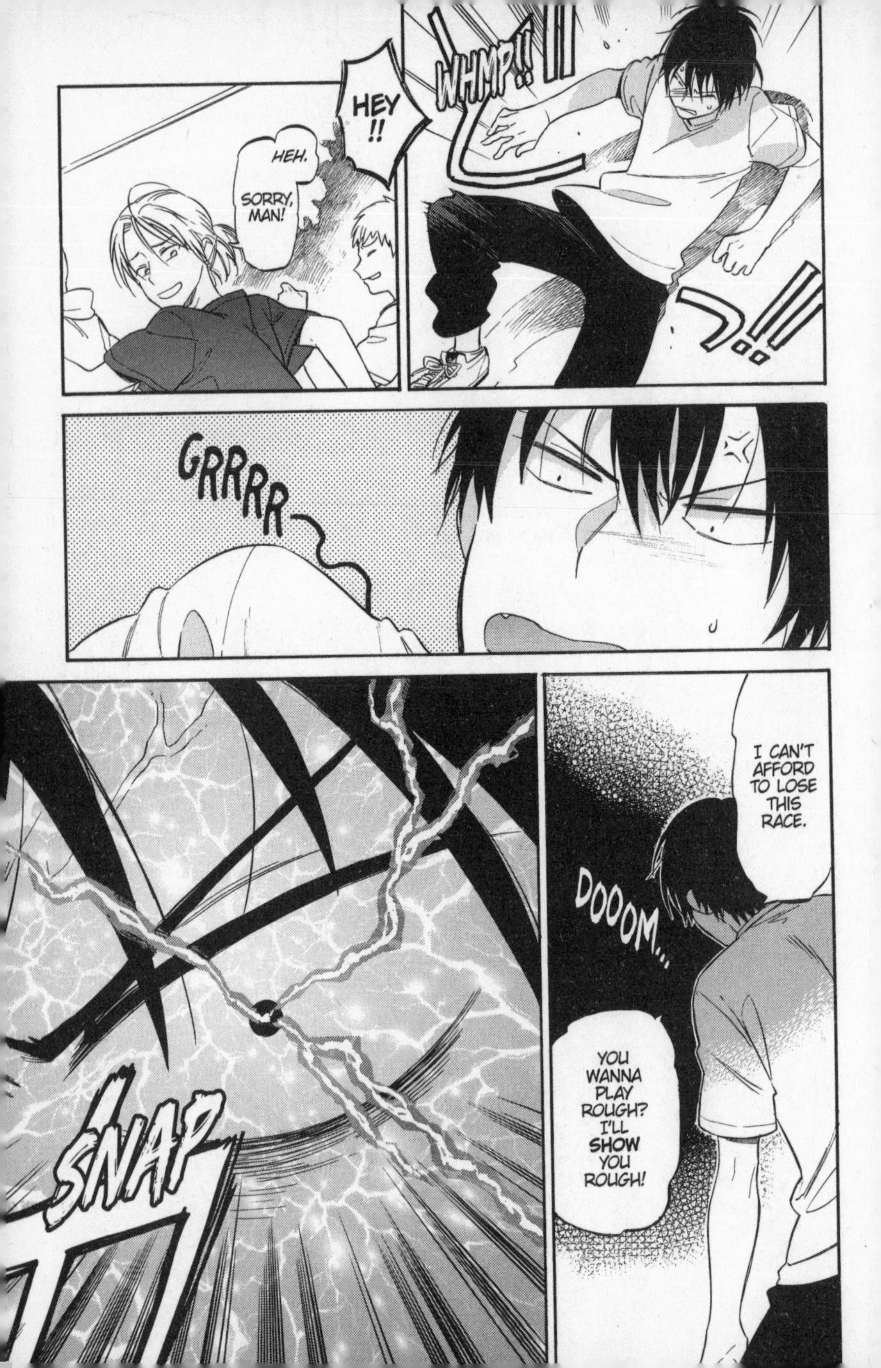
WHMP!!
HEY!!
HEH.
SORRY, MAN!
GRRRR
I CAN'T AFFORD TO LOSE THIS RACE.
DOOOM...
YOU WANNA PLAY ROUGH? I'LL **SHOW** YOU ROUGH!
SNAP

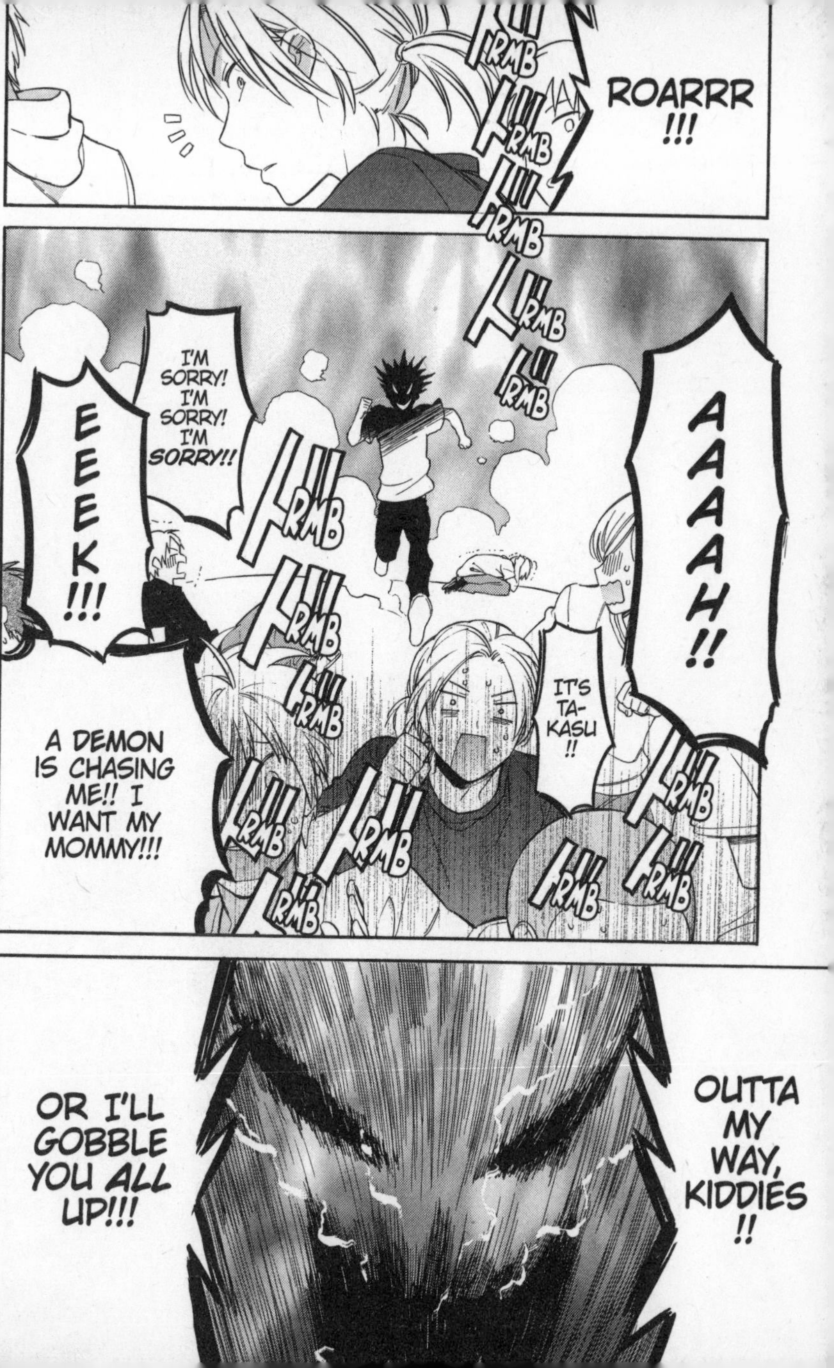
RMB
RMB
RMB
ROARRR!!!
RMB
RMB
RMB
AAAAAH!!
IT'S TA-KASU!!
I'M SORRY! I'M SORRY! I'M SORRY!!
EEEEK!!!
RMB
RMB
RMB
RMB
RMB
RMB
RMB
RMB
A DEMON IS CHASING ME!! I WANT MY MOMMY!!!
OUTTA MY WAY, KIDDIES!!
OR I'LL GOBBLE YOU ALL UP!!!

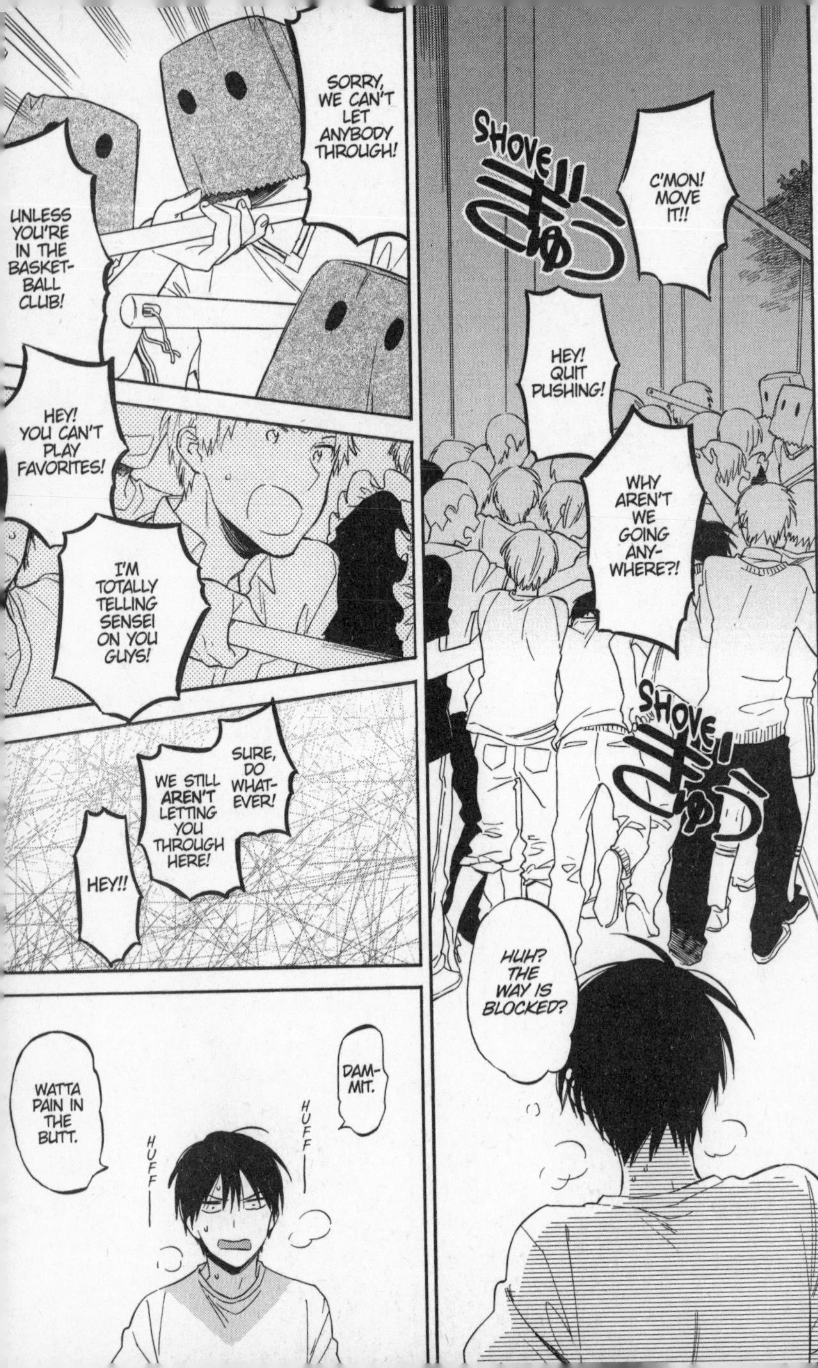
C'MON! MOVE IT!!
SHOVE
ぎゅう
HEY! QUIT PUSHING!
WHY AREN'T WE GOING ANY-WHERE?!
SHOVE
ぎゅう
HUH? THE WAY IS BLOCKED?
SORRY, WE CAN'T LET ANYBODY THROUGH!
UNLESS YOU'RE IN THE BASKET-BALL CLUB!
HEY! YOU CAN'T PLAY FAVORITES!
I'M TOTALLY TELLING SENSEI ON YOU GUYS!
SURE, DO WHAT-EVER!
WE STILL AREN'T LETTING YOU THROUGH HERE!
HEY!!
DAM-MIT.
HUFF
HUFF
WATTA PAIN IN THE BUTT.

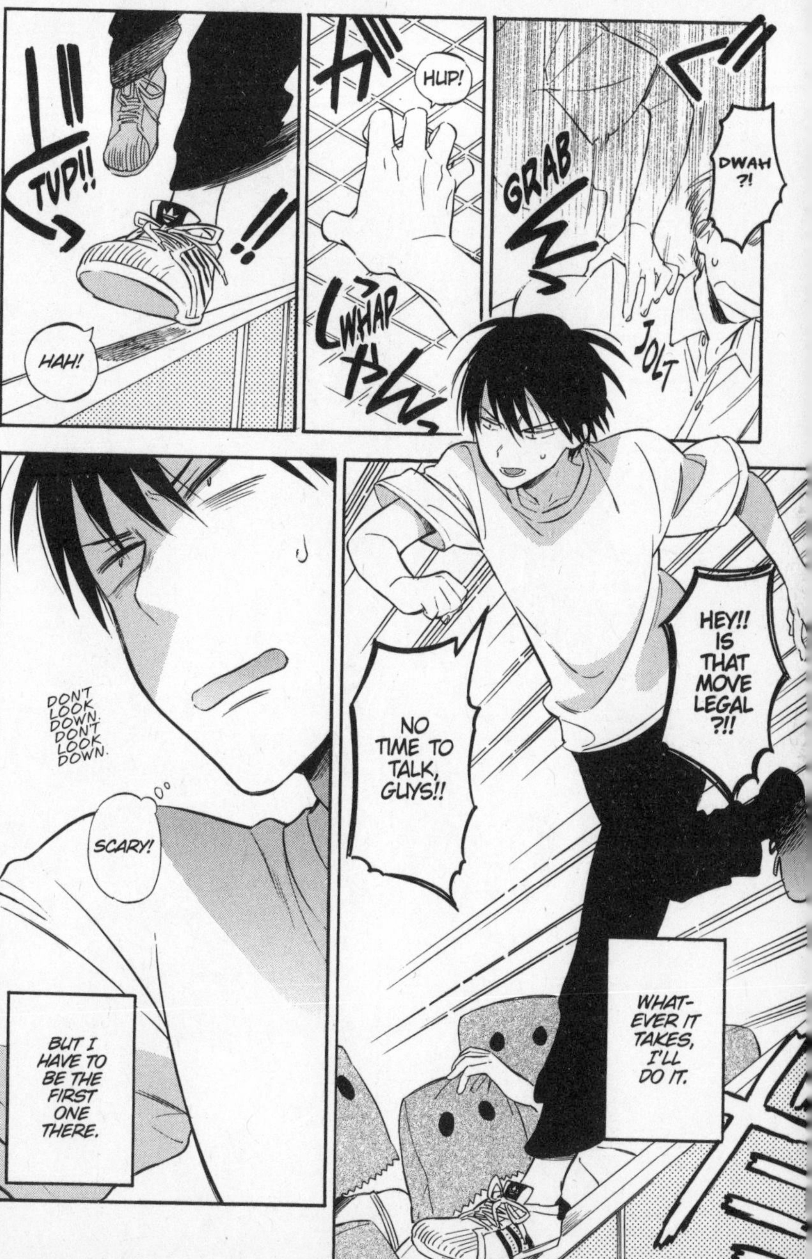
DWAH ?!
GRAB
JOLT
HUP!
WHAP
TUP!!
HAH!
HEY!! IS THAT MOVE LEGAL ?!!
NO TIME TO TALK, GUYS!!
WHAT-EVER IT TAKES, I'LL DO IT.
DON'T LOOK DOWN. DON'T LOOK DOWN.
SCARY!
BUT I HAVE TO BE THE FIRST ONE THERE.

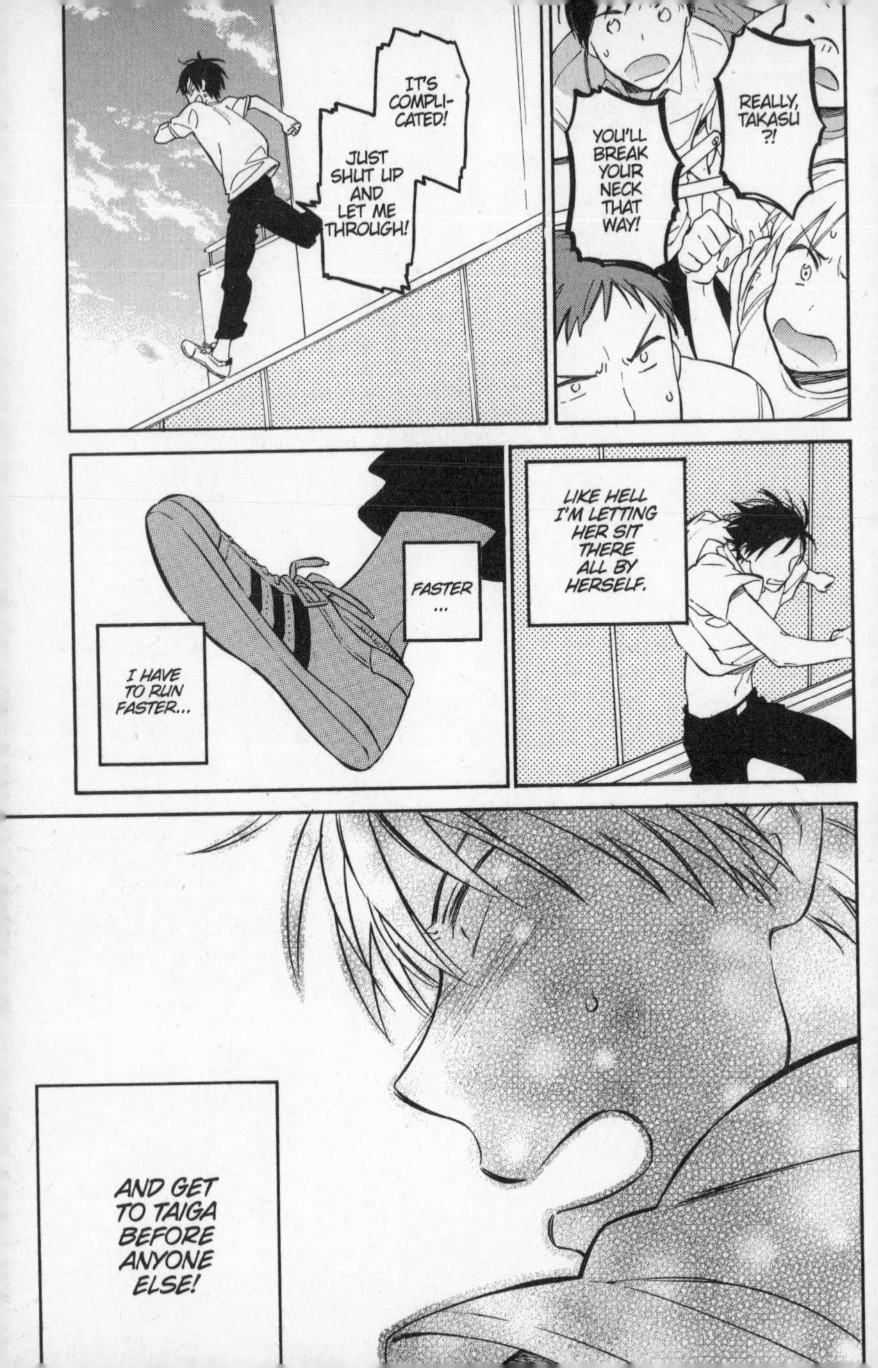
REALLY, TAKASU?!
YOU'LL BREAK YOUR NECK THAT WAY!
IT'S COMPLICATED!
JUST SHUT UP AND LET ME THROUGH!
LIKE HELL I'M LETTING HER SIT THERE ALL BY HERSELF.
FASTER...
I HAVE TO RUN FASTER...
AND GET TO TAIGA BEFORE ANYONE ELSE!

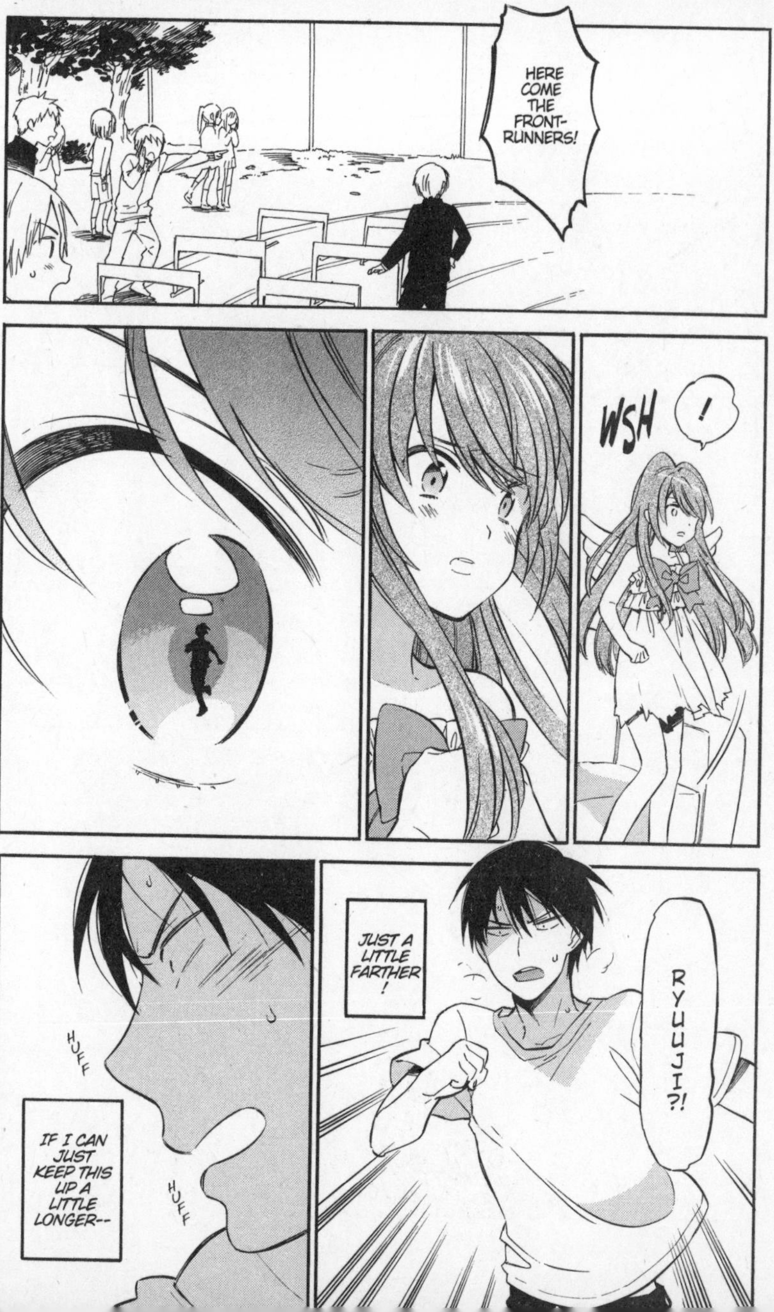
HERE COME THE FRONT-RUNNERS!
WSH
!
RYUUJI?!
JUST A LITTLE FARTHER!
HUFF
IF I CAN JUST KEEP THIS UP A LITTLE LONGER--
HUFF

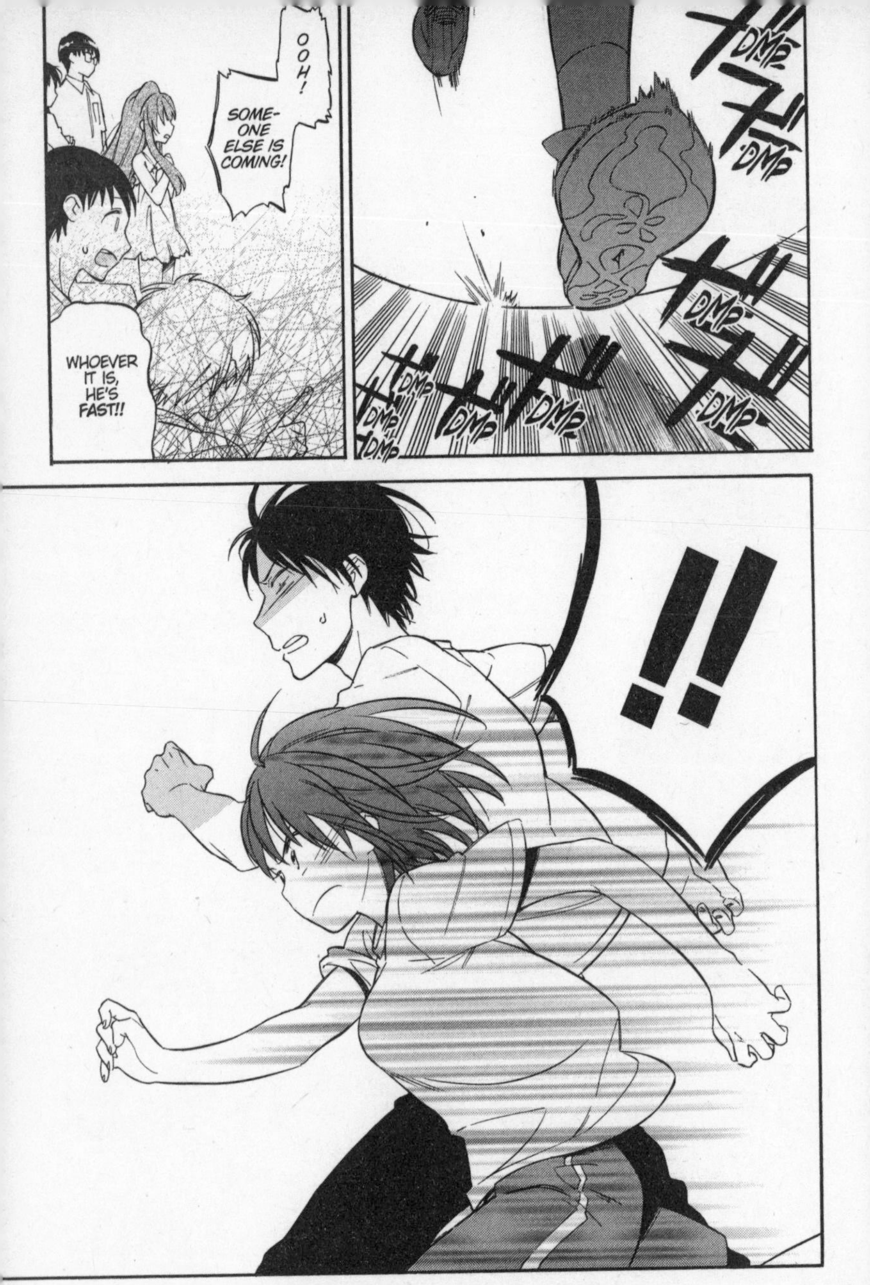
DMP
DMP
DMP
DMP
DMP
DMP
DMP
DMP
DMP
OOH!
SOME-ONE ELSE IS COMING!
WHOEVER IT IS, HE'S FAST!!
!!

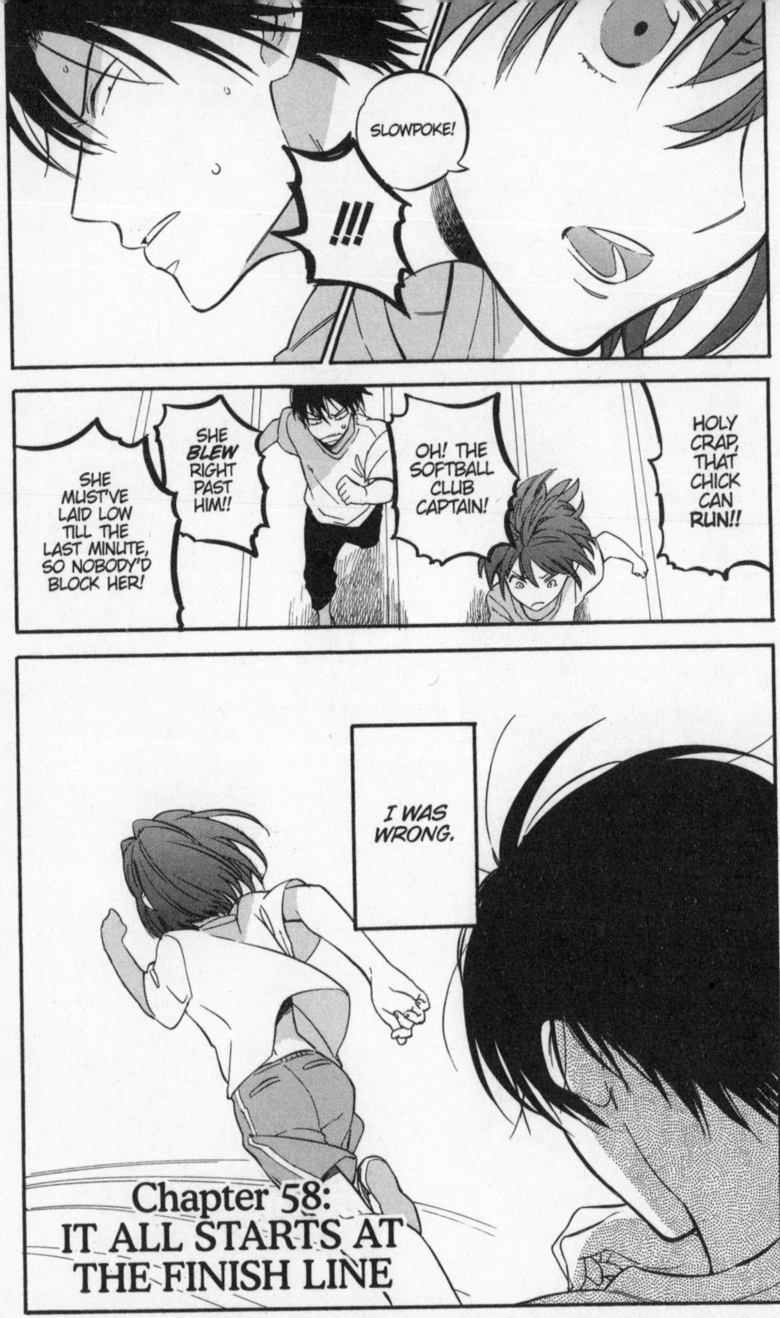
SLOWPOKE!
!!!
HOLY CRAP, THAT CHICK CAN RUN!!
OH! THE SOFTBALL CLUB CAPTAIN!
SHE *BLEW* RIGHT PAST HIM!!
SHE MUST'VE LAID LOW TILL THE LAST MINUTE, SO NOBODY'D BLOCK HER!
I WAS WRONG.
Chapter 58: IT ALL STARTS AT THE FINISH LINE

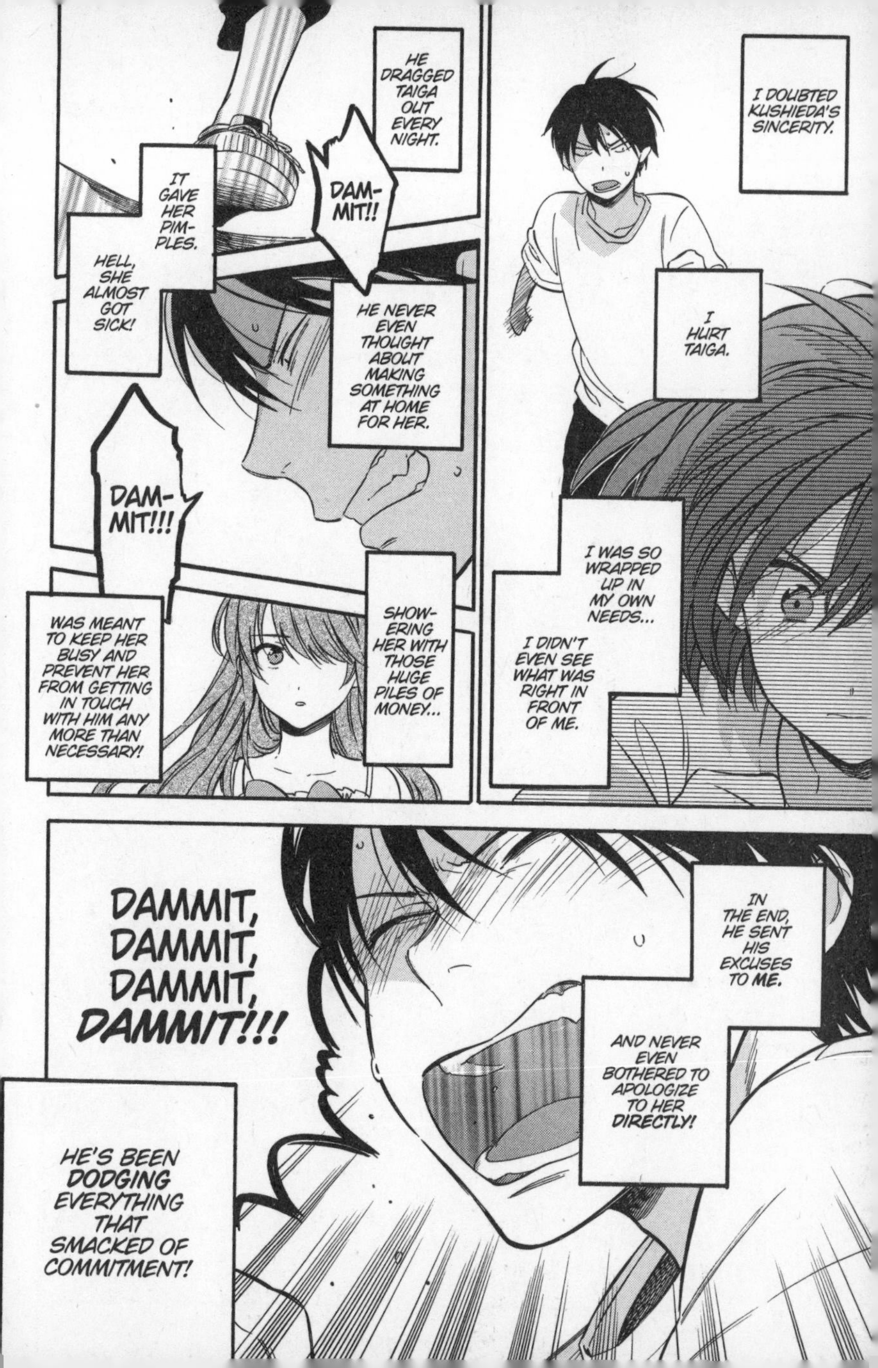
I DOUBTED KUSHIEDA'S SINCERITY.
I HURT TAIGA.
I WAS SO WRAPPED UP IN MY OWN NEEDS...
I DIDN'T EVEN SEE WHAT WAS RIGHT IN FRONT OF ME.
HE DRAGGED TAIGA OUT EVERY NIGHT.
DAM-MIT!!
IT GAVE HER PIM-PLES.
HELL, SHE ALMOST GOT SICK!
HE NEVER EVEN THOUGHT ABOUT MAKING SOMETHING AT HOME FOR HER.
DAM-MIT!!!
SHOW-ERING HER WITH THOSE HUGE PILES OF MONEY...
WAS MEANT TO KEEP HER BUSY AND PREVENT HER FROM GETTING IN TOUCH WITH HIM ANY MORE THAN NECESSARY!
IN THE END, HE SENT HIS EXCUSES TO ME.
AND NEVER EVEN BOTHERED TO APOLOGIZE TO HER DIRECTLY!
DAMMIT, DAMMIT, DAMMIT, DAMMIT!!!
HE'S BEEN DODGING EVERYTHING THAT SMACKED OF COMMITMENT!

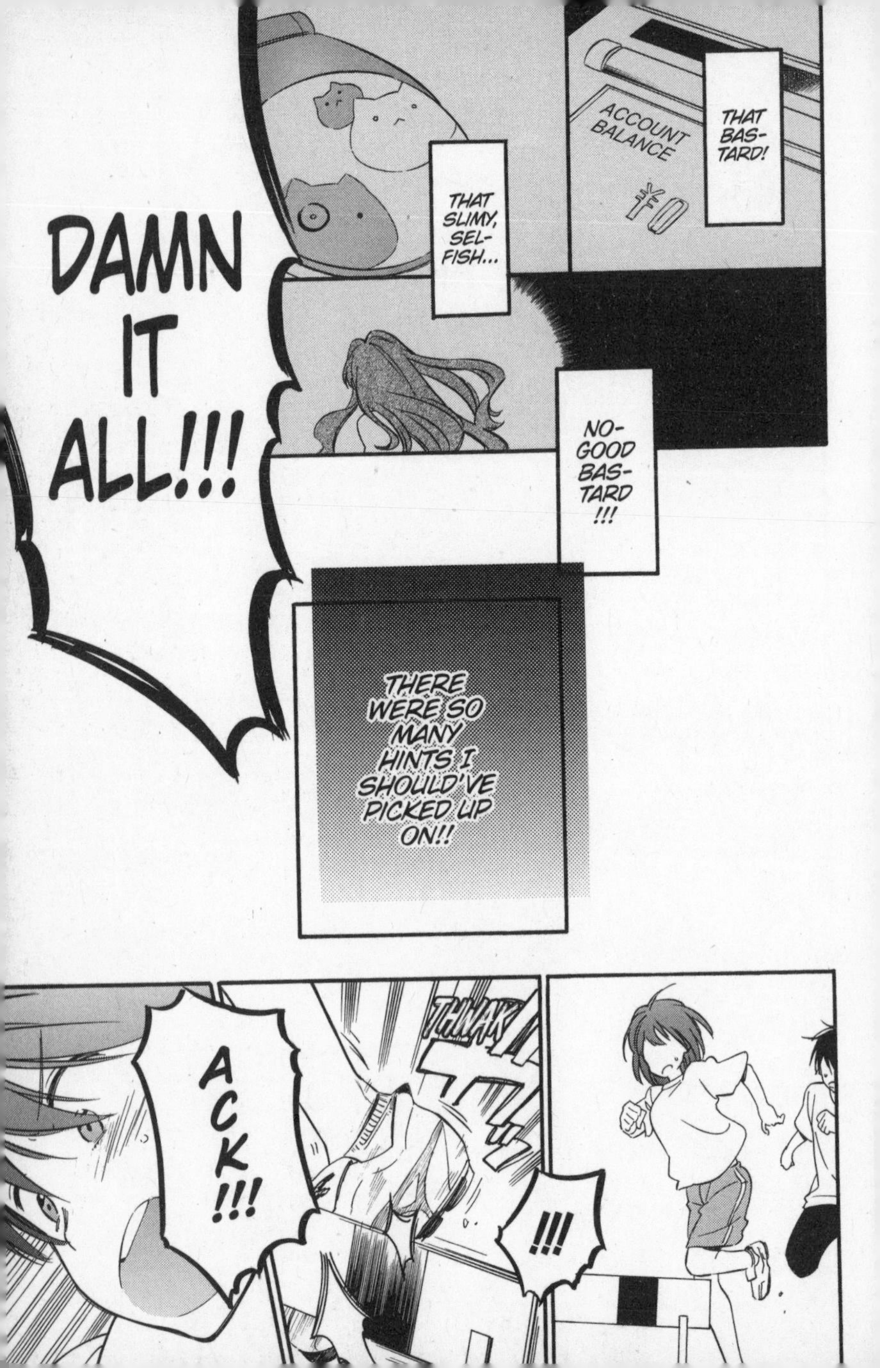
ACCOUNT BALANCE
¥0
THAT BASTARD!
THAT SLIMY, SELFISH...
NO-GOOD BASTARD!!!
THERE WERE SO MANY HINTS I SHOULD'VE PICKED UP ON!!
DAMN IT ALL!!!
THWAK
!!!
ACK!!!

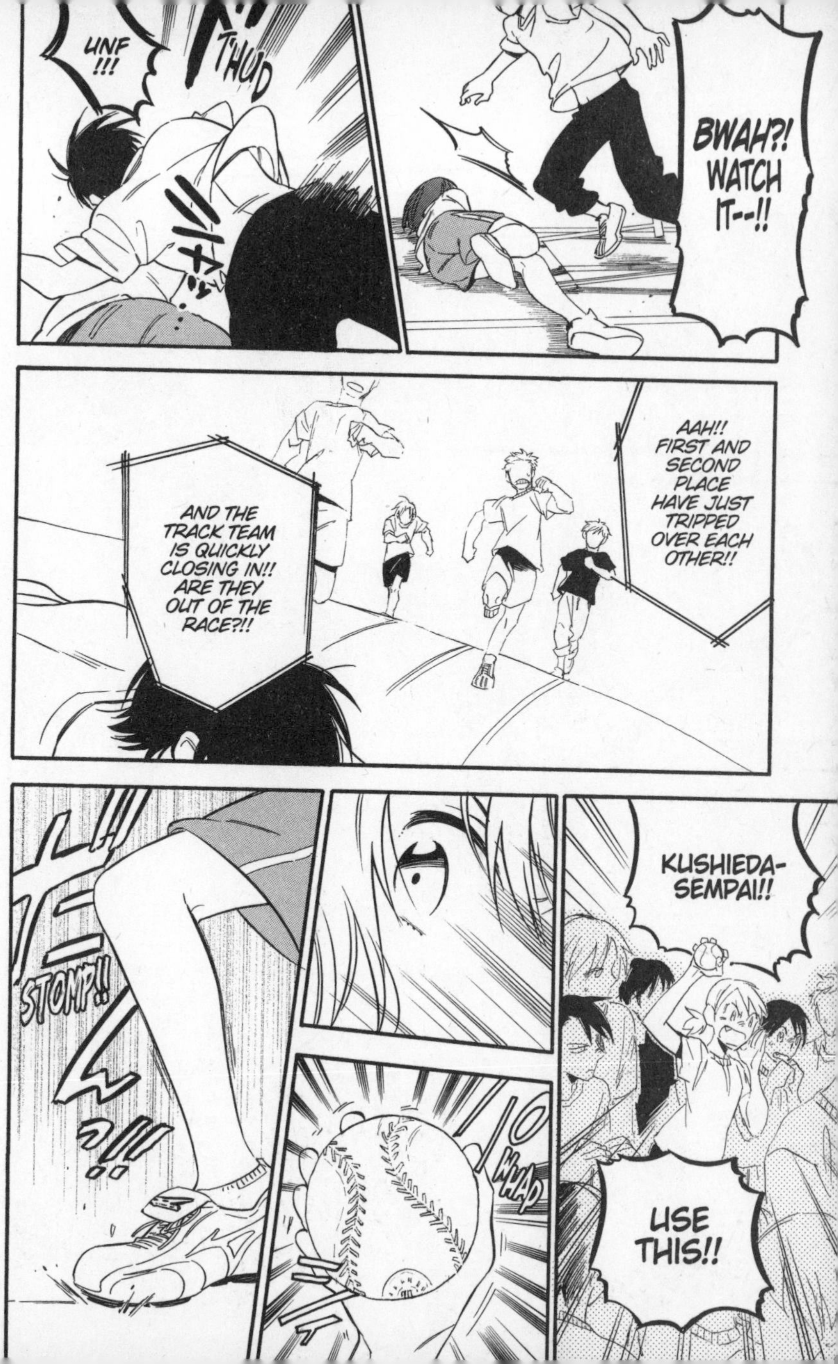
BWAH?! WATCH IT--!!
UNF !!!
THUD
AAH!! FIRST AND SECOND PLACE HAVE JUST TRIPPED OVER EACH OTHER!!
AND THE TRACK TEAM IS QUICKLY CLOSING IN!! ARE THEY OUT OF THE RACE?!!
KUSHIEDA-SEMPAI!!
USE THIS!!
WHAP
STOMP!!

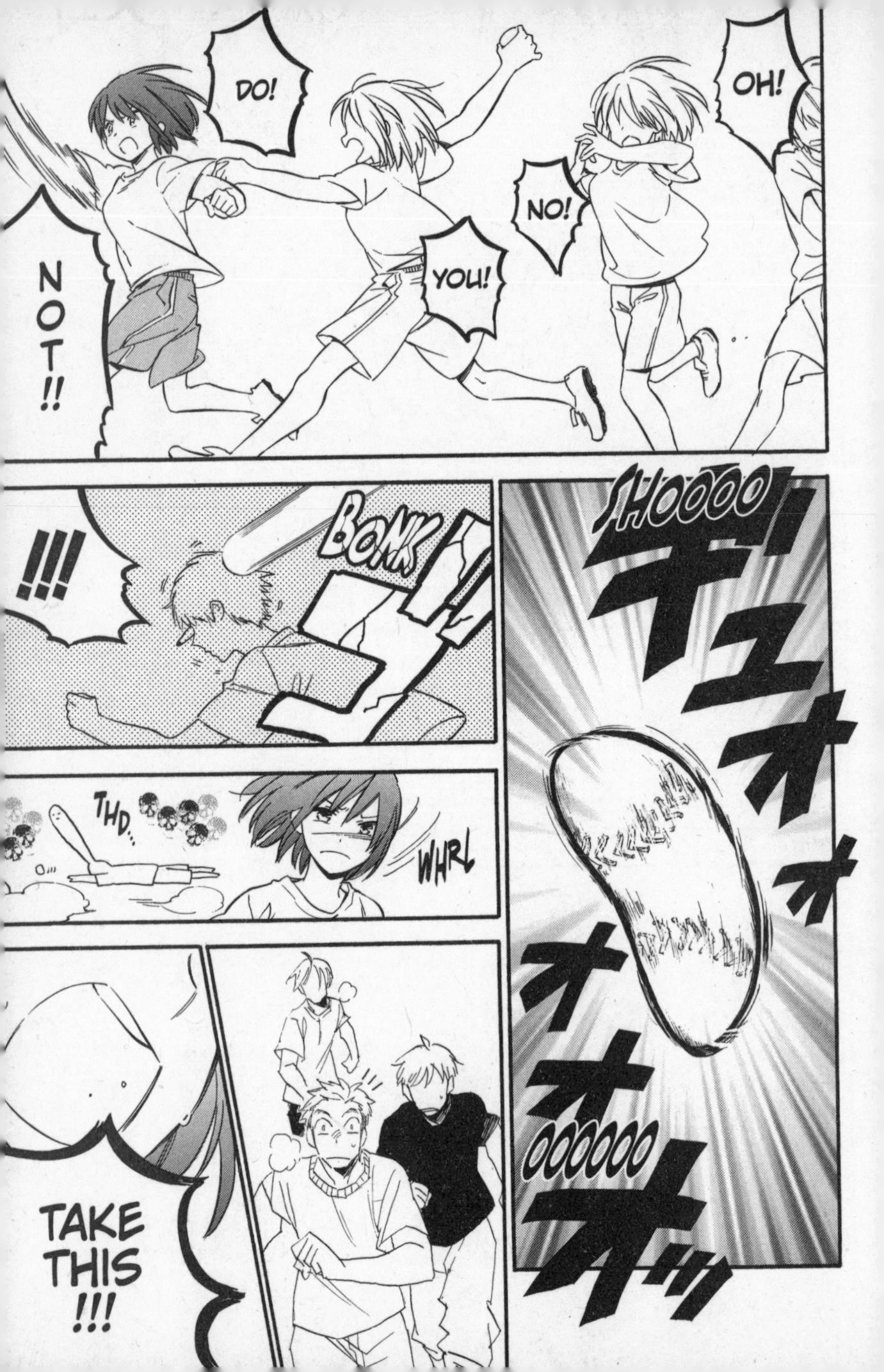
OH!
NO!
YOU!
DO!
NOT!!
SHOOOO
ギュオォォォォォッ
OOOOOO
BONK
!!!
WHRL
THD...
TAKE THIS!!!

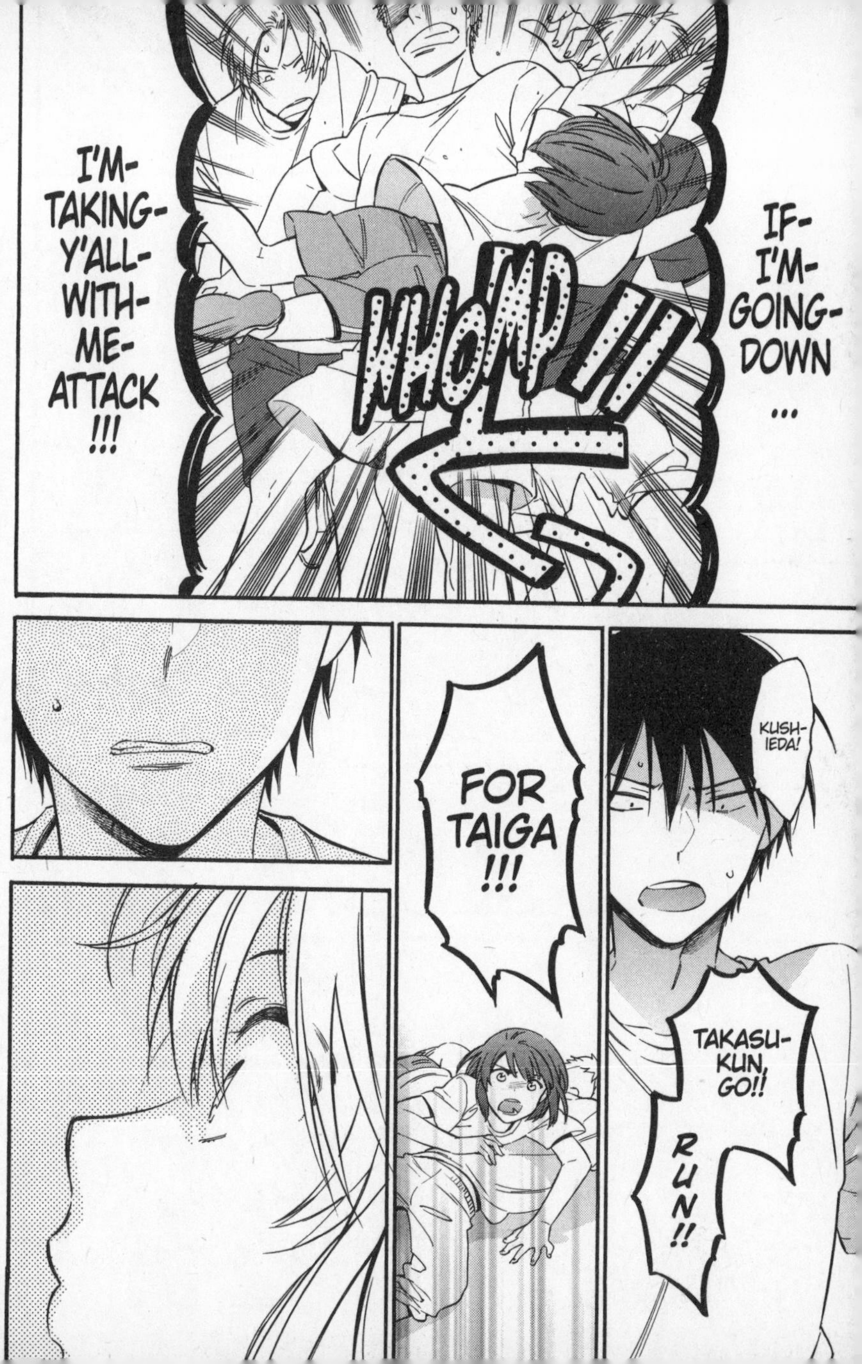
IF-I'M-GOING-DOWN...
WHOMP!!
I'M-TAKING-Y'ALL-WITH-ME-ATTACK!!!
KUSH-IEDA!
TAKASU-KUN, GO!!
RUN!!
FOR TAIGA!!!

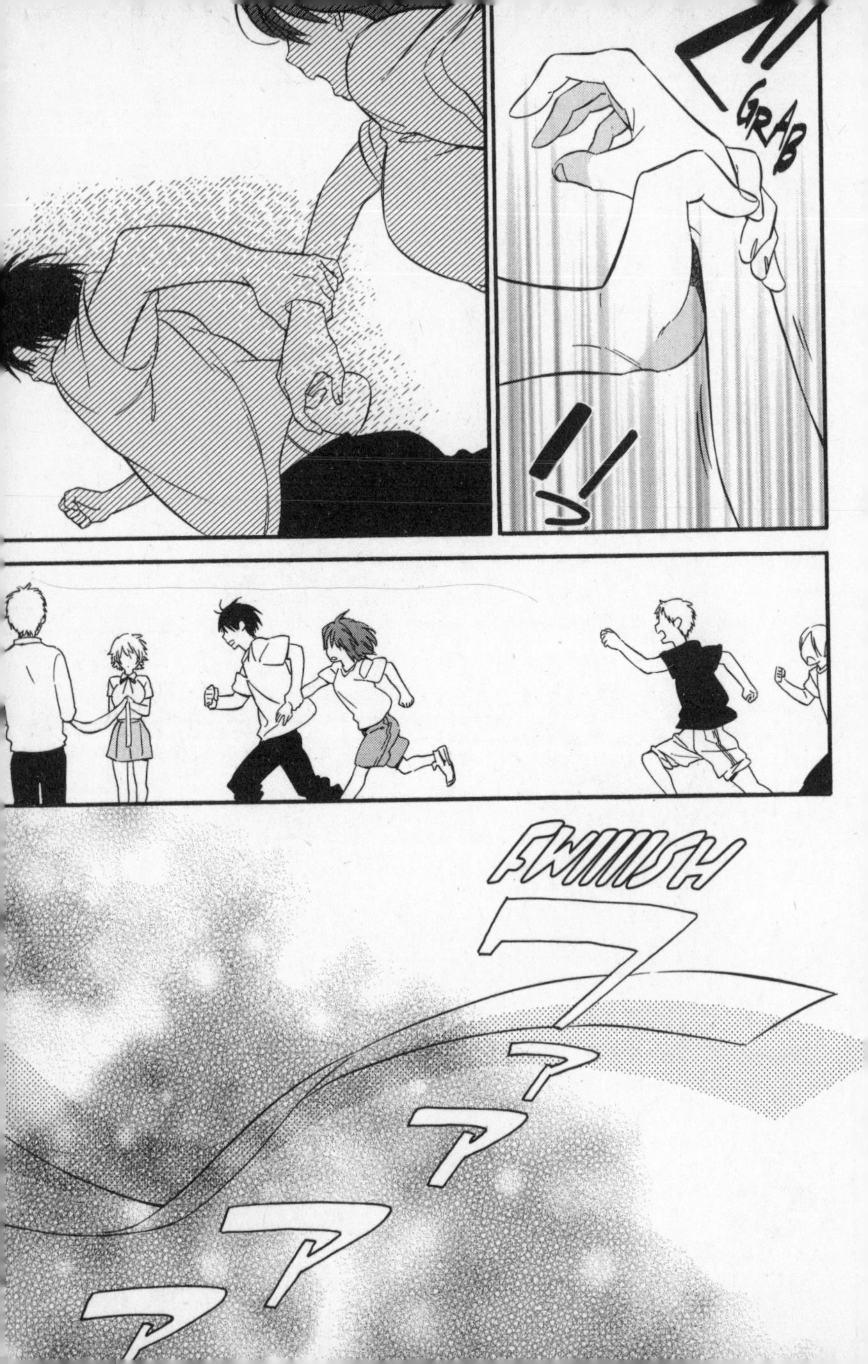
GRAB
FWIIISH

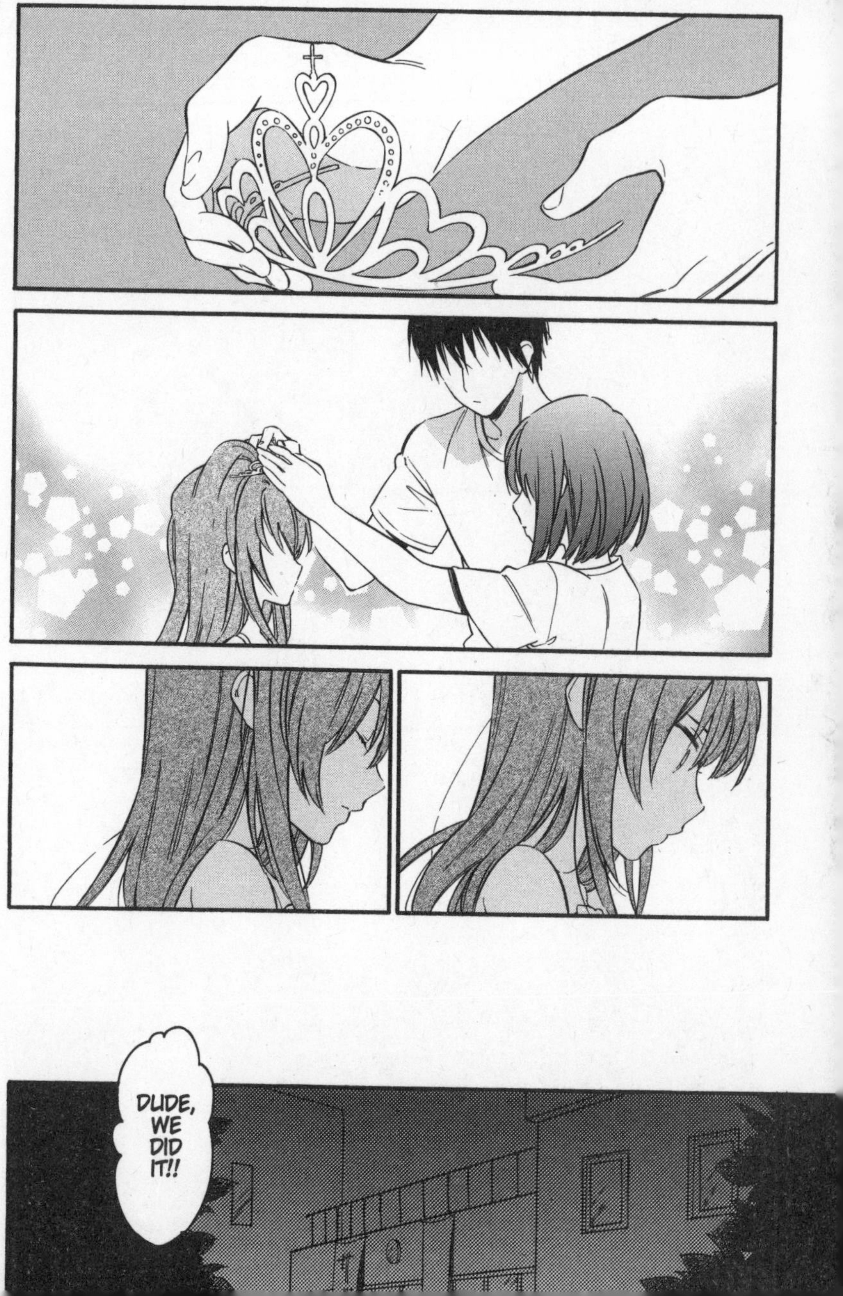
DUDE, WE DID IT!!

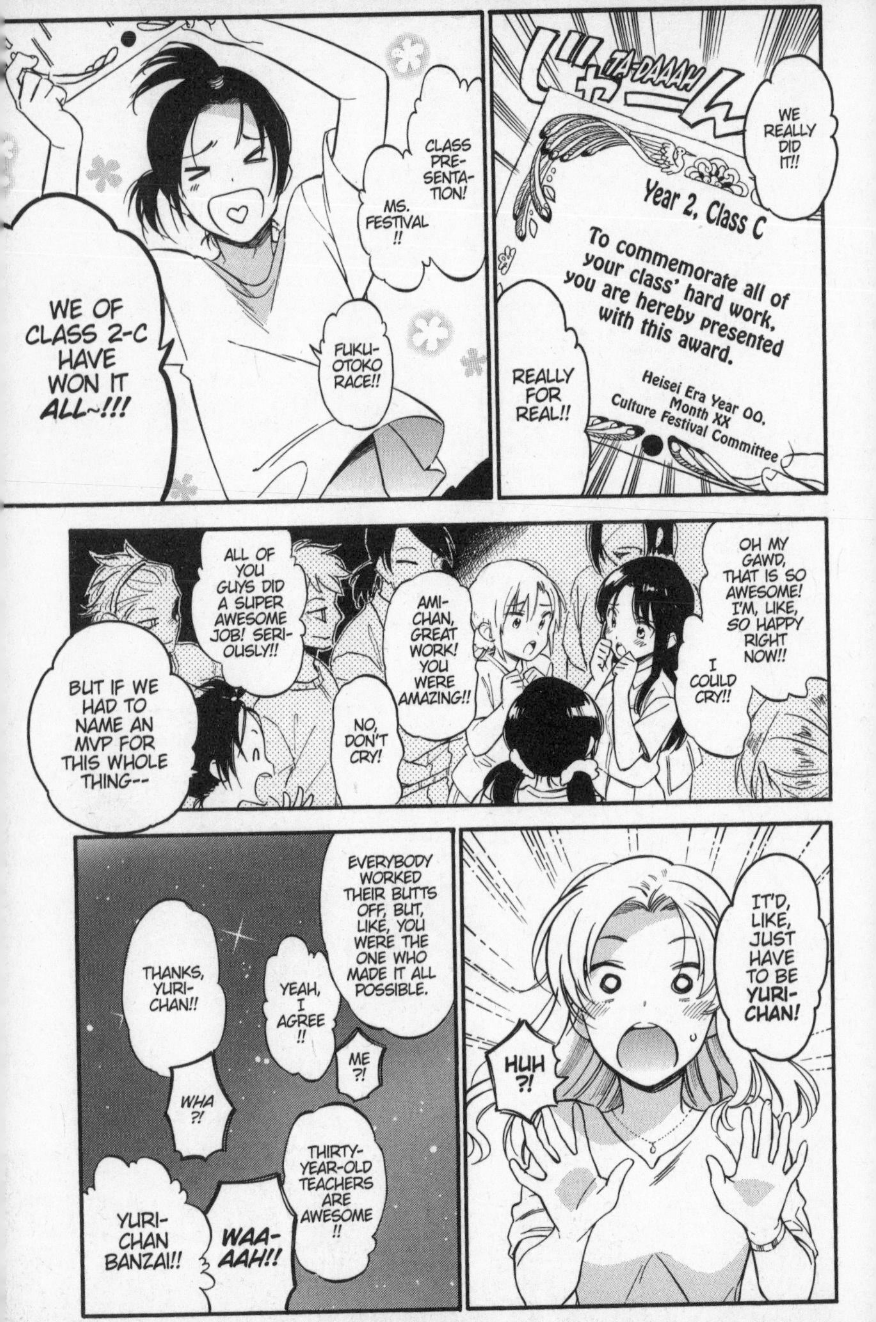
TA-DAAAH
WE REALLY DID IT!!
Year 2, Class C
To commemorate all of your class' hard work, you are hereby presented with this award.
Heisei Era Year OO. Month XX Culture Festival Committee
REALLY FOR REAL!!
CLASS PRESENTATION!
MS. FESTIVAL!!
FUKU-OTOKO RACE!!
WE OF CLASS 2-C HAVE WON IT ALL~!!!
OH MY GAWD, THAT IS SO AWESOME! I'M, LIKE, SO HAPPY RIGHT NOW!!
I COULD CRY!!
AMI-CHAN, GREAT WORK! YOU WERE AMAZING!!
NO, DON'T CRY!
ALL OF YOU GUYS DID A SUPER AWESOME JOB! SERIOUSLY!!
BUT IF WE HAD TO NAME AN MVP FOR THIS WHOLE THING--
IT'D, LIKE, JUST HAVE TO BE YURI-CHAN!
HUH ?!
EVERYBODY WORKED THEIR BUTTS OFF, BUT, LIKE, YOU WERE THE ONE WHO MADE IT ALL POSSIBLE.
YEAH, I AGREE !!
THANKS, YURI-CHAN!!
ME ?!
WHA ?!
THIRTY-YEAR-OLD TEACHERS ARE AWESOME !!
WAA-AAH!!
YURI-CHAN BANZAI!!

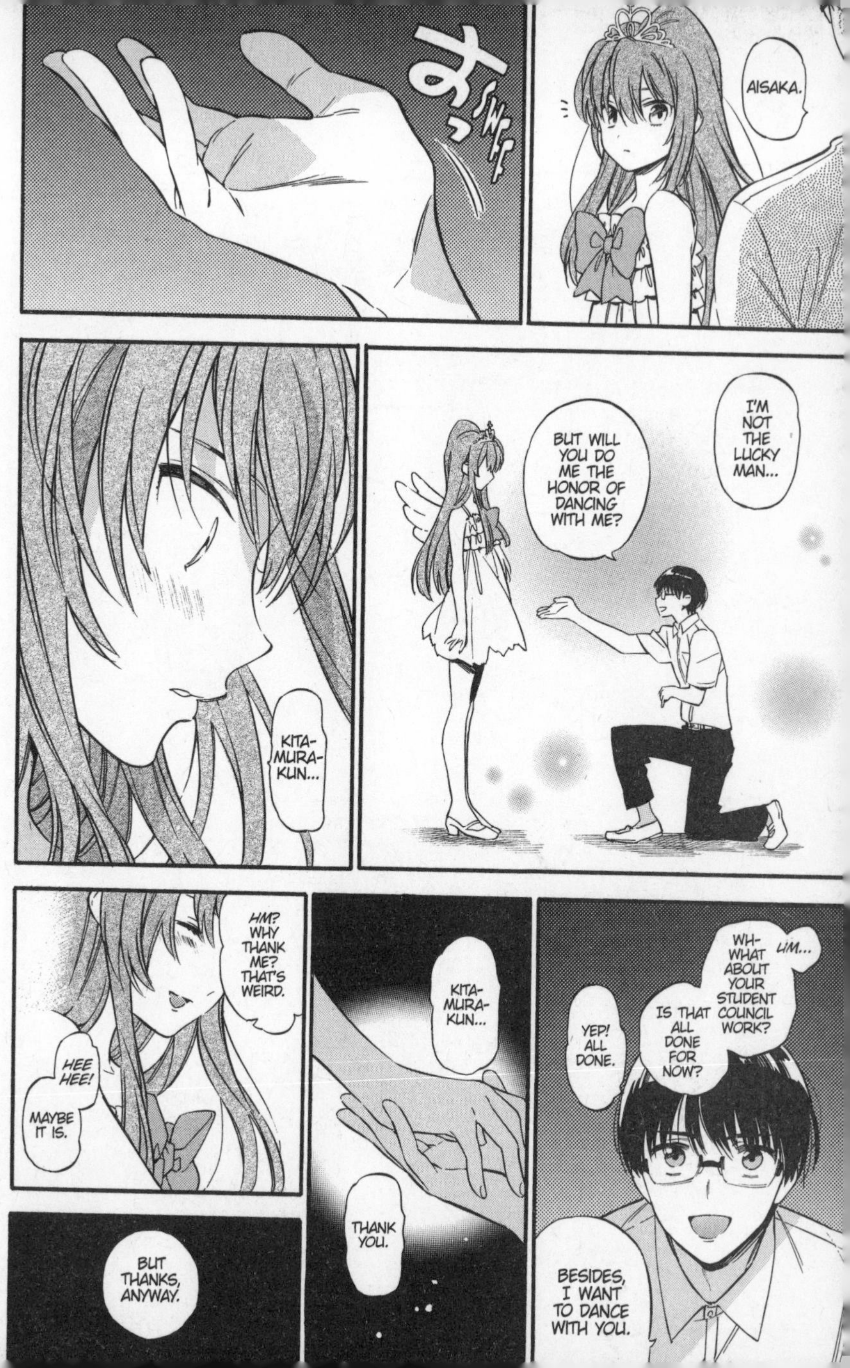
AISAKA.
SWEEP
I'M NOT THE LUCKY MAN...
BUT WILL YOU DO ME THE HONOR OF DANCING WITH ME?
KITA-MURA-KUN...
UM...
WH-WHAT ABOUT YOUR STUDENT COUNCIL WORK?
IS THAT ALL DONE FOR NOW?
YEP! ALL DONE.
BESIDES, I WANT TO DANCE WITH YOU.
KITA-MURA-KUN...
THANK YOU.
HM? WHY THANK ME? THAT'S WEIRD.
HEE HEE!
MAYBE IT IS.
BUT THANKS, ANYWAY.

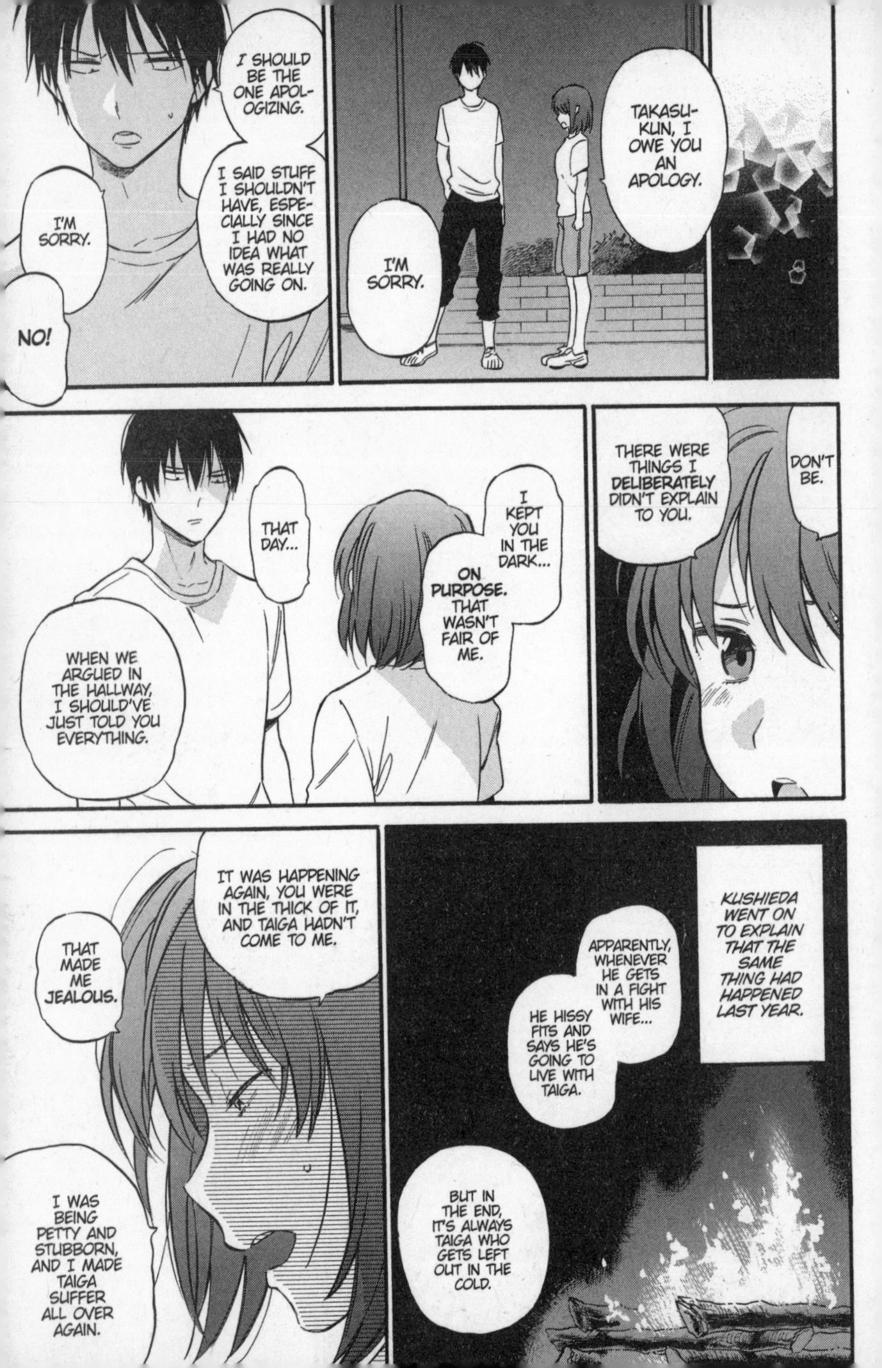
TAKASU-KUN, I OWE YOU AN APOLOGY.
I'M SORRY.
I SHOULD BE THE ONE APOLOGIZING.
I SAID STUFF I SHOULDN'T HAVE, ESPECIALLY SINCE I HAD NO IDEA WHAT WAS REALLY GOING ON.
I'M SORRY.
NO!
DON'T BE.
THERE WERE THINGS I DELIBERATELY DIDN'T EXPLAIN TO YOU.
I KEPT YOU IN THE DARK...
ON PURPOSE. THAT WASN'T FAIR OF ME.
THAT DAY...
WHEN WE ARGUED IN THE HALLWAY, I SHOULD'VE JUST TOLD YOU EVERYTHING.
KUSHIEDA WENT ON TO EXPLAIN THAT THE SAME THING HAD HAPPENED LAST YEAR.
APPARENTLY, WHENEVER HE GETS IN A FIGHT WITH HIS WIFE...
HE HISSY FITS AND SAYS HE'S GOING TO LIVE WITH TAIGA.
BUT IN THE END, IT'S ALWAYS TAIGA WHO GETS LEFT OUT IN THE COLD.
IT WAS HAPPENING AGAIN, YOU WERE IN THE THICK OF IT, AND TAIGA HADN'T COME TO ME.
THAT MADE ME JEALOUS.
I WAS BEING PETTY AND STUBBORN, AND I MADE TAIGA SUFFER ALL OVER AGAIN.

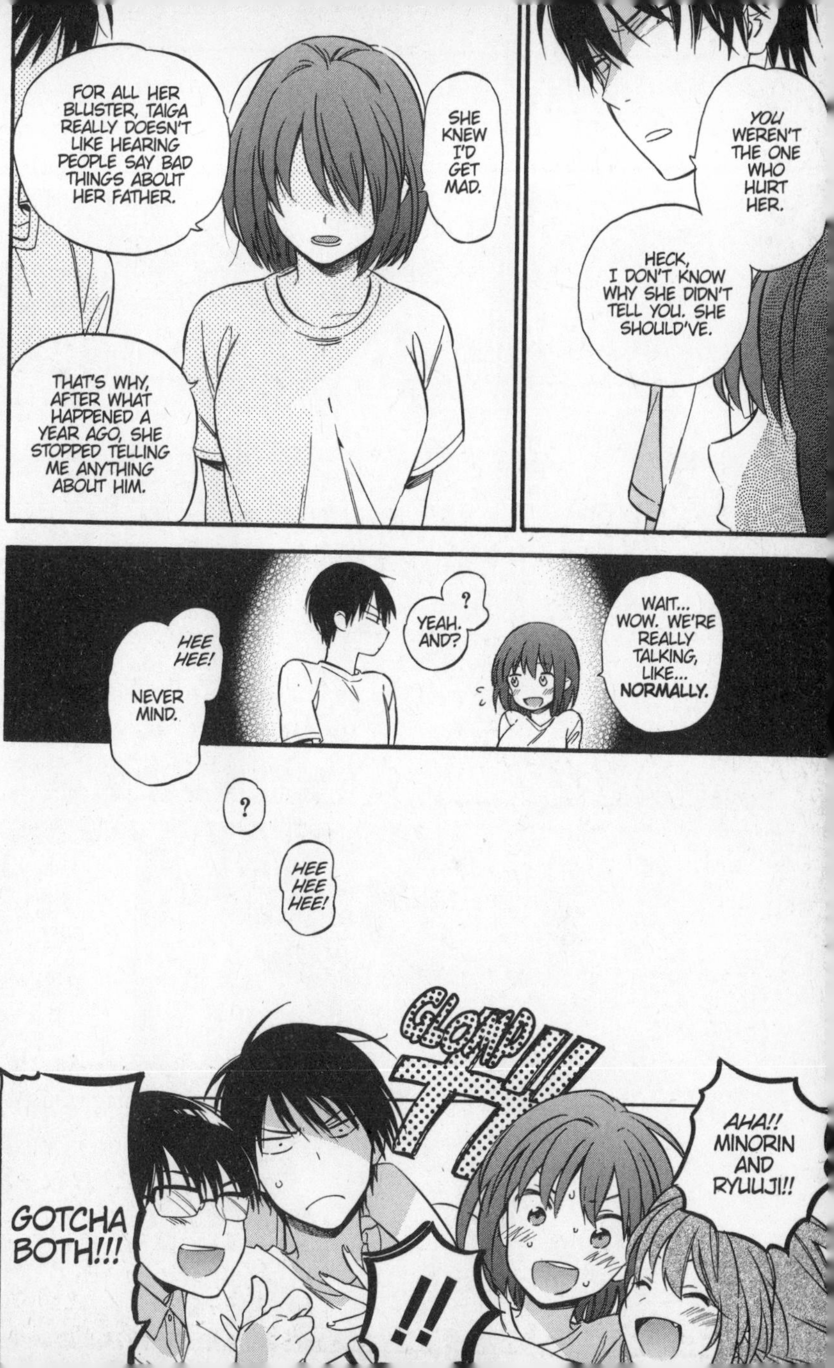
YOU WEREN'T THE ONE WHO HURT HER.
HECK, I DON'T KNOW WHY SHE DIDN'T TELL YOU. SHE SHOULD'VE.
SHE KNEW I'D GET MAD.
FOR ALL HER BLUSTER, TAIGA REALLY DOESN'T LIKE HEARING PEOPLE SAY BAD THINGS ABOUT HER FATHER.
THAT'S WHY, AFTER WHAT HAPPENED A YEAR AGO, SHE STOPPED TELLING ME ANYTHING ABOUT HIM.
WAIT... WOW. WE'RE REALLY TALKING, LIKE... NORMALLY.
?
YEAH. AND?
HEE HEE!
NEVER MIND.
?
HEE HEE HEE!
AHA!! MINORIN AND RYUUJI!!
GLOMP!!
!!
GOTCHA BOTH!!!

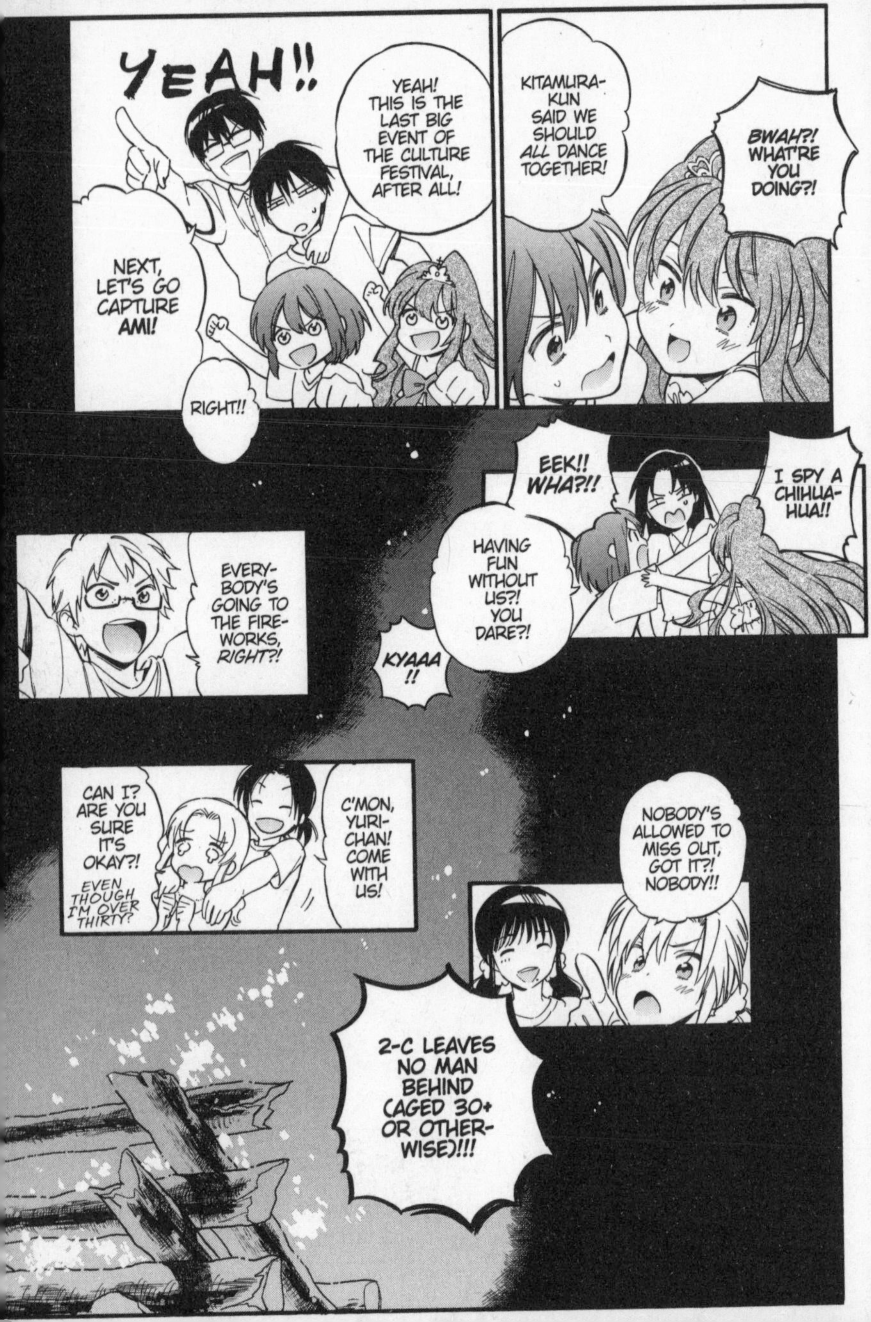
BWAH?! WHAT'RE YOU DOING?!
KITAMURA-KUN SAID WE SHOULD ALL DANCE TOGETHER!
YEAH! THIS IS THE LAST BIG EVENT OF THE CULTURE FESTIVAL, AFTER ALL!
YEAH!!
NEXT, LET'S GO CAPTURE AMI!
RIGHT!!
I SPY A CHIHUAHUA!!
EEK!! WHA?!!
HAVING FUN WITHOUT US?! YOU DARE?!
KYAAA!!
EVERYBODY'S GOING TO THE FIREWORKS, RIGHT?!
NOBODY'S ALLOWED TO MISS OUT, GOT IT?! NOBODY!!
C'MON, YURI-CHAN! COME WITH US!
CAN I? ARE YOU SURE IT'S OKAY?!
EVEN THOUGH I'M OVER THIRTY?
2-C LEAVES NO MAN BEHIND (AGED 30+ OR OTHERWISE)!!!

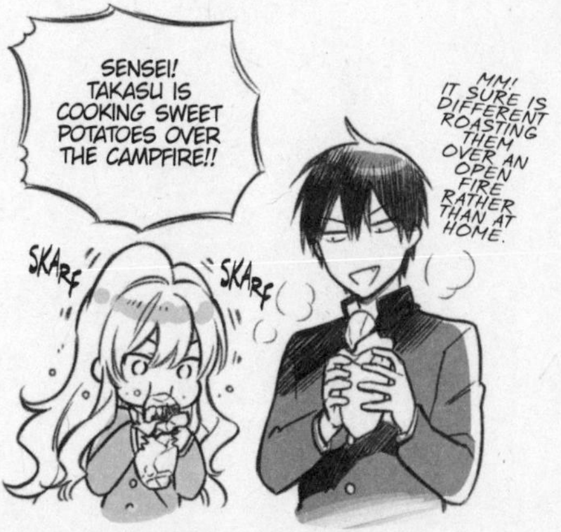
MM! IT SURE IS DIFFERENT ROASTING THEM OVER AN OPEN FIRE RATHER THAN AT HOME.
SENSEI! TAKASU IS COOKING SWEET POTATOES OVER THE CAMPFIRE!!
SKARF
SKARF

Chapter 59: THE TWO IN THE PICTURE

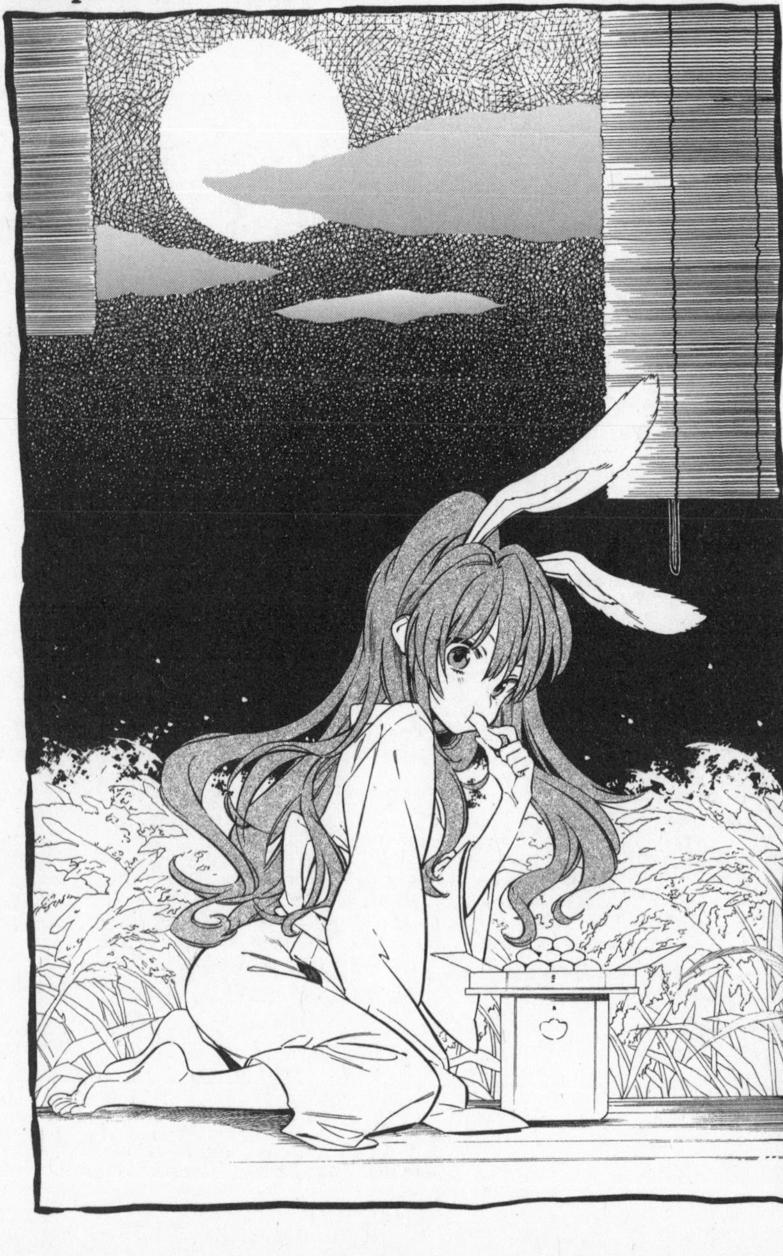

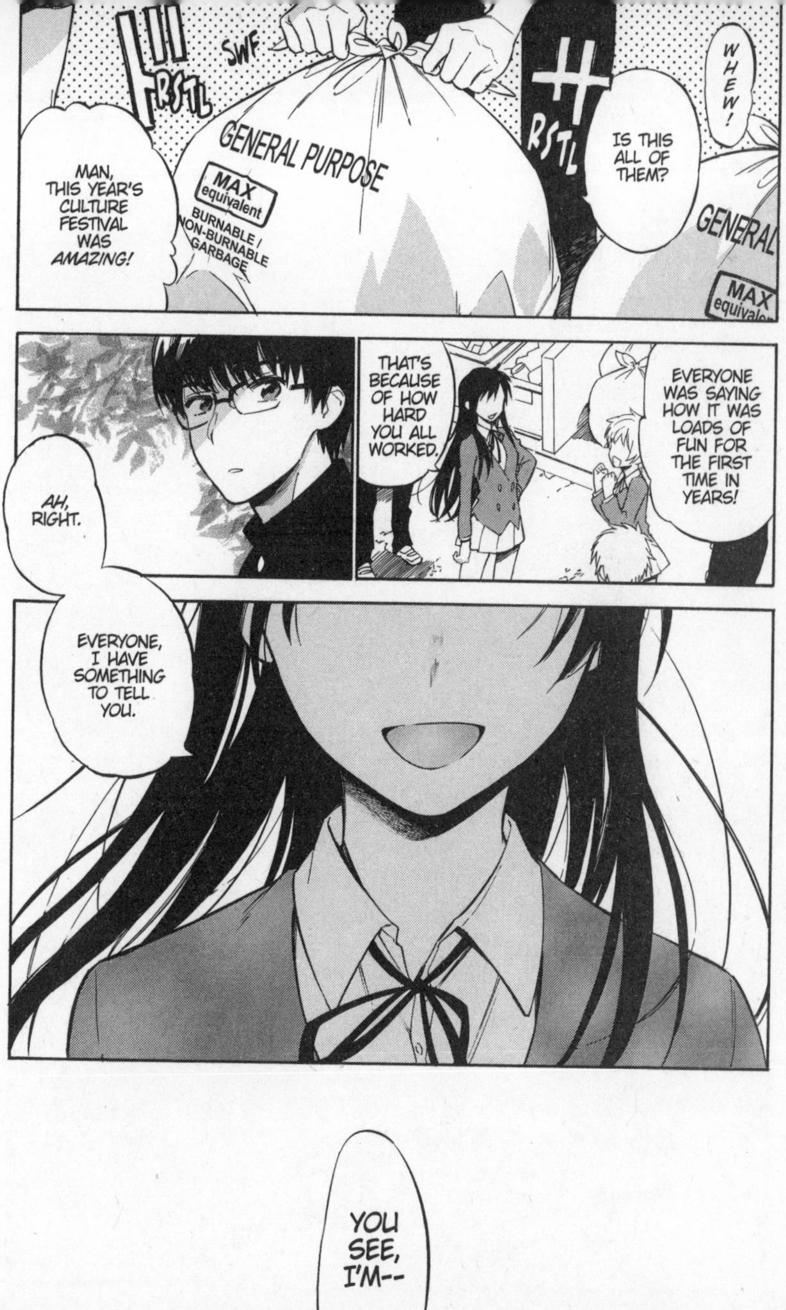
WHEW!
IS THIS ALL OF THEM?
RSTL
GENERAL
MAX equivalent
SWF
GENERAL PURPOSE
MAX equivalent
BURNABLE / NON-BURNABLE GARBAGE
RSTL
MAN, THIS YEAR'S CULTURE FESTIVAL WAS *AMAZING!*
EVERYONE WAS SAYING HOW IT WAS LOADS OF FUN FOR THE FIRST TIME IN YEARS!
THAT'S BECAUSE OF HOW HARD YOU ALL WORKED.
AH, RIGHT.
EVERYONE, I HAVE SOMETHING TO TELL YOU.
YOU SEE, I'M--

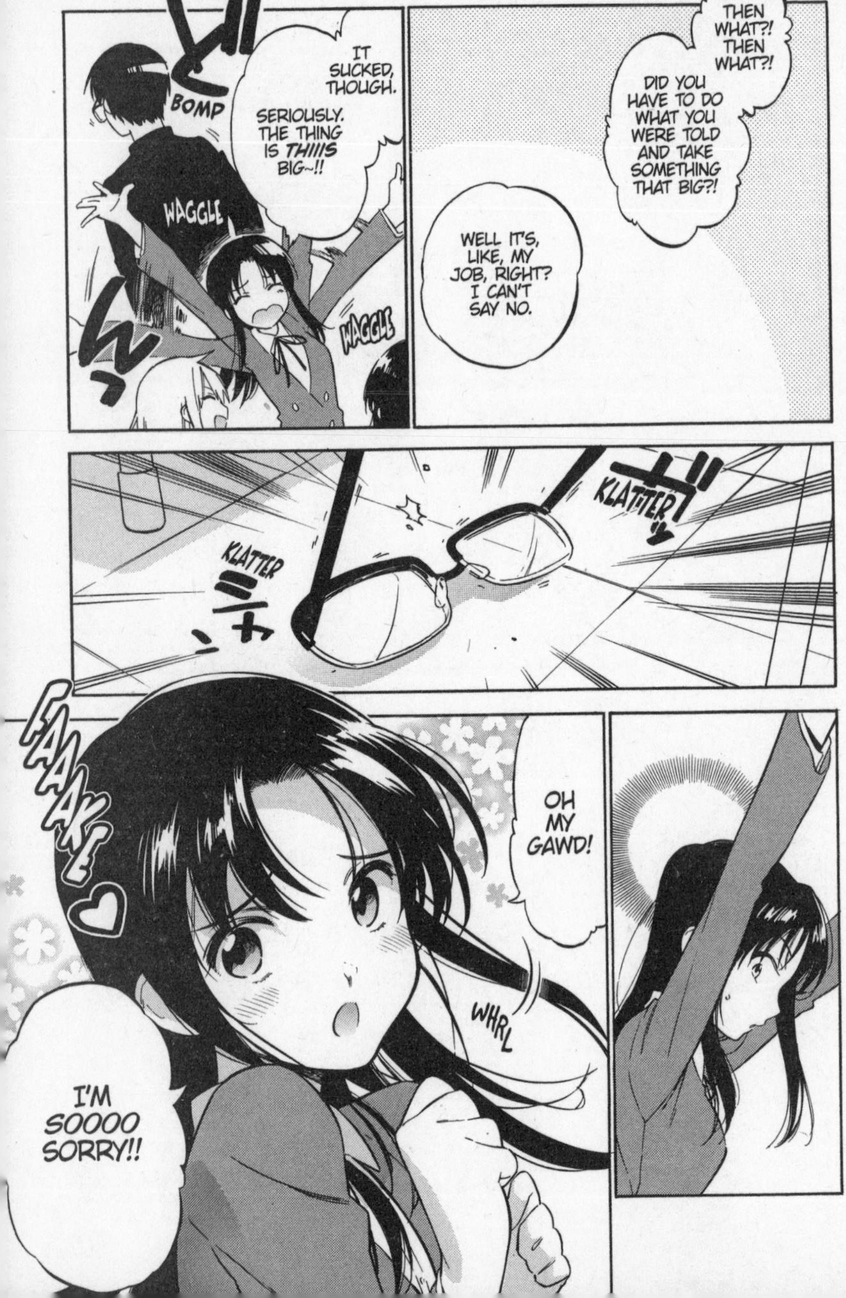
THEN WHAT?! THEN WHAT?!
DID YOU HAVE TO DO WHAT YOU WERE TOLD AND TAKE SOMETHING THAT BIG?!
WELL IT'S, LIKE, MY JOB, RIGHT? I CAN'T SAY NO.
IT SUCKED, THOUGH.
SERIOUSLY. THE THING IS THIIIS BIG~!!
BOMP
WAGGLE
WAGGLE
KLATTER
KLATTER
OH MY GAWD!
FAAAKE
WHRL
I'M SOOOO SORRY!!

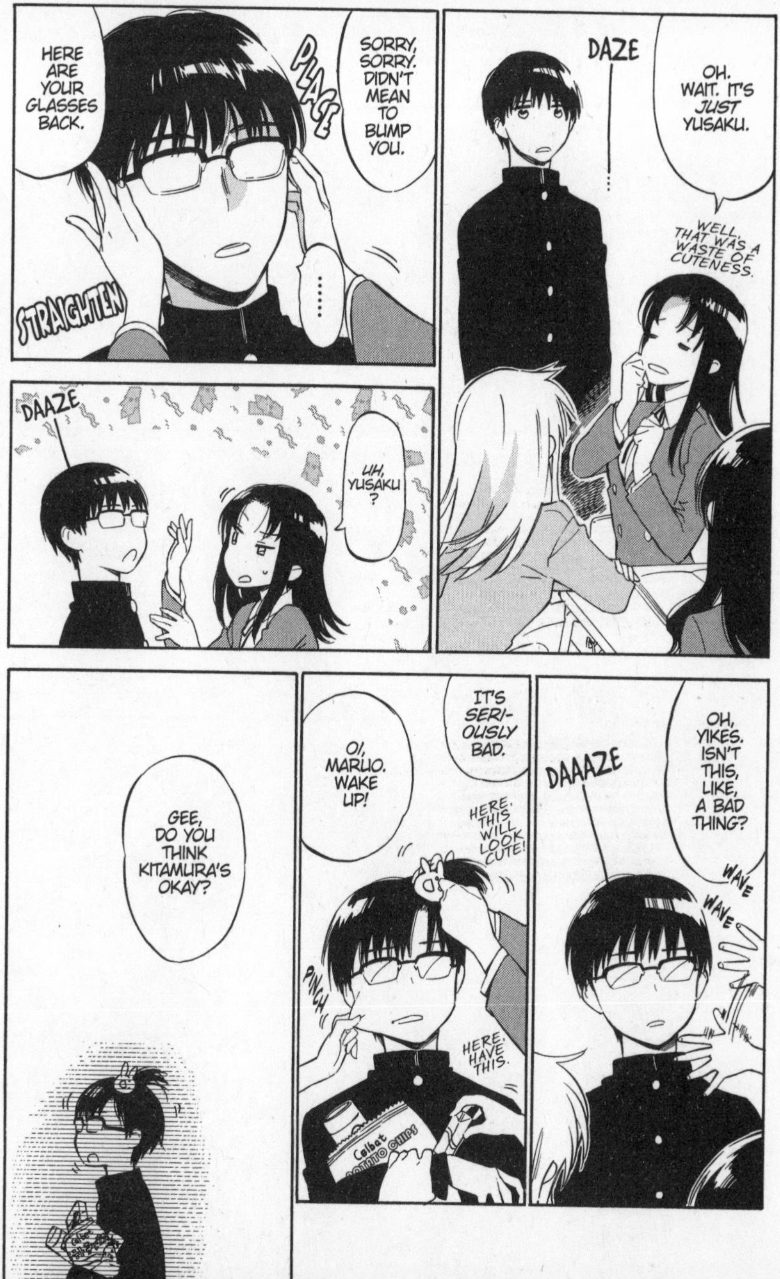
DAZE
OH. WAIT. IT'S JUST YUSAKU.
WELL, THAT WAS A WASTE OF CUTENESS.
SORRY, SORRY. DIDN'T MEAN TO BUMP YOU.
PLACE
HERE ARE YOUR GLASSES BACK.
......
STRAIGHTEN
UH, YUSAKU?
DAAZE
OH, YIKES. ISN'T THIS, LIKE, A BAD THING?
DAAAZE
WAVE
WAVE
IT'S SERIOUSLY BAD.
OI, MARUO. WAKE UP!
HERE. THIS WILL LOOK CUTE!
PINCH
HERE, HAVE THIS.
GEE, DO YOU THINK KITAMURA'S OKAY?

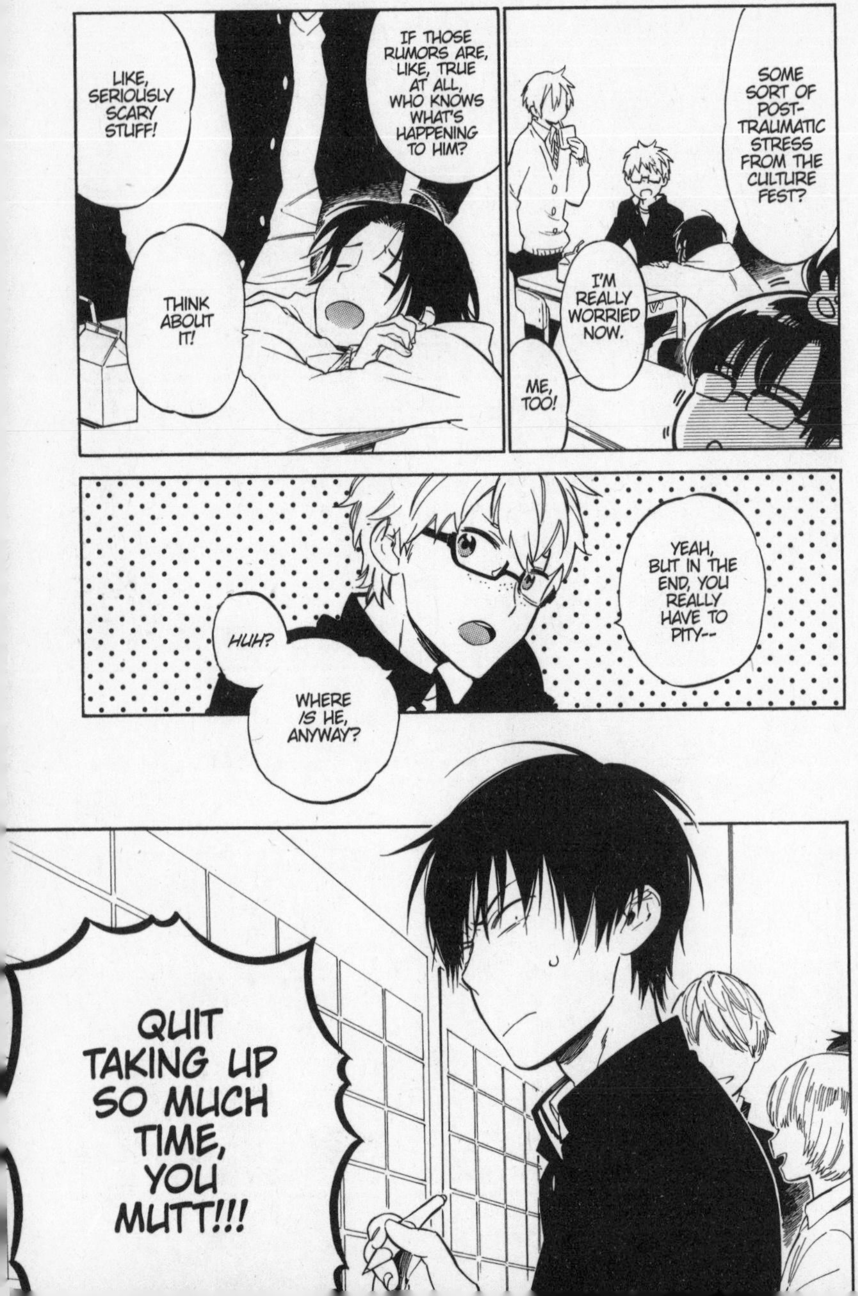
SOME SORT OF POST-TRAUMATIC STRESS FROM THE CULTURE FEST?
I'M REALLY WORRIED NOW.
ME, TOO!
IF THOSE RUMORS ARE, LIKE, TRUE AT ALL, WHO KNOWS WHAT'S HAPPENING TO HIM?
LIKE, SERIOUSLY SCARY STUFF!
THINK ABOUT IT!
YEAH, BUT IN THE END, YOU REALLY HAVE TO PITY--
HUH?
WHERE IS HE, ANYWAY?
QUIT TAKING UP SO MUCH TIME, YOU MUTT!!!

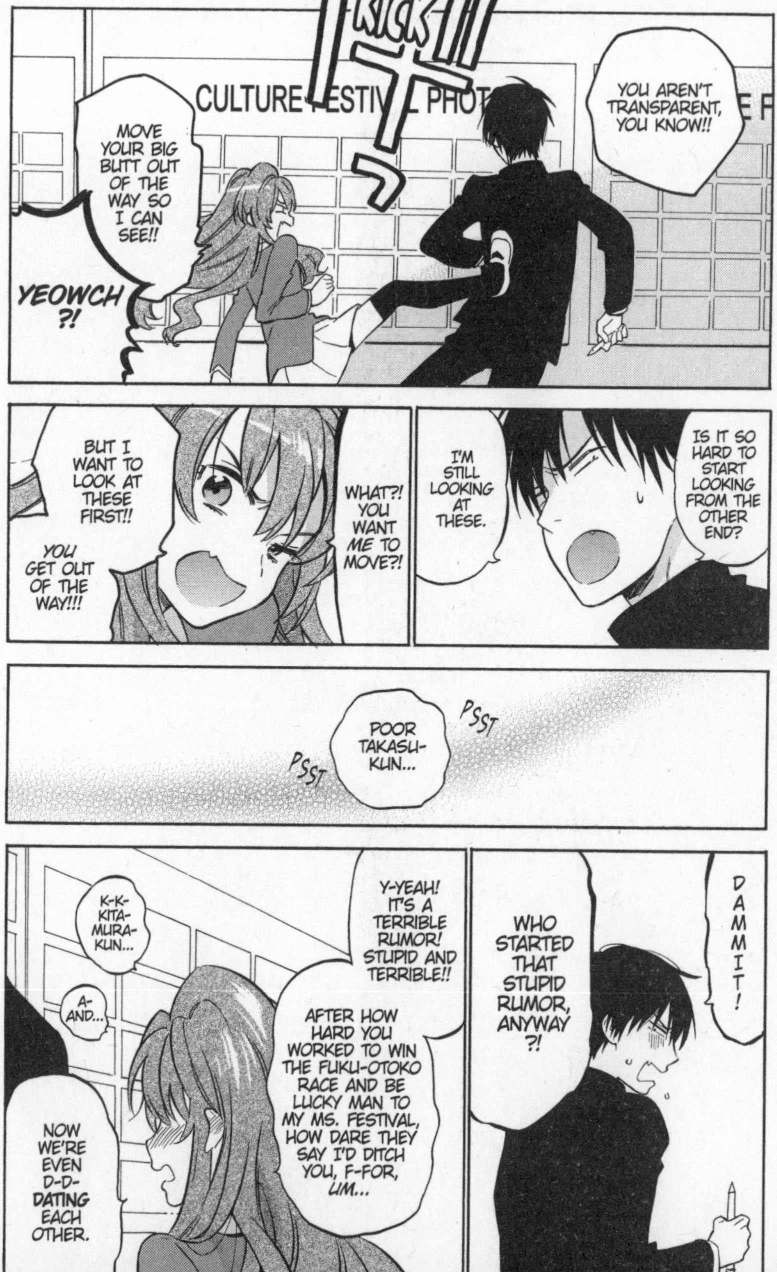
KICK
YOU AREN'T TRANSPARENT, YOU KNOW!!
MOVE YOUR BIG BUTT OUT OF THE WAY SO I CAN SEE!!
YEOWCH ?!
IS IT SO HARD TO START LOOKING FROM THE OTHER END?
I'M STILL LOOKING AT THESE.
WHAT?! YOU WANT *ME* TO MOVE?!
BUT I WANT TO LOOK AT THESE FIRST!!
YOU GET OUT OF THE WAY!!!
PSST
POOR TAKASU-KUN...
PSST
DAMMIT!
WHO STARTED THAT STUPID RUMOR, ANYWAY ?!
Y-YEAH! IT'S A TERRIBLE RUMOR! STUPID AND TERRIBLE!!
K-K-KITAMURA-KUN...
AFTER HOW HARD YOU WORKED TO WIN THE FUKU-OTOKO RACE AND BE LUCKY MAN TO MY MS. FESTIVAL, HOW DARE THEY SAY I'D DITCH YOU, F-FOR, *UM*...
A-AND...
NOW WE'RE EVEN D-D-DATING EACH OTHER.

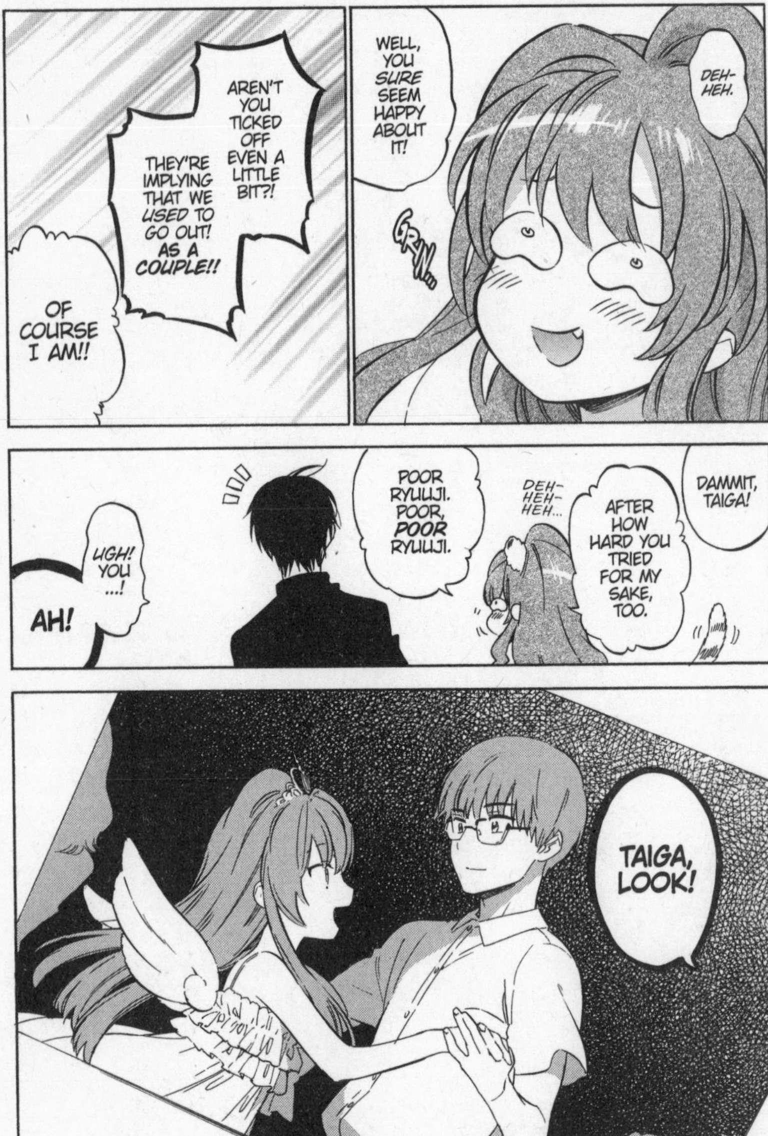
DEH-HEH.
WELL, YOU SURE SEEM HAPPY ABOUT IT!
GRIN...
AREN'T YOU TICKED OFF EVEN A LITTLE BIT?!
THEY'RE IMPLYING THAT WE USED TO GO OUT! AS A COUPLE!!
OF COURSE I AM!!
DAMMIT, TAIGA!
AFTER HOW HARD YOU TRIED FOR MY SAKE, TOO.
DEH-HEH-HEH...
POOR RYUUJI. POOR, POOR RYUUJI.
UGH! YOU ...!
AH!
TAIGA, LOOK!

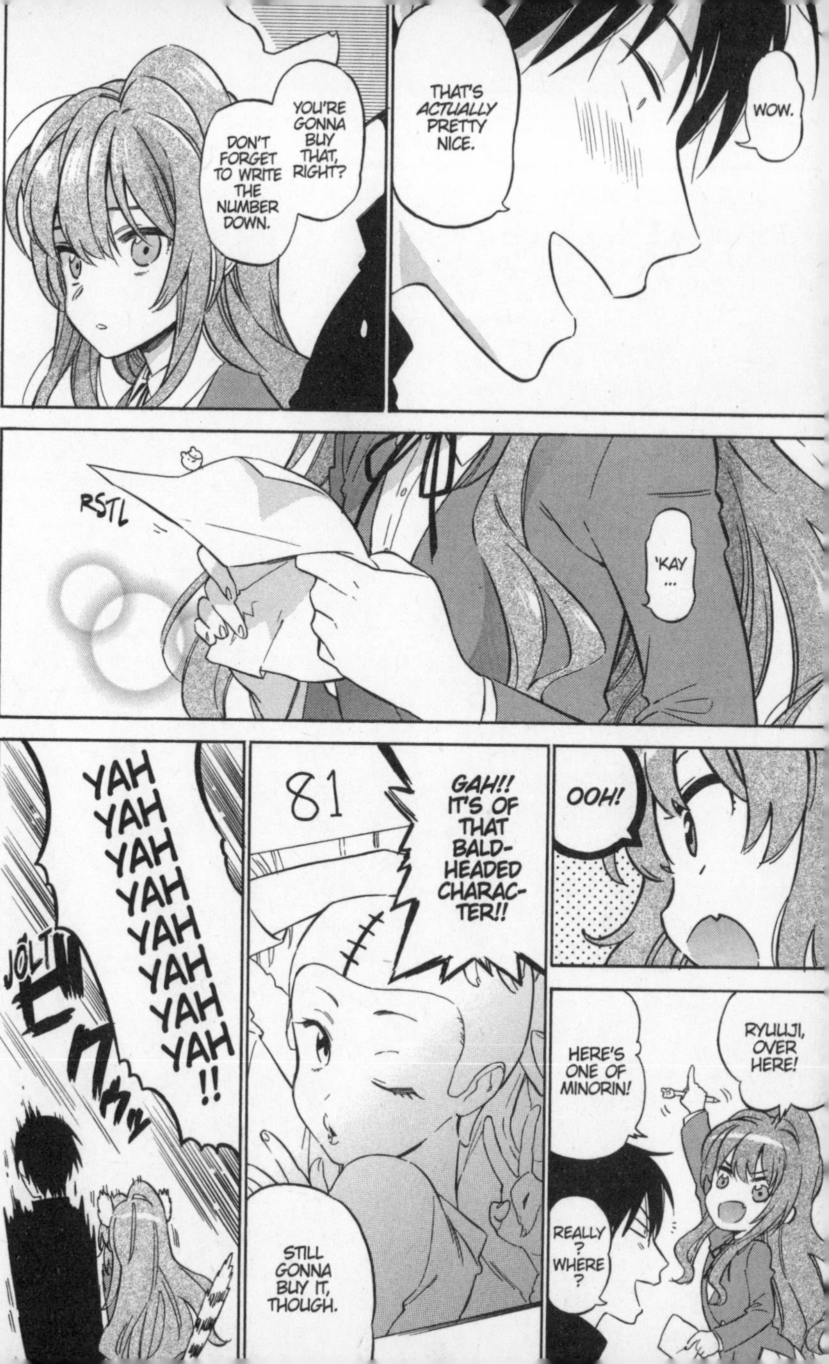
WOW.
THAT'S ACTUALLY PRETTY NICE.
YOU'RE GONNA BUY THAT, RIGHT?
DON'T FORGET TO WRITE THE NUMBER DOWN.
'KAY...
RSTL
OOH!
RYUUJI, OVER HERE!
HERE'S ONE OF MINORIN!
REALLY? WHERE?
81
GAH!! IT'S OF THAT BALD-HEADED CHARACTER!!
STILL GONNA BUY IT, THOUGH.
YAH YAH YAH YAH YAH YAH YAH YAH!!
JOLT

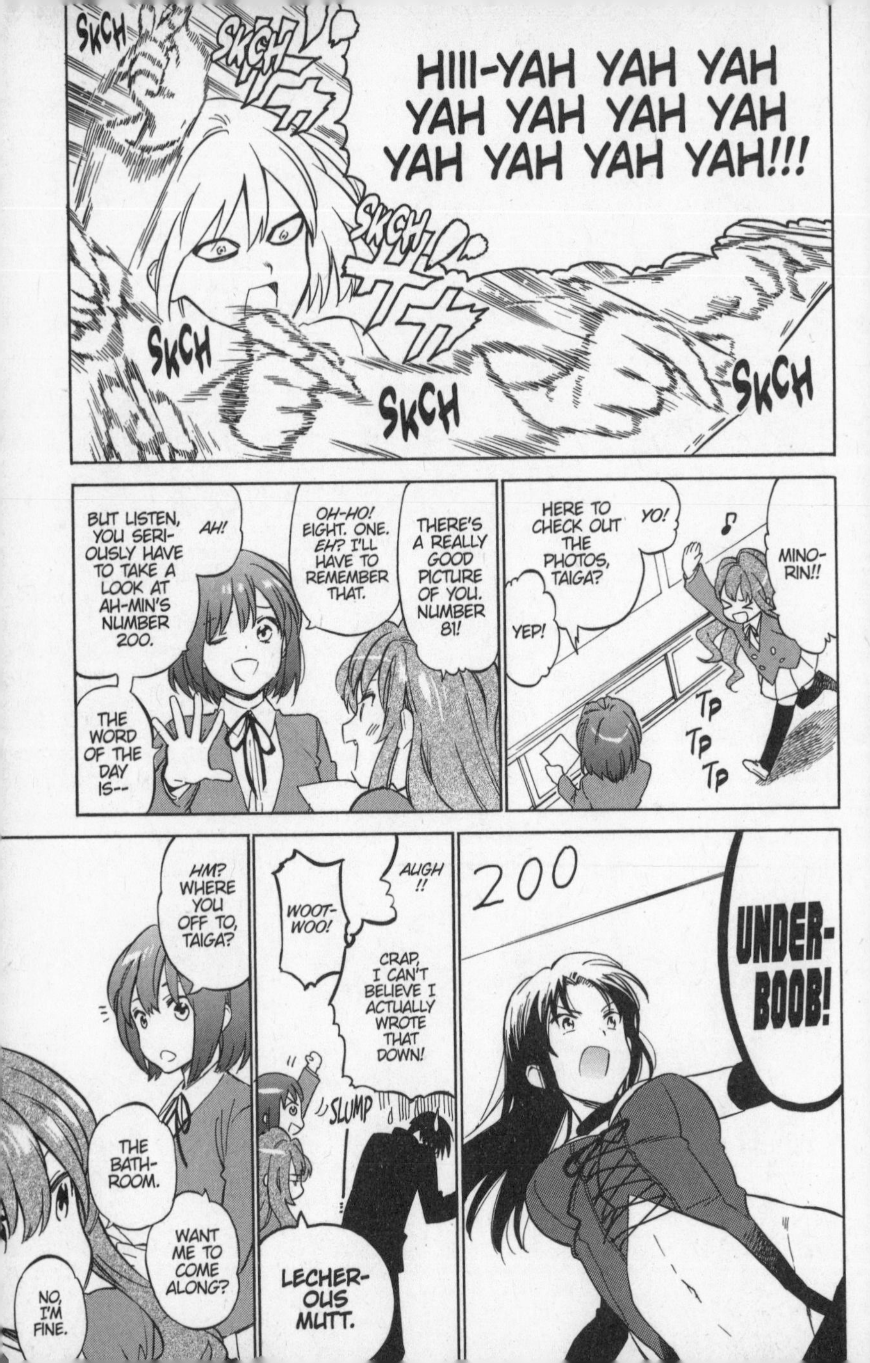

HIII-YAH YAH YAH YAH YAH YAH YAH YAH YAH YAH YAH!!!
SKCH
SKCH
SKCH
SKCH
SKCH
SKCH
MINO-RIN!!
YO!
HERE TO CHECK OUT THE PHOTOS, TAIGA?
YEP!
TP TP TP
THERE'S A REALLY GOOD PICTURE OF YOU. NUMBER 81!
OH-HO! EIGHT. ONE. EH? I'LL HAVE TO REMEMBER THAT.
AH!
BUT LISTEN, YOU SERIOUSLY HAVE TO TAKE A LOOK AT AH-MIN'S NUMBER 200.
THE WORD OF THE DAY IS--
200
UNDER-BOOB!
AUGH!!
WOOT-WOO!
CRAP, I CAN'T BELIEVE I ACTUALLY WROTE THAT DOWN!
SLUMP
LECHEROUS MUTT.
HM? WHERE YOU OFF TO, TAIGA?
THE BATHROOM.
WANT ME TO COME ALONG?
NO, I'M FINE.

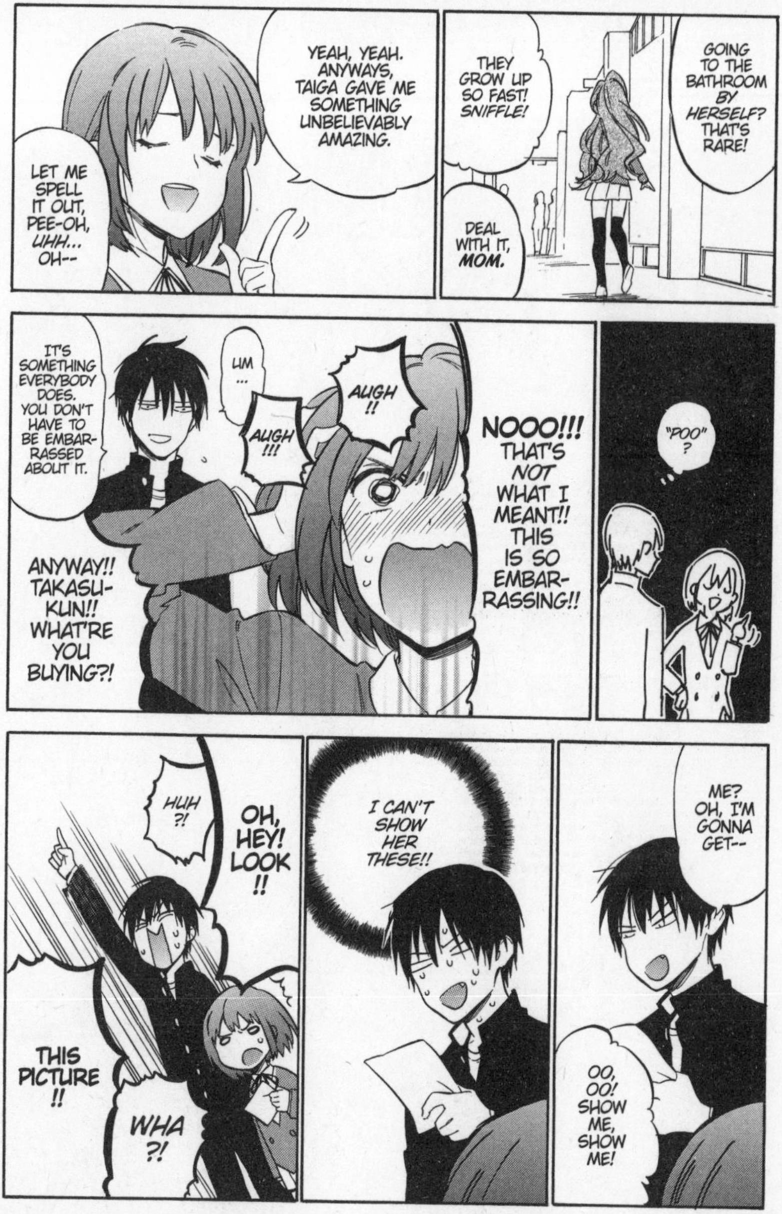
GOING TO THE BATHROOM BY HERSELF? THAT'S RARE!
THEY GROW UP SO FAST! SNIFFLE!
DEAL WITH IT, MOM.
YEAH, YEAH. ANYWAYS, TAIGA GAVE ME SOMETHING UNBELIEVABLY AMAZING.
LET ME SPELL IT OUT, PEE-OH, UHH... OH--
"POO"?
NOOO!!! THAT'S NOT WHAT I MEANT!! THIS IS SO EMBARRASSING!!
AUGH!!
AUGH!!!
UM...
IT'S SOMETHING EVERYBODY DOES. YOU DON'T HAVE TO BE EMBARRASSED ABOUT IT.
ANYWAY!! TAKASU-KUN!! WHAT'RE YOU BUYING?!
ME? OH, I'M GONNA GET--
OO, OO! SHOW ME, SHOW ME!
I CAN'T SHOW HER THESE!!
OH, HEY! LOOK!!
HUH?!
THIS PICTURE!!
WHA?!

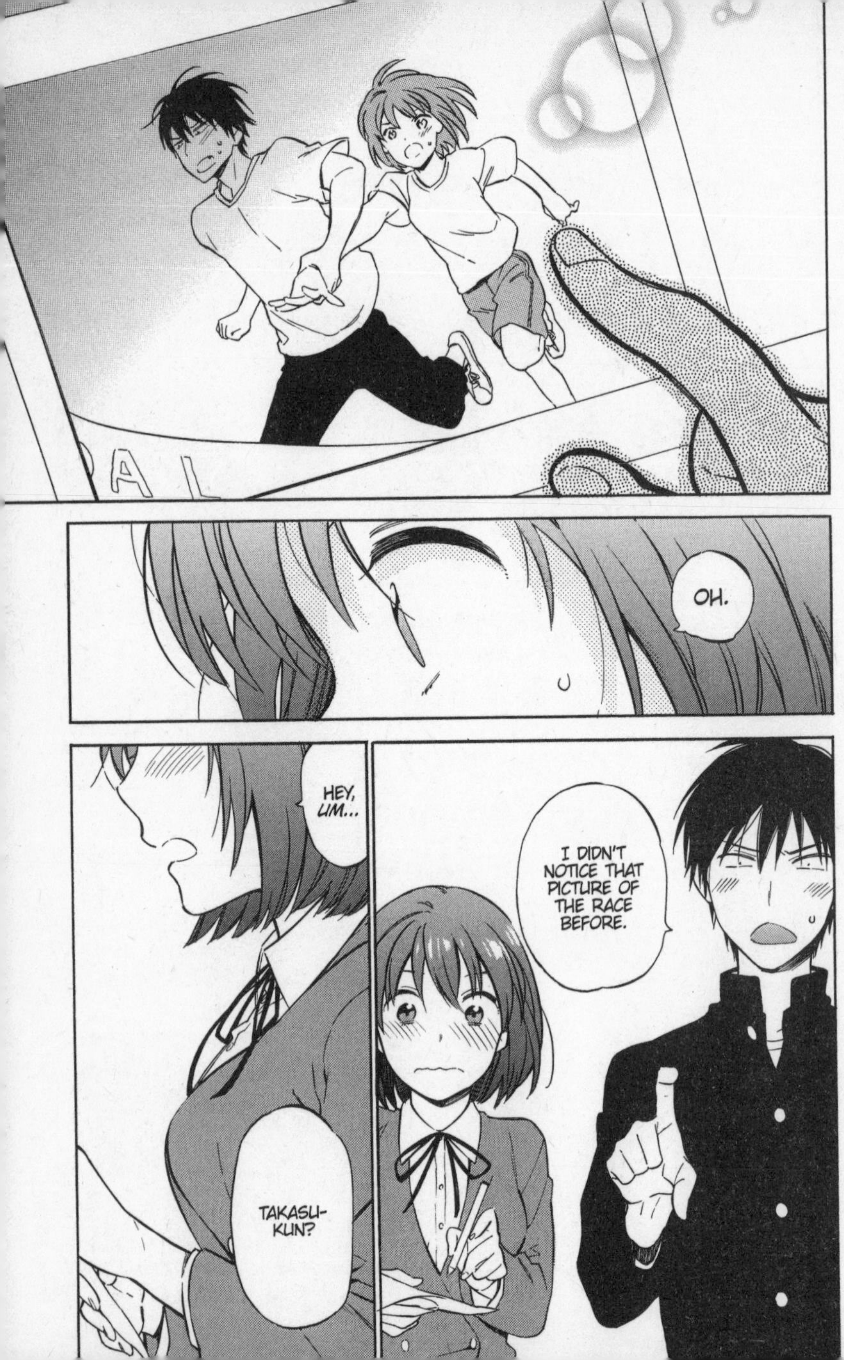
OH.
I DIDN'T NOTICE THAT PICTURE OF THE RACE BEFORE.
HEY, UM...
TAKASU-KUN?

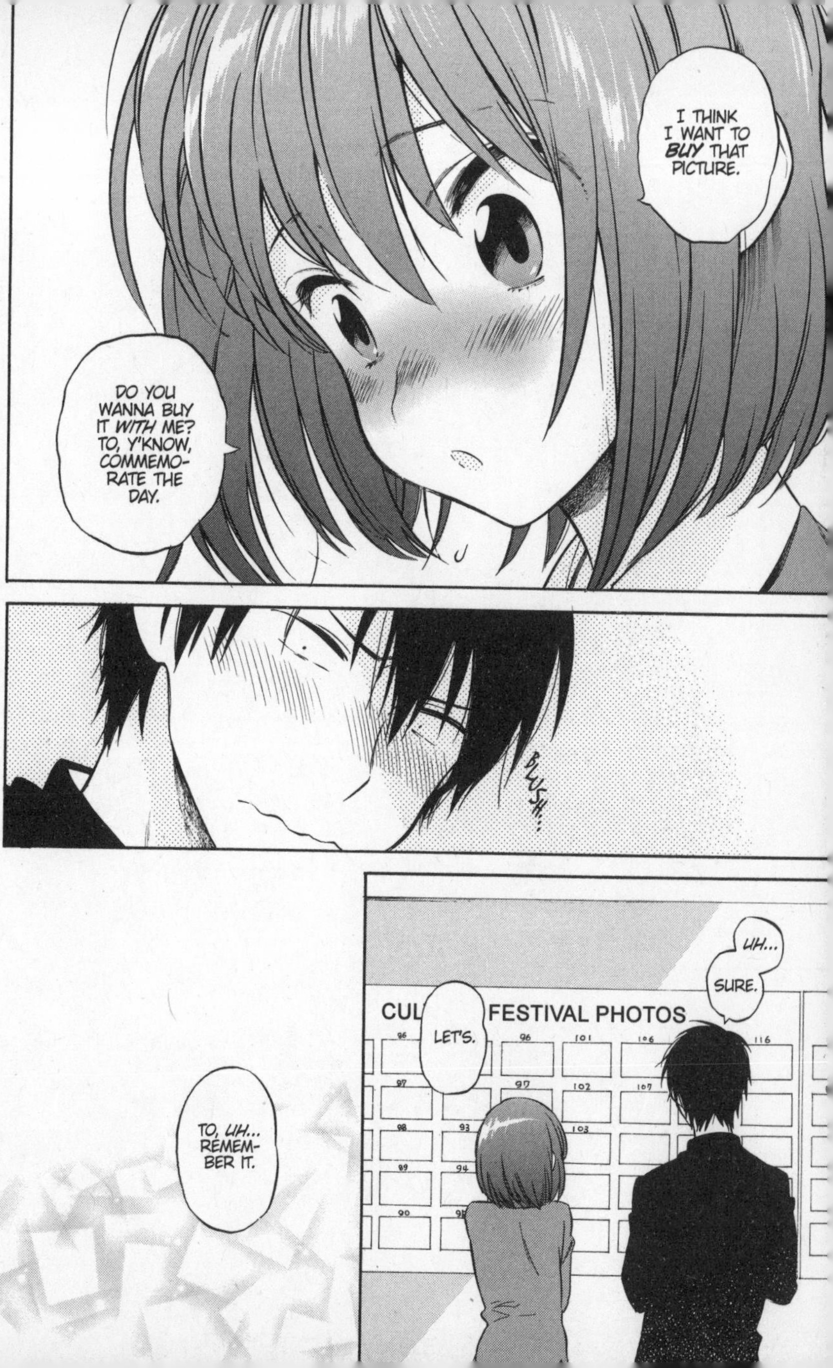
I THINK I WANT TO *BUY* THAT PICTURE.
DO YOU WANNA BUY IT *WITH* ME? TO, Y'KNOW, COMMEMO-RATE THE DAY.
BLUSH...
UH... SURE.
LET'S.
CUL FESTIVAL PHOTOS
TO, *UH*... REMEMB-BER IT.

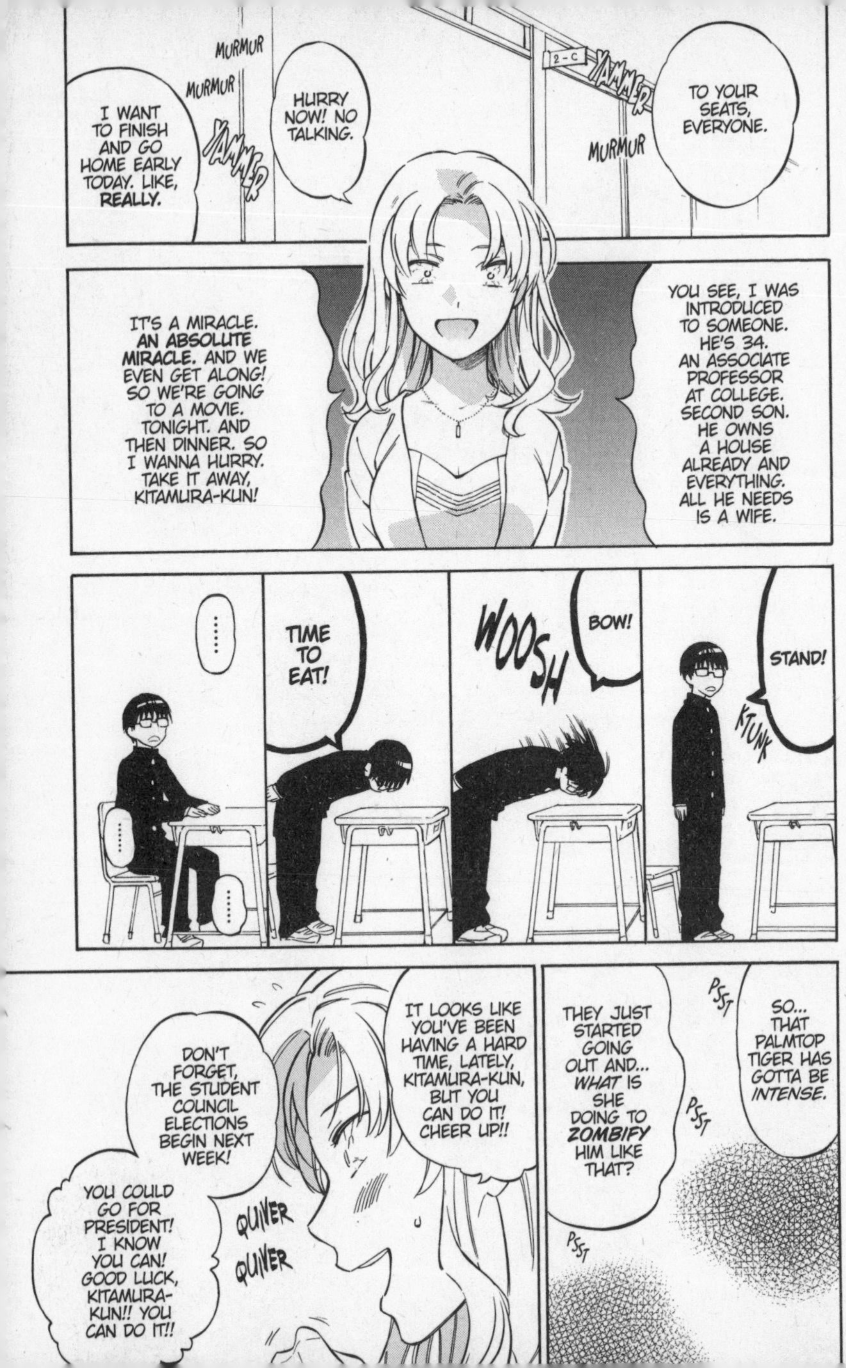
TO YOUR SEATS, EVERYONE.
2-C
YAMMER
MURMUR
HURRY NOW! NO TALKING.
MURMUR
MURMUR
YAMMER
I WANT TO FINISH AND GO HOME EARLY TODAY. LIKE, **REALLY.**
YOU SEE, I WAS INTRODUCED TO SOMEONE. HE'S 34. AN ASSOCIATE PROFESSOR AT COLLEGE. SECOND SON. HE OWNS A HOUSE ALREADY AND EVERYTHING. ALL HE NEEDS IS A WIFE.
IT'S A MIRACLE. **AN ABSOLUTE MIRACLE.** AND WE EVEN GET ALONG! SO WE'RE GOING TO A MOVIE. TONIGHT. AND THEN DINNER. SO I WANNA HURRY. TAKE IT AWAY, KITAMURA-KUN!
STAND!
KTUNK
BOW!
WOOSH
TIME TO EAT!
......
......
......
PSST
SO... THAT PALMTOP TIGER HAS GOTTA BE *INTENSE.*
THEY JUST STARTED GOING OUT AND... *WHAT* IS SHE DOING TO **ZOMBIFY** HIM LIKE THAT?
PSST
PSST
IT LOOKS LIKE YOU'VE BEEN HAVING A HARD TIME, LATELY, KITAMURA-KUN, BUT YOU CAN DO IT! CHEER UP!!
DON'T FORGET, THE STUDENT COUNCIL ELECTIONS BEGIN NEXT WEEK!
QUIVER
QUIVER
YOU COULD GO FOR PRESIDENT! I KNOW YOU CAN! GOOD LUCK, KITAMURA-KUN!! YOU CAN DO IT!!

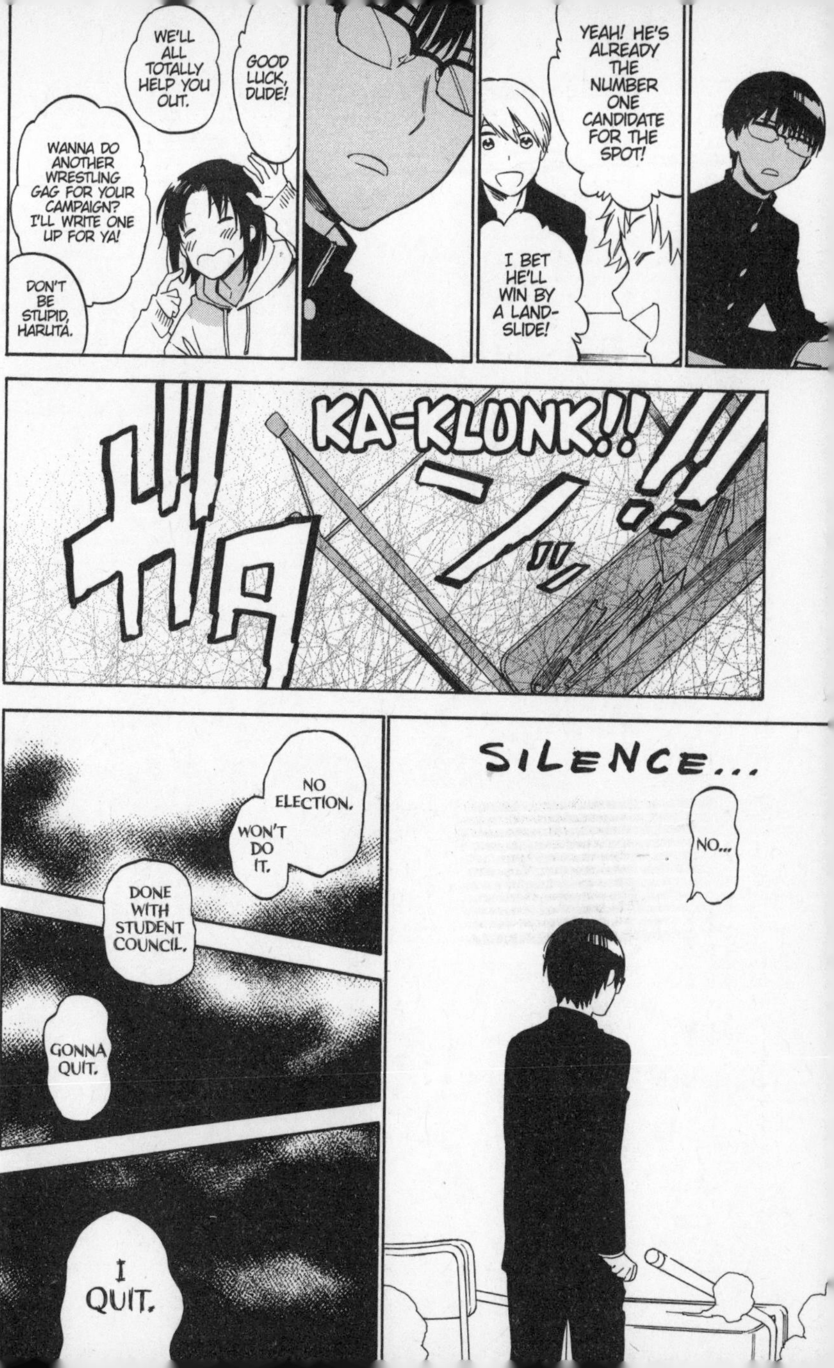
YEAH! HE'S ALREADY THE NUMBER ONE CANDIDATE FOR THE SPOT!
I BET HE'LL WIN BY A LAND-SLIDE!
GOOD LUCK, DUDE!
WE'LL ALL TOTALLY HELP YOU OUT.
WANNA DO ANOTHER WRESTLING GAG FOR YOUR CAMPAIGN? I'LL WRITE ONE UP FOR YA!
DON'T BE STUPID, HARUTA.
KA-KLUNK!!
SILENCE...
NO...
NO ELECTION.
WON'T DO IT.
DONE WITH STUDENT COUNCIL.
GONNA QUIT.
I QUIT.

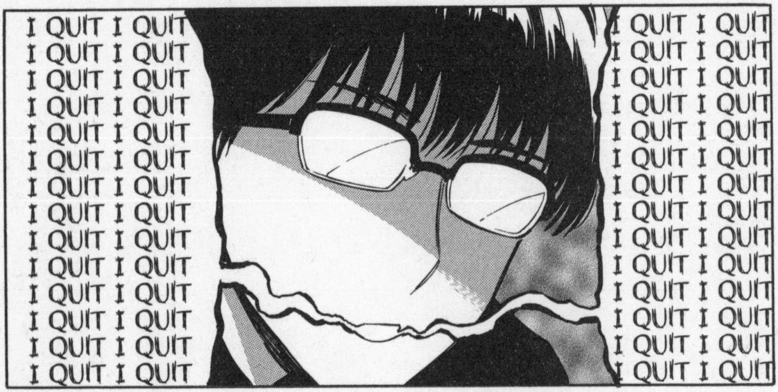
I QUIT I QUIT
I QUIT I QUIT
I QUIT I QUIT
I QUIT I QUIT
I QUIT I QUIT
I QUIT I QUIT
I QUIT I QUIT
I QUIT I QUIT
I QUIT I QUIT
I QUIT I QUIT
I QUIT I QUIT
I QUIT I QUIT
I QUIT I QUIT
I QUIT I QUIT
I QUIT I QUIT
I QUIT I QUIT
I QUIT I QUIT
I QUIT I QUIT
I QUIT I QUIT
I QUIT I QUIT
I QUIT I QUIT
I QUIT I QUIT
I QUIT I QUIT
I QUIT I QUIT
I QUIT I QUIT
I QUIT I QUIT
I QUIT I QUIT
I QUIT I QUIT

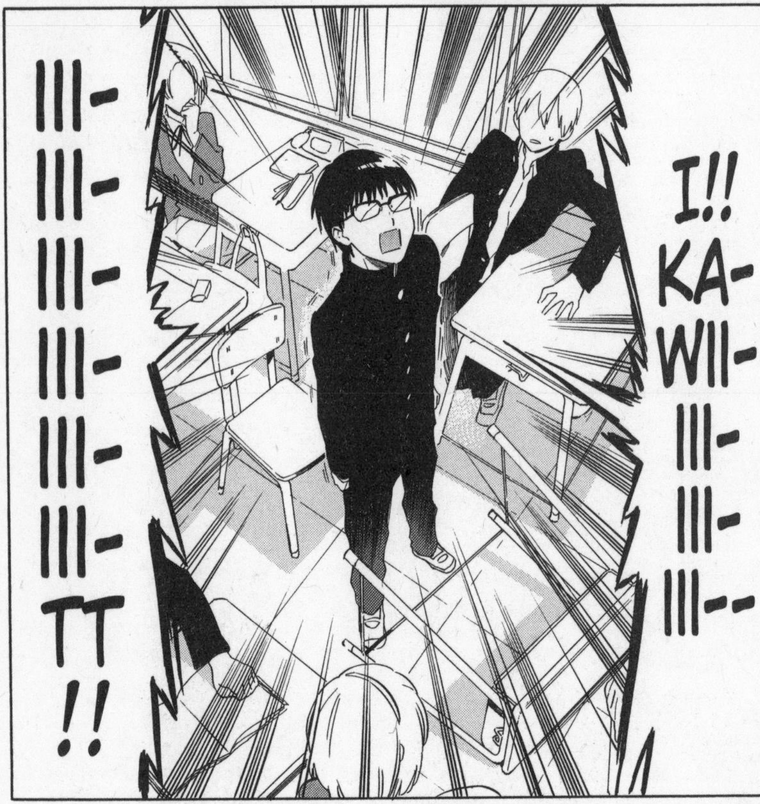
I!! KA-WII-III-III-III--
III-III-III-III-III-III-TT!!

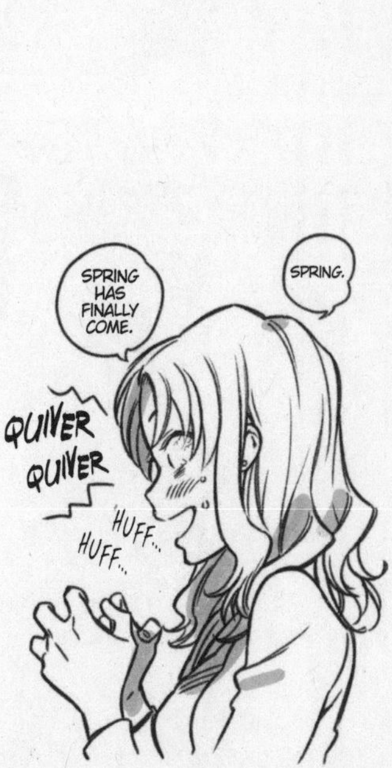
SPRING.
SPRING HAS FINALLY COME.
QUIVER QUIVER
HUFF... HUFF...

Chapter 60: YOU LOOK STUPID

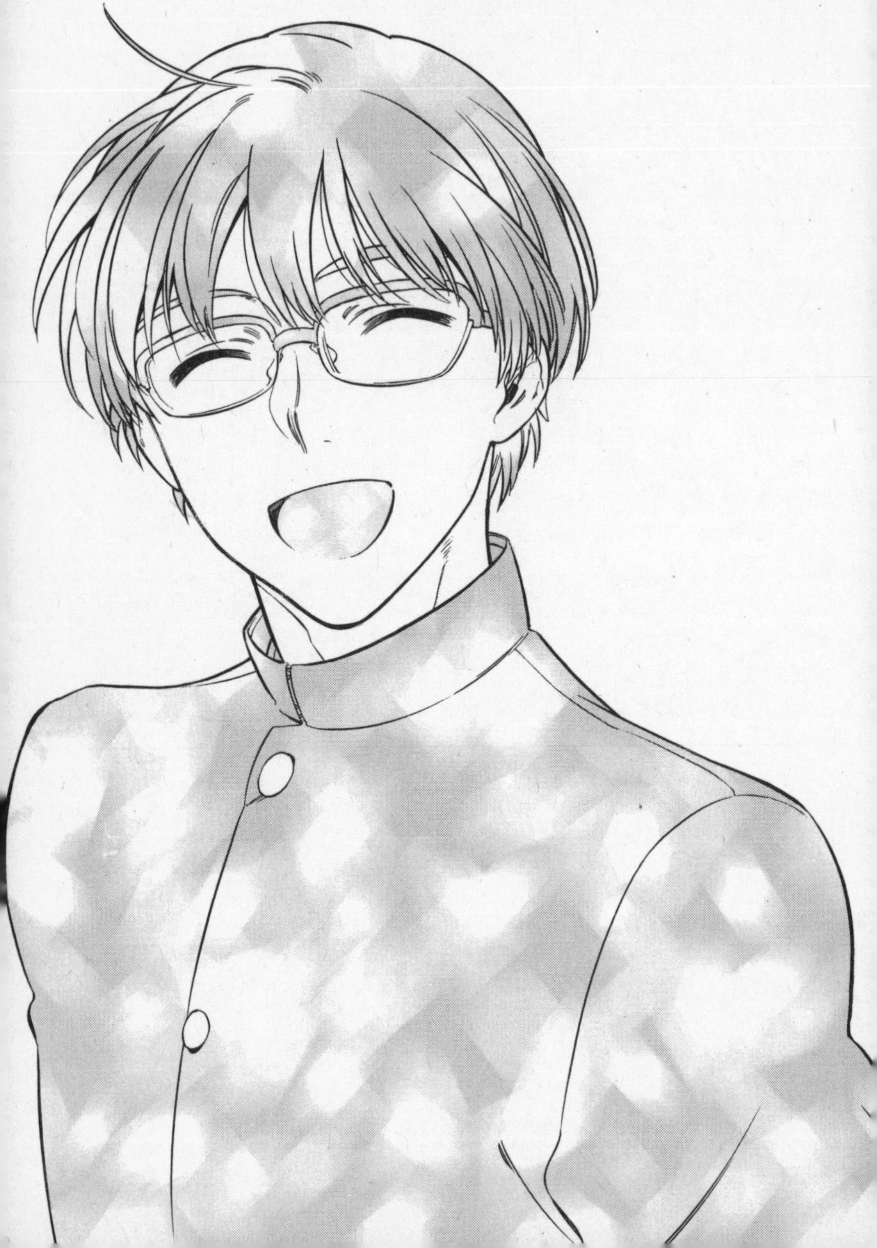

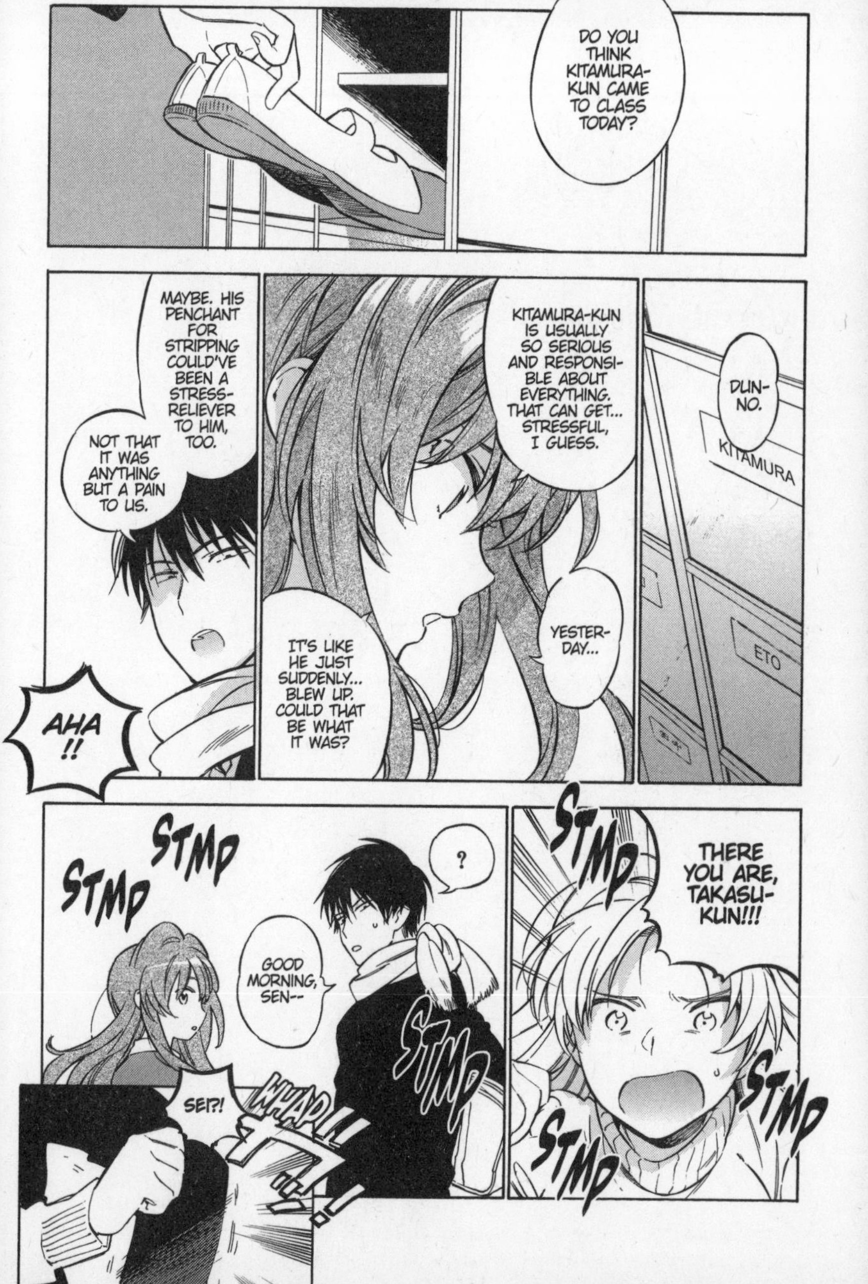
DO YOU THINK KITAMURA-KUN CAME TO CLASS TODAY?
DUN-NO.
KITAMURA
ETO
KITAMURA-KUN IS USUALLY SO SERIOUS AND RESPONSIBLE ABOUT EVERYTHING. THAT CAN GET... STRESSFUL, I GUESS.
YESTERDAY...
IT'S LIKE HE JUST SUDDENLY... BLEW UP. COULD THAT BE WHAT IT WAS?
MAYBE. HIS PENCHANT FOR STRIPPING COULD'VE BEEN A STRESS-RELIEVER TO HIM, TOO.
NOT THAT IT WAS ANYTHING BUT A PAIN TO US.
AHA!!
STMP
THERE YOU ARE, TAKASU-KUN!!!
STMP
STMP
?
STMP
STMP
GOOD MORNING, SEN--
STMP
SEI?!
WHAP!!

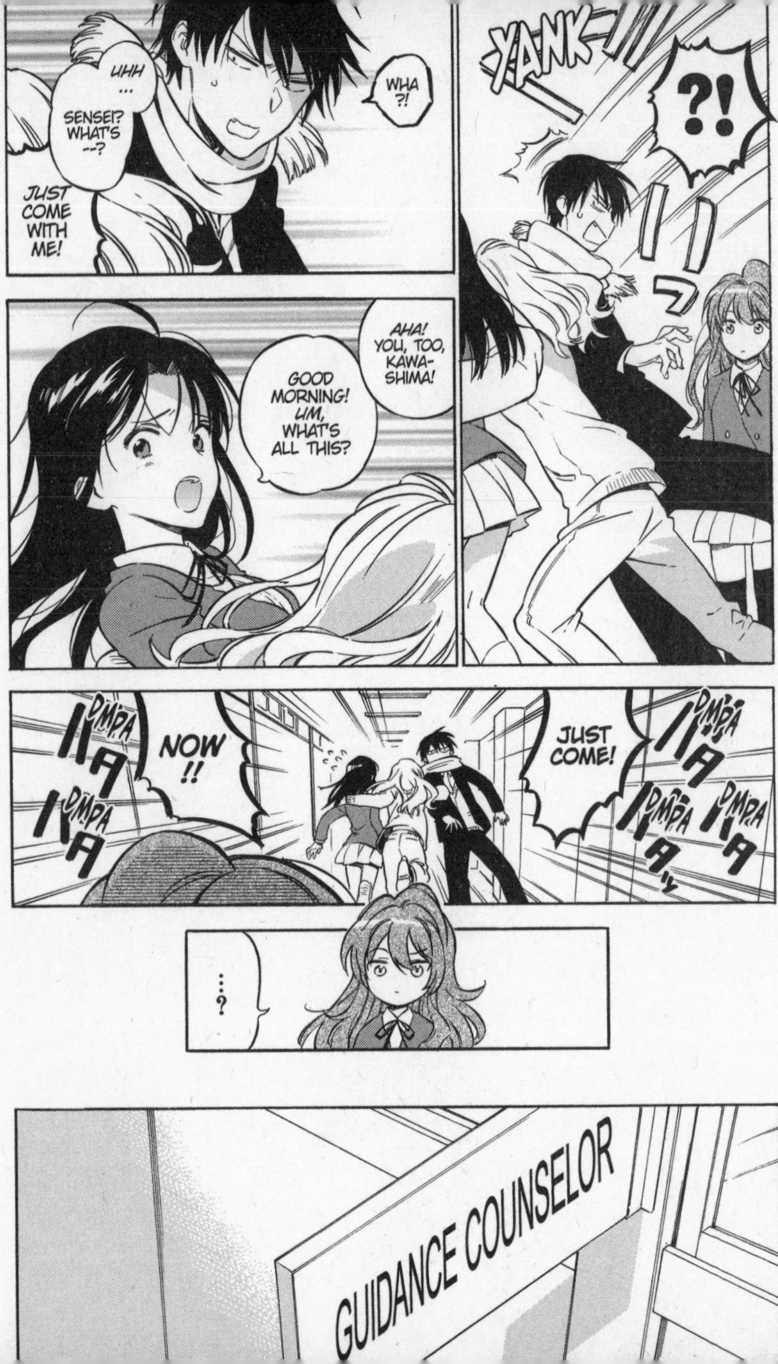
YANK
?!
WHA ?!
UHH ... SENSEI? WHAT'S --?
JUST COME WITH ME!
AHA! YOU, TOO, KAWA-SHIMA!
GOOD MORNING! UM, WHAT'S ALL THIS?
JUST COME!
DMPA
DMPA
DMPA
NOW !!
DMPA
DMPA
...?
GUIDANCE COUNSELOR

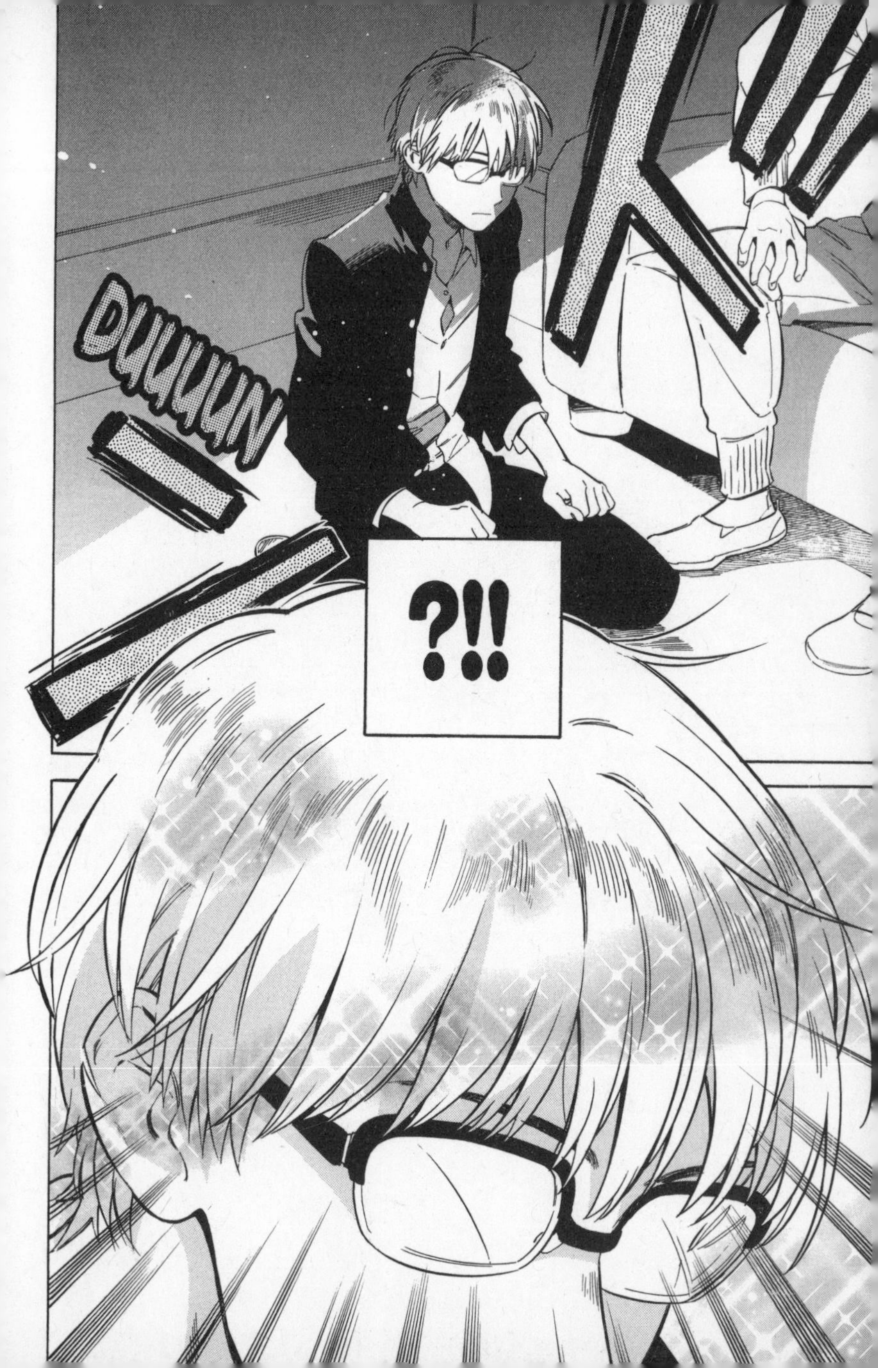
DUUUUN
?!!

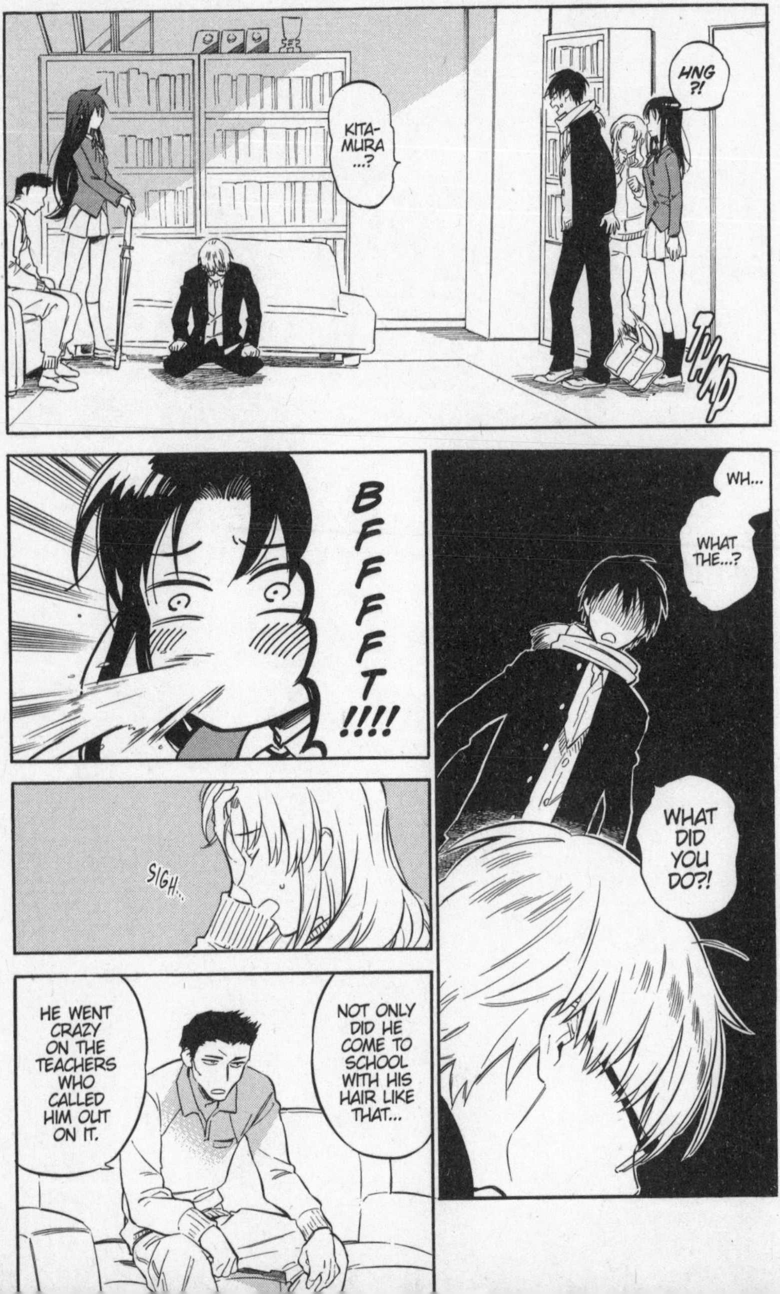
HNG ?!
THMP
KITA-MURA ...?
WH...
WHAT THE...?
WHAT DID YOU DO?!
BFFFFT !!!!
SIGH...
NOT ONLY DID HE COME TO SCHOOL WITH HIS HAIR LIKE THAT...
HE WENT CRAZY ON THE TEACHERS WHO CALLED HIM OUT ON IT.

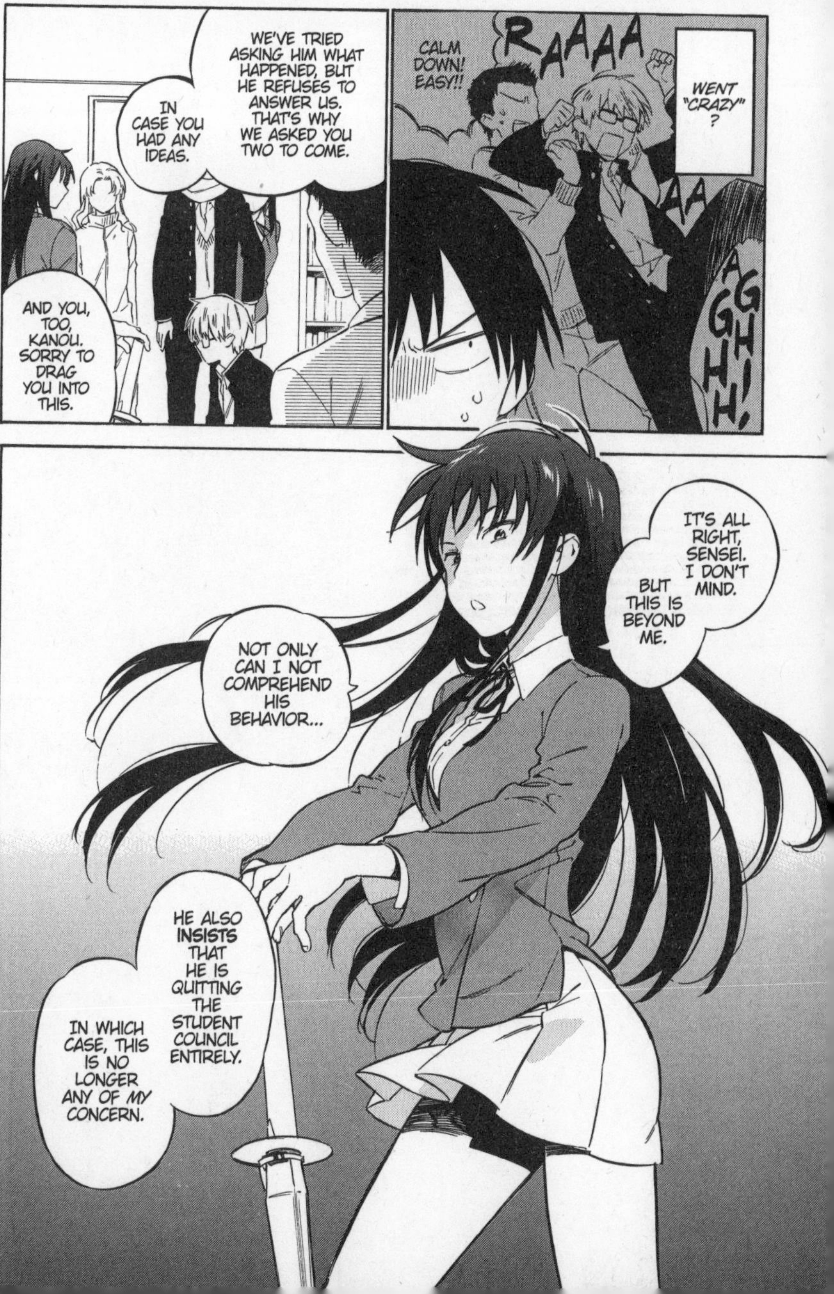
WENT "CRAZY"?
CALM DOWN! EASY!!
RAAAA
AA
AGGHHHH!
WE'VE TRIED ASKING HIM WHAT HAPPENED, BUT HE REFUSES TO ANSWER US. THAT'S WHY WE ASKED YOU TWO TO COME.
IN CASE YOU HAD ANY IDEAS.
AND YOU, TOO, KANOU. SORRY TO DRAG YOU INTO THIS.
IT'S ALL RIGHT, SENSEI. I DON'T MIND.
BUT THIS IS BEYOND ME.
NOT ONLY CAN I NOT COMPREHEND HIS BEHAVIOR...
HE ALSO INSISTS THAT HE IS QUITTING THE STUDENT COUNCIL ENTIRELY.
IN WHICH CASE, THIS IS NO LONGER ANY OF MY CONCERN.

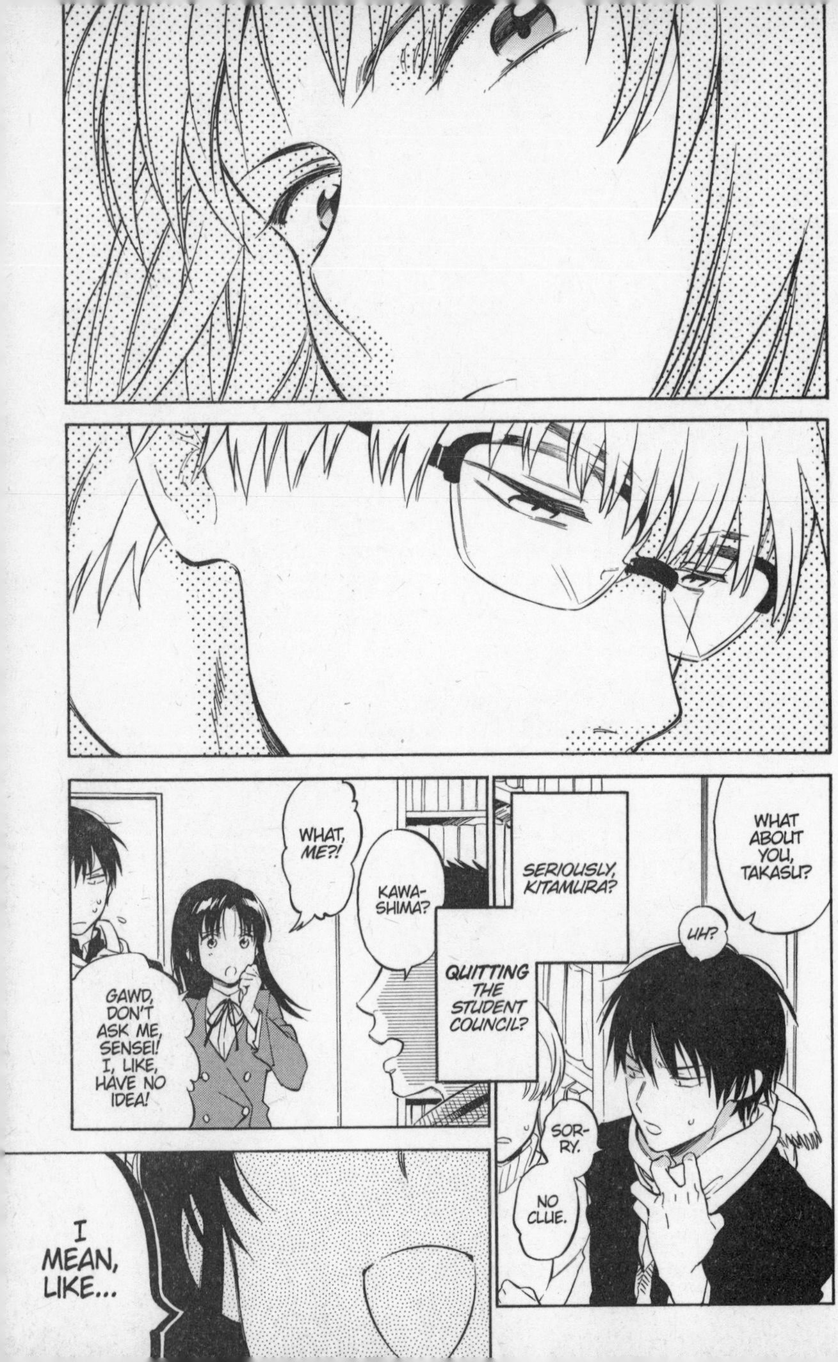
WHAT ABOUT YOU, TAKASU?
UH?
SERIOUSLY, KITAMURA?
QUITTING THE STUDENT COUNCIL?
SORRY.
NO CLUE.
KAWA-SHIMA?
WHAT, ME?!
GAWD, DON'T ASK ME, SENSEI! I, LIKE, HAVE NO IDEA!
I MEAN, LIKE...

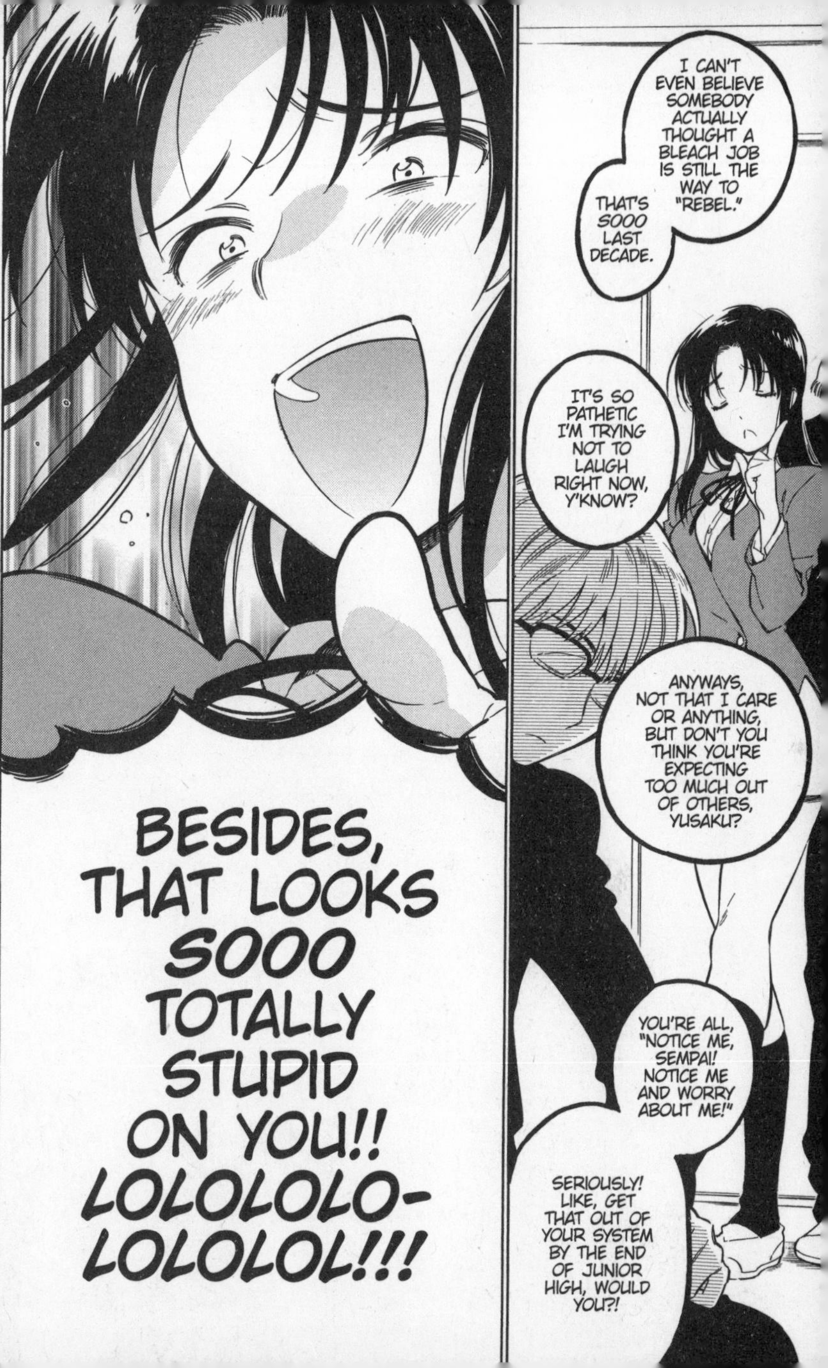
I CAN'T EVEN BELIEVE SOMEBODY ACTUALLY THOUGHT A BLEACH JOB IS STILL THE WAY TO "REBEL."
THAT'S SOOO LAST DECADE.
IT'S SO PATHETIC I'M TRYING NOT TO LAUGH RIGHT NOW, Y'KNOW?
ANYWAYS, NOT THAT I CARE OR ANYTHING, BUT DON'T YOU THINK YOU'RE EXPECTING TOO MUCH OUT OF OTHERS, YUSAKU?
YOU'RE ALL, "NOTICE ME, SEMPAI! NOTICE ME AND WORRY ABOUT ME!"
SERIOUSLY! LIKE, GET THAT OUT OF YOUR SYSTEM BY THE END OF JUNIOR HIGH, WOULD YOU?!
BESIDES, THAT LOOKS *SOOO* TOTALLY STUPID ON YOU!! *LOLOLOLO-LOLOLOL!!!*

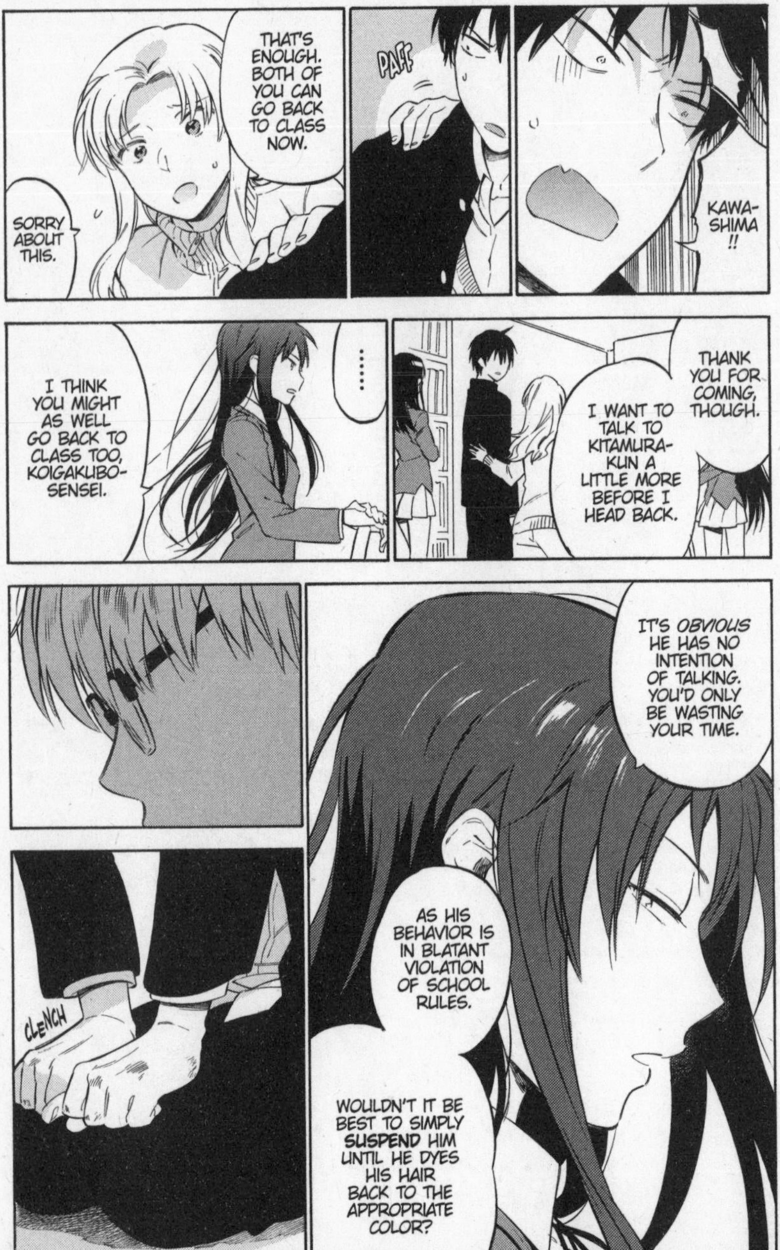
KAWA-SHIMA!!
PAFF
THAT'S ENOUGH. BOTH OF YOU CAN GO BACK TO CLASS NOW.
SORRY ABOUT THIS.
THANK YOU FOR COMING, THOUGH.
I WANT TO TALK TO KITAMURA-KUN A LITTLE MORE BEFORE I HEAD BACK.
......
I THINK YOU MIGHT AS WELL GO BACK TO CLASS TOO, KOIGAKUBO-SENSEI.
IT'S *OBVIOUS* HE HAS NO INTENTION OF TALKING. YOU'D ONLY BE WASTING YOUR TIME.
AS HIS BEHAVIOR IS IN BLATANT VIOLATION OF SCHOOL RULES.
WOULDN'T IT BE BEST TO SIMPLY **SUSPEND** HIM UNTIL HE DYES HIS HAIR BACK TO THE APPROPRIATE COLOR?
CLENCH

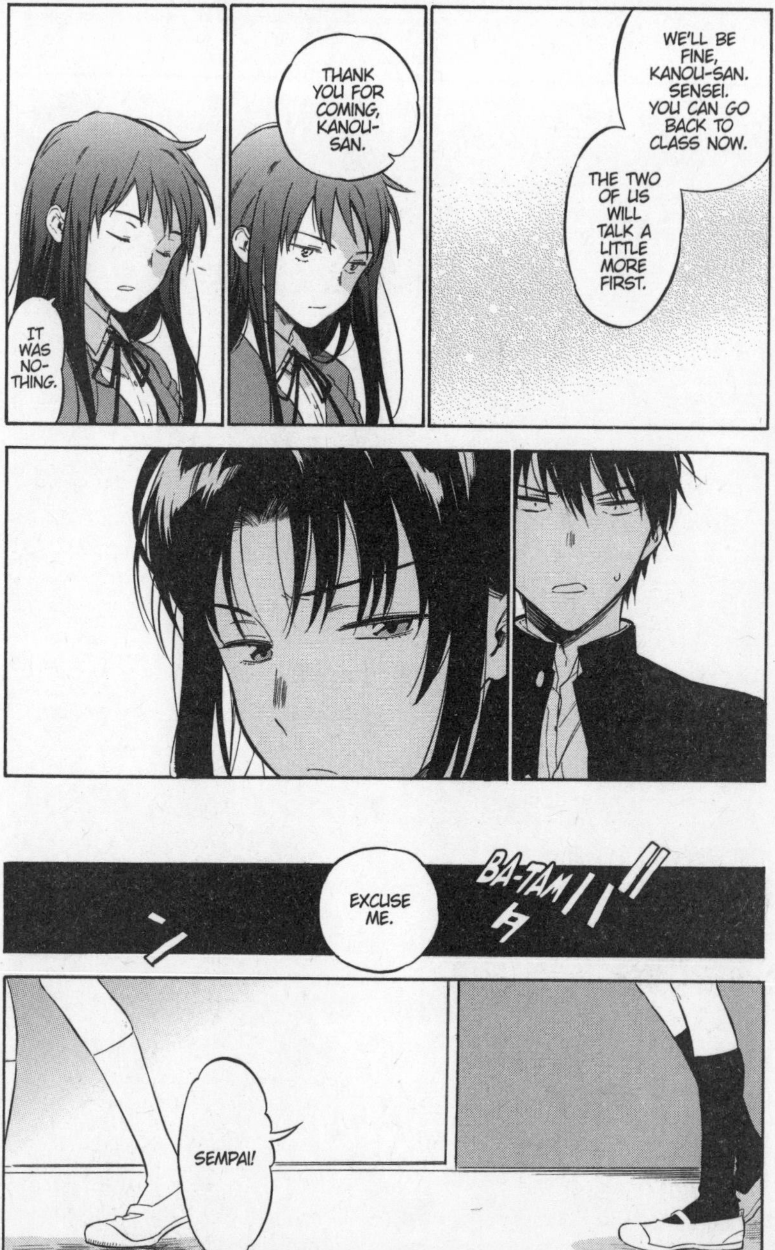
WE'LL BE FINE, KANOU-SAN. SENSEI. YOU CAN GO BACK TO CLASS NOW.
THE TWO OF US WILL TALK A LITTLE MORE FIRST.
THANK YOU FOR COMING, KANOU-SAN.
IT WAS NOTHING.
BA-TAM
EXCUSE ME.
SEMPAI!

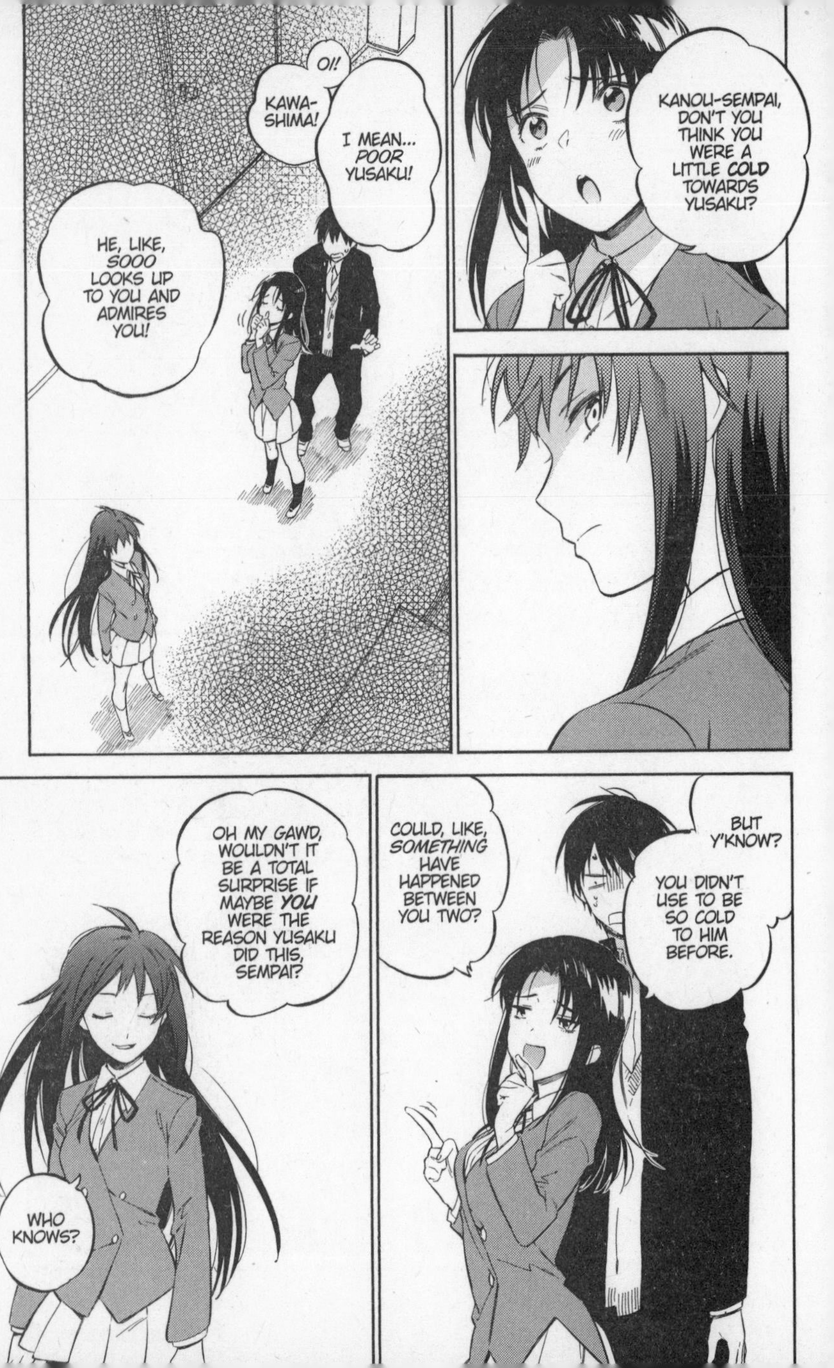
KANOU-SEMPAI, DON'T YOU THINK YOU WERE A LITTLE COLD TOWARDS YUSAKU?
OI!
KAWA-SHIMA!
I MEAN... POOR YUSAKU!
HE, LIKE, SOOO LOOKS UP TO YOU AND ADMIRES YOU!
BUT Y'KNOW?
YOU DIDN'T USE TO BE SO COLD TO HIM BEFORE.
COULD, LIKE, SOMETHING HAVE HAPPENED BETWEEN YOU TWO?
OH MY GAWD, WOULDN'T IT BE A TOTAL SURPRISE IF MAYBE YOU WERE THE REASON YUSAKU DID THIS, SEMPAI?
WHO KNOWS?

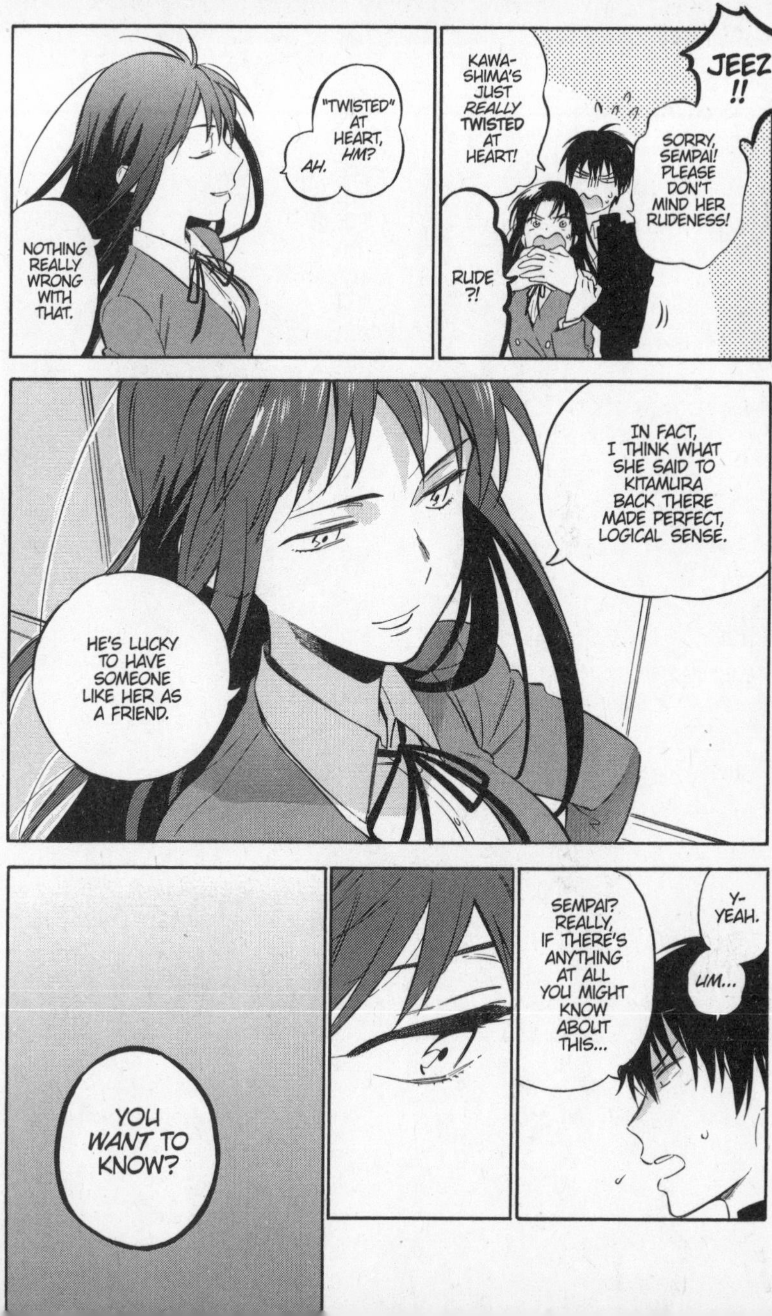
JEEZ !!
KAWA-SHIMA'S JUST *REALLY* TWISTED AT HEART!
SORRY, SEMPAI! PLEASE DON'T MIND HER RUDENESS!
RUDE ?!
"TWISTED" AT HEART, *HM?*
AH.
NOTHING REALLY WRONG WITH THAT.
IN FACT, I THINK WHAT SHE SAID TO KITAMURA BACK THERE MADE PERFECT, LOGICAL SENSE.
HE'S LUCKY TO HAVE SOMEONE LIKE HER AS A FRIEND.
Y-YEAH.
UM...
SEMPAI? REALLY, IF THERE'S ANYTHING AT ALL YOU MIGHT KNOW ABOUT THIS...
YOU *WANT* TO KNOW?

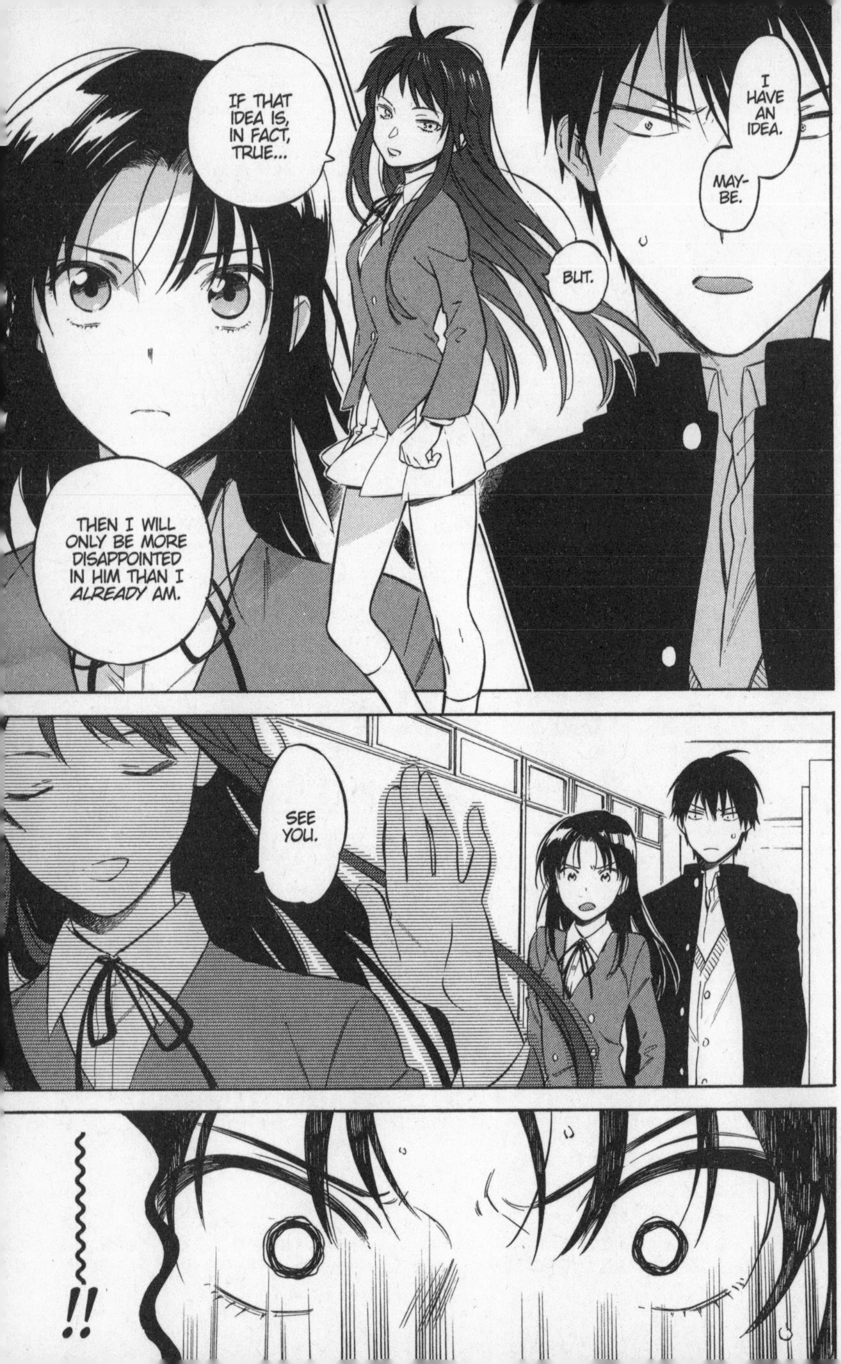
I HAVE AN IDEA.
MAY-BE.
BUT.
IF THAT IDEA IS, IN FACT, TRUE...
THEN I WILL ONLY BE MORE DISAPPOINTED IN HIM THAN I *ALREADY* AM.
SEE YOU.
!!

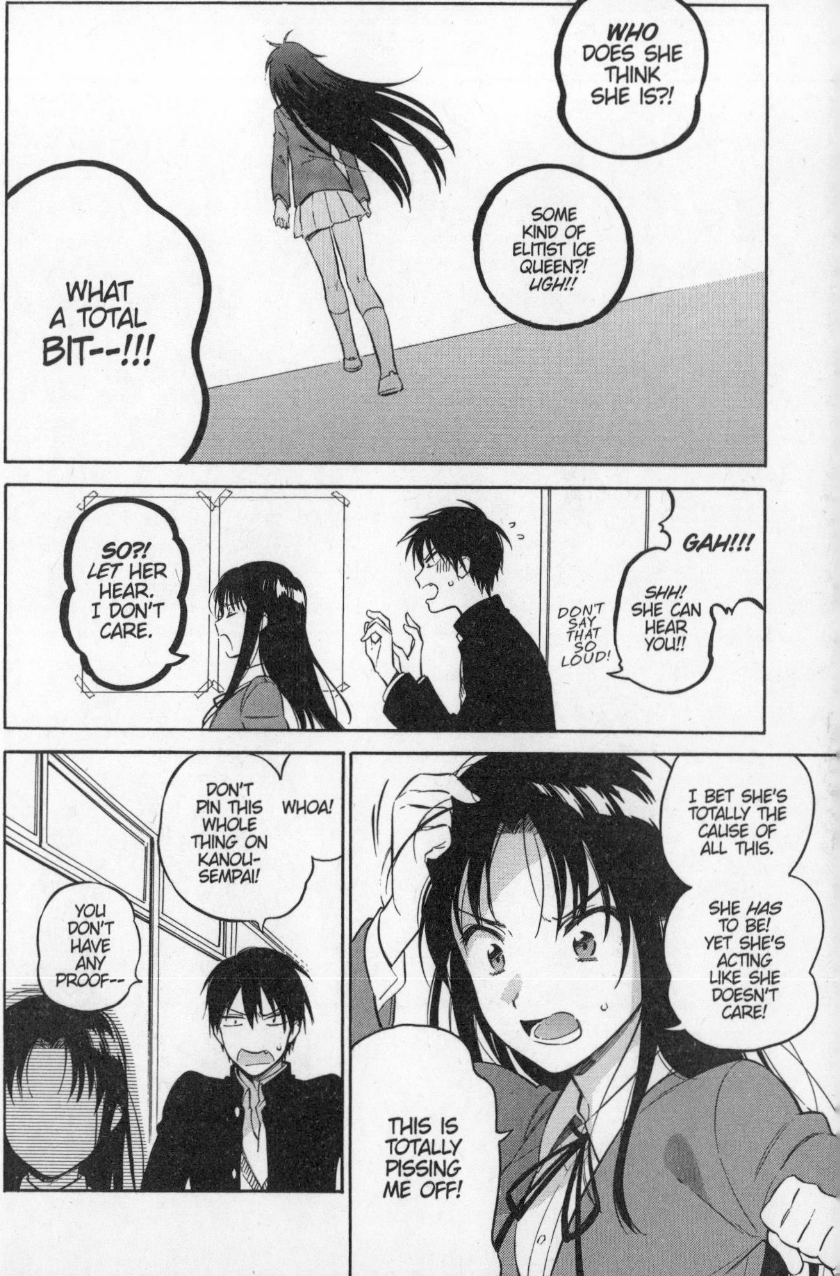
WHO DOES SHE THINK SHE IS?!
SOME KIND OF ELITIST ICE QUEEN?! UGH!!
WHAT A TOTAL BIT--!!!
GAH!!!
SHH! SHE CAN HEAR YOU!!
DON'T SAY THAT SO LOUD!
SO?! LET HER HEAR. I DON'T CARE.
I BET SHE'S TOTALLY THE CAUSE OF ALL THIS.
SHE *HAS* TO BE! YET SHE'S ACTING LIKE SHE DOESN'T CARE!
THIS IS TOTALLY PISSING ME OFF!
WHOA!
DON'T PIN THIS WHOLE THING ON KANOU-SEMPAI!
YOU DON'T HAVE ANY PROOF--

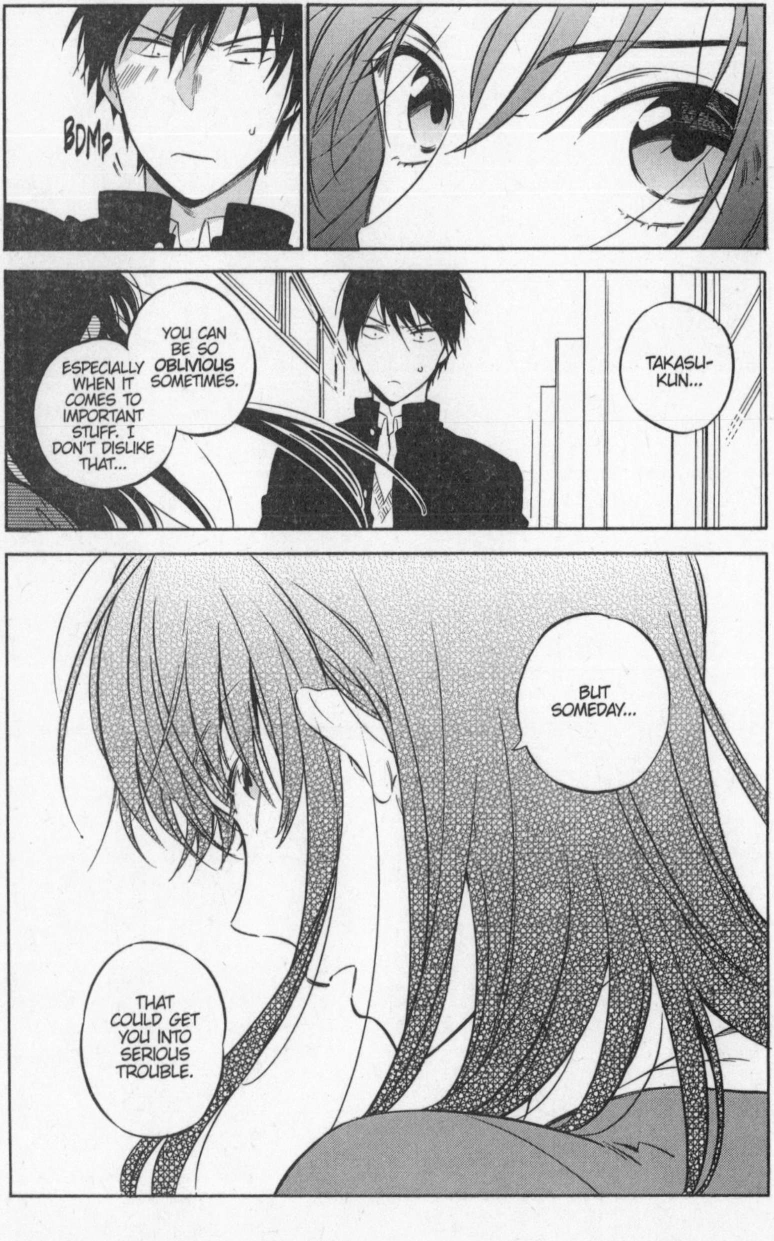
BDMP
TAKASU-KUN...
YOU CAN BE SO OBLIVIOUS SOMETIMES.
ESPECIALLY WHEN IT COMES TO IMPORTANT STUFF. I DON'T DISLIKE THAT...
BUT SOMEDAY...
THAT COULD GET YOU INTO SERIOUS TROUBLE.

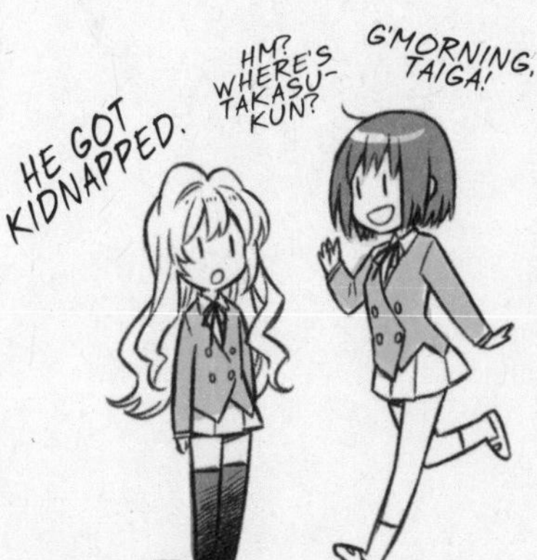
G'MORNING, TAIGA!
HM? WHERE'S TAKASU-KUN?
HE GOT KIDNAPPED.

Chapter 61: I WANT TO KNOW

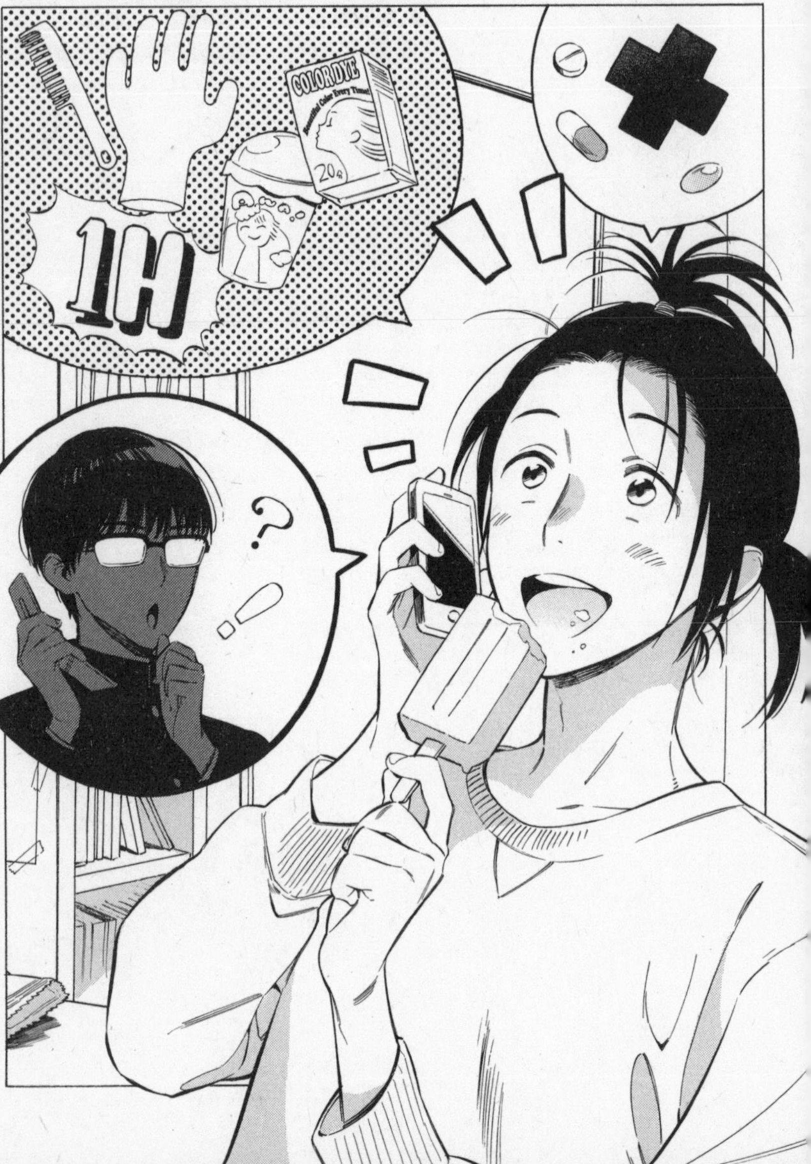
COLOR DYE
Beautiful Color Every Time!
1H

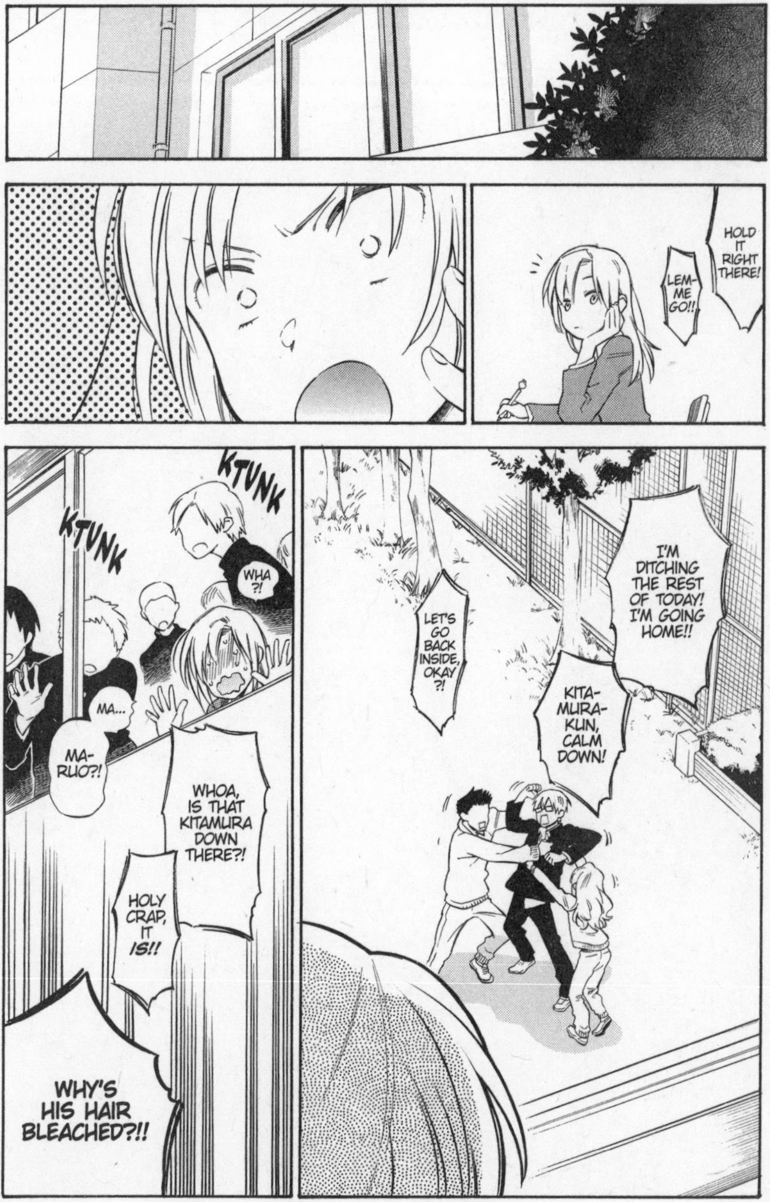
HOLD IT RIGHT THERE!
LEM-ME GO!!
I'M DITCHING THE REST OF TODAY! I'M GOING HOME!!
KITA-MURA-KUN, CALM DOWN!
LET'S GO BACK INSIDE, OKAY?!
KTUNK
KTUNK
WHA?!
MA...
MA-RUO?!
WHOA, IS THAT KITAMURA DOWN THERE?!
HOLY CRAP, IT *IS*!!
WHY'S HIS HAIR BLEACHED?!!

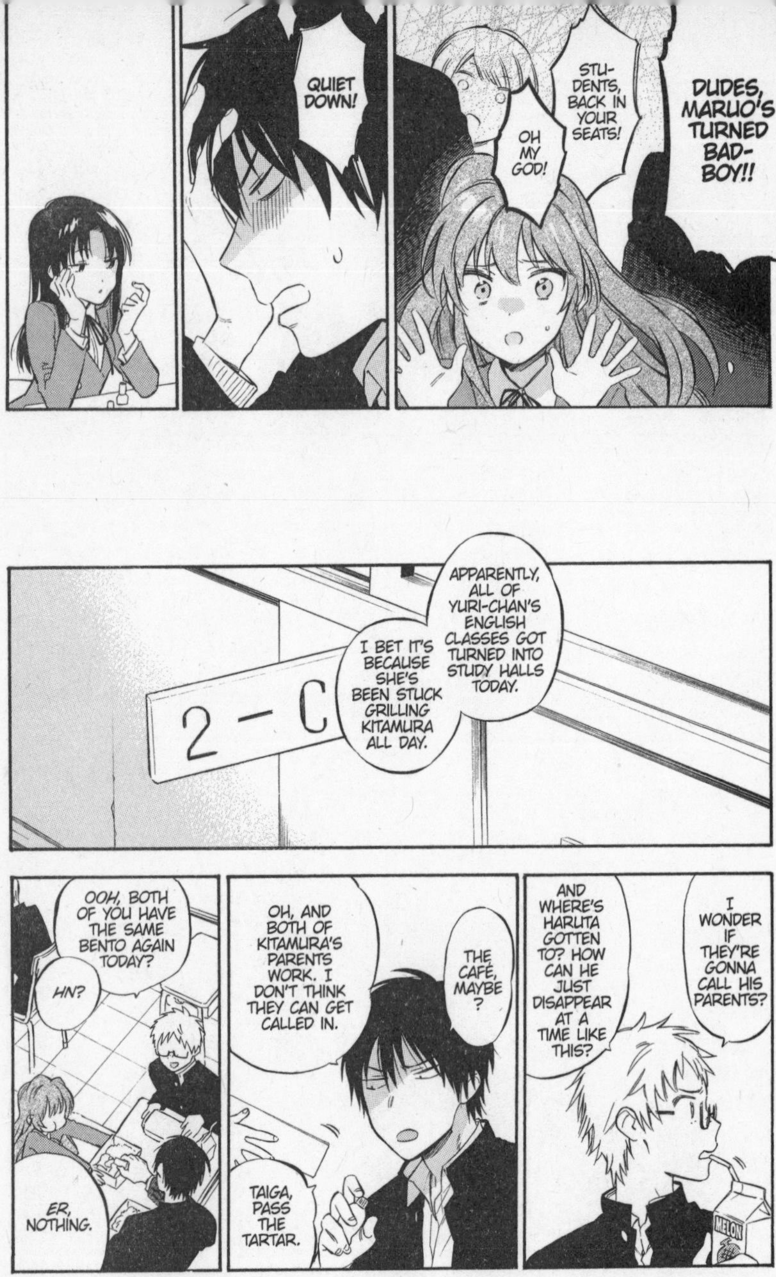
DUDES, MARUO'S TURNED BAD-BOY!!
STU-DENTS, BACK IN YOUR SEATS!
OH MY GOD!
QUIET DOWN!
APPARENTLY, ALL OF YURI-CHAN'S ENGLISH CLASSES GOT TURNED INTO STUDY HALLS TODAY.
I BET IT'S BECAUSE SHE'S BEEN STUCK GRILLING KITAMURA ALL DAY.
2-C
I WONDER IF THEY'RE GONNA CALL HIS PARENTS?
AND WHERE'S HARUTA GOTTEN TO? HOW CAN HE JUST DISAPPEAR AT A TIME LIKE THIS?
MELON
THE CAFÉ, MAYBE?
OH, AND BOTH OF KITAMURA'S PARENTS WORK. I DON'T THINK THEY CAN GET CALLED IN.
TAIGA, PASS THE TARTAR.
OOH, BOTH OF YOU HAVE THE SAME BENTO AGAIN TODAY?
HN?
ER, NOTHING.

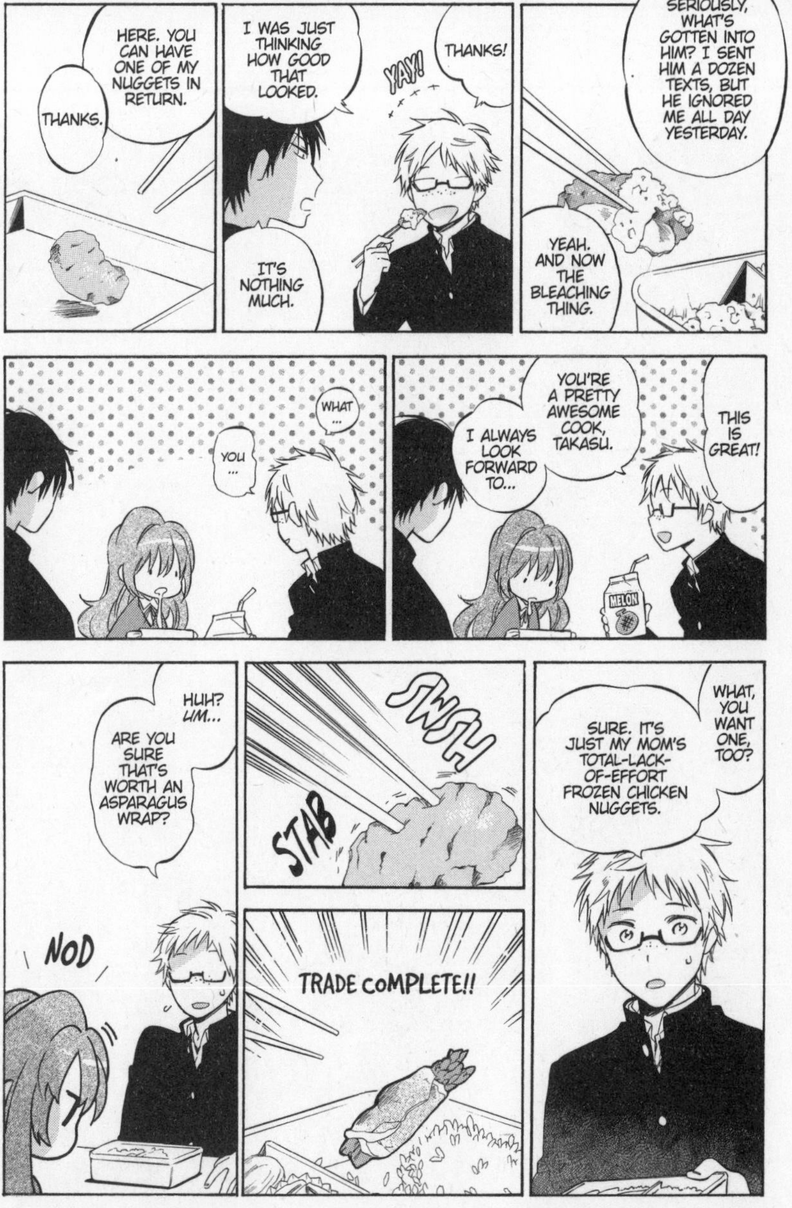
SERIOUSLY, WHAT'S GOTTEN INTO HIM? I SENT HIM A DOZEN TEXTS, BUT HE IGNORED ME ALL DAY YESTERDAY.
YEAH. AND NOW THE BLEACHING THING.
THANKS!
YAY!
I WAS JUST THINKING HOW GOOD THAT LOOKED.
IT'S NOTHING MUCH.
HERE. YOU CAN HAVE ONE OF MY NUGGETS IN RETURN.
THANKS.
THIS IS GREAT!
YOU'RE A PRETTY AWESOME COOK, TAKASU.
I ALWAYS LOOK FORWARD TO...
MELON
WHAT ...
YOU ...
WHAT, YOU WANT ONE, TOO?
SURE. IT'S JUST MY MOM'S TOTAL-LACK-OF-EFFORT FROZEN CHICKEN NUGGETS.
SWSH
STAB
TRADE COMPLETE!!
HUH? UM...
ARE YOU SURE THAT'S WORTH AN ASPARAGUS WRAP?
NOD

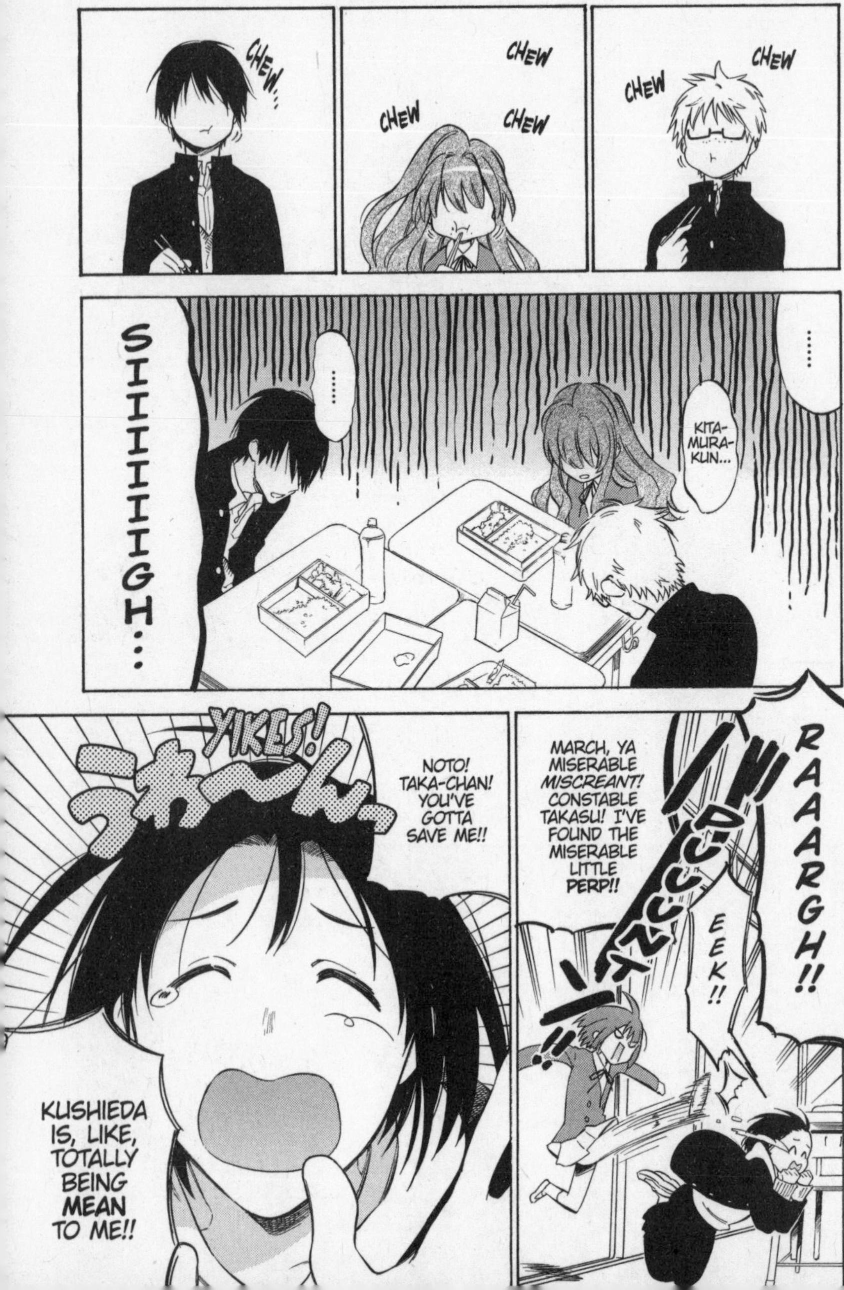
CHEW
CHEW
CHEW
CHEW
CHEW
CHEW...
......
KITA-MURA-KUN...
......
SIIIIIIIIIGH...
RAAAARGH!!
MARCH, YA MISERABLE MISCREANT! CONSTABLE TAKASU! I'VE FOUND THE MISERABLE LITTLE PERP!!
EEK!!
YIKES!
NOTO! TAKA-CHAN! YOU'VE GOTTA SAVE ME!!
KUSHIEDA IS, LIKE, TOTALLY BEING MEAN TO ME!!

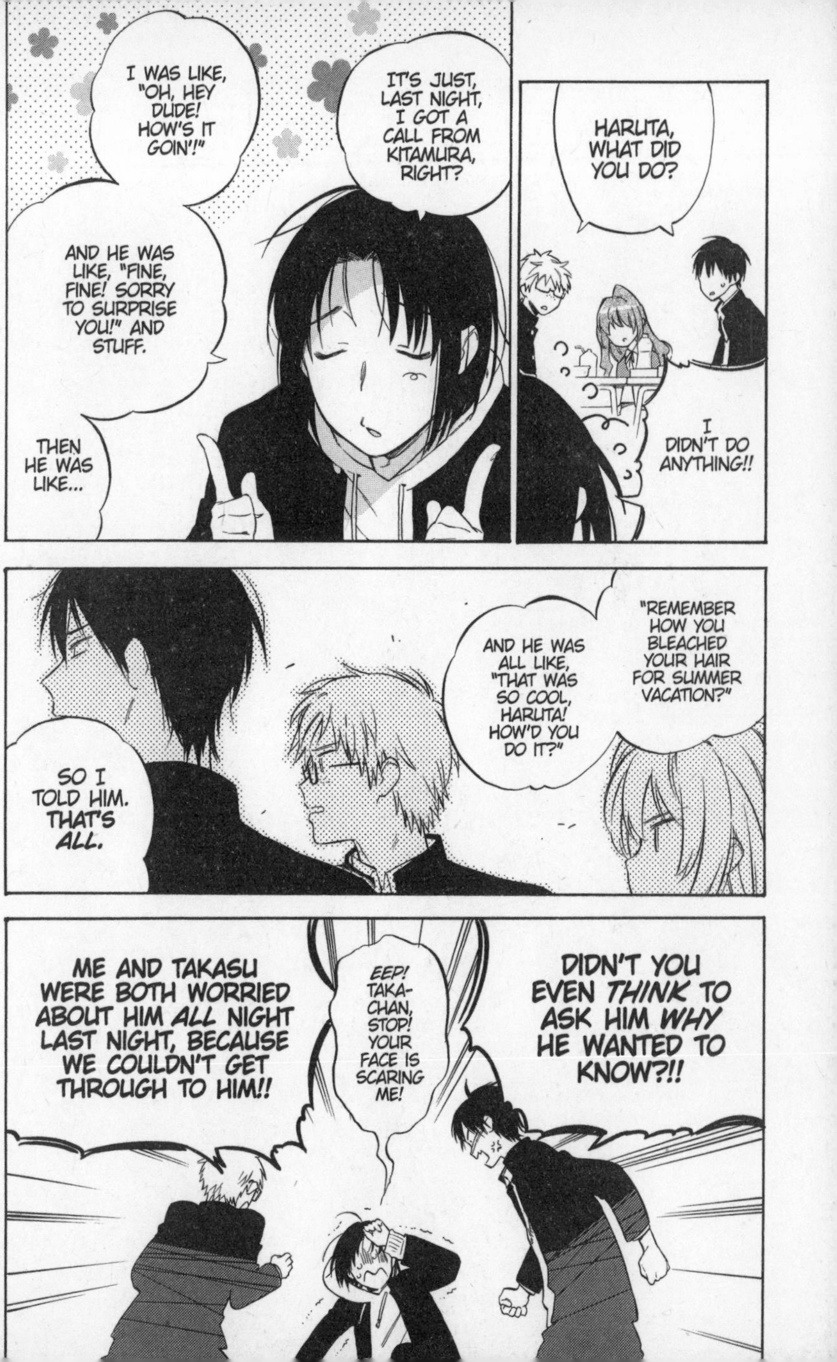
HARUTA, WHAT DID YOU DO?
I DIDN'T DO ANYTHING!!
IT'S JUST, LAST NIGHT, I GOT A CALL FROM KITAMURA, RIGHT?
I WAS LIKE, "OH, HEY DUDE! HOW'S IT GOIN'!"
AND HE WAS LIKE, "FINE, FINE! SORRY TO SURPRISE YOU!" AND STUFF.
THEN HE WAS LIKE...
"REMEMBER HOW YOU BLEACHED YOUR HAIR FOR SUMMER VACATION?"
AND HE WAS ALL LIKE, "THAT WAS SO COOL, HARUTA! HOW'D YOU DO IT?"
SO I TOLD HIM. THAT'S *ALL*.
DIDN'T YOU EVEN *THINK* TO ASK HIM *WHY* HE WANTED TO KNOW?!!
EEP! TAKA-CHAN, STOP! YOUR FACE IS SCARING ME!
ME AND TAKASU WERE BOTH WORRIED ABOUT HIM *ALL* NIGHT LAST NIGHT, BECAUSE WE COULDN'T GET THROUGH TO HIM!!

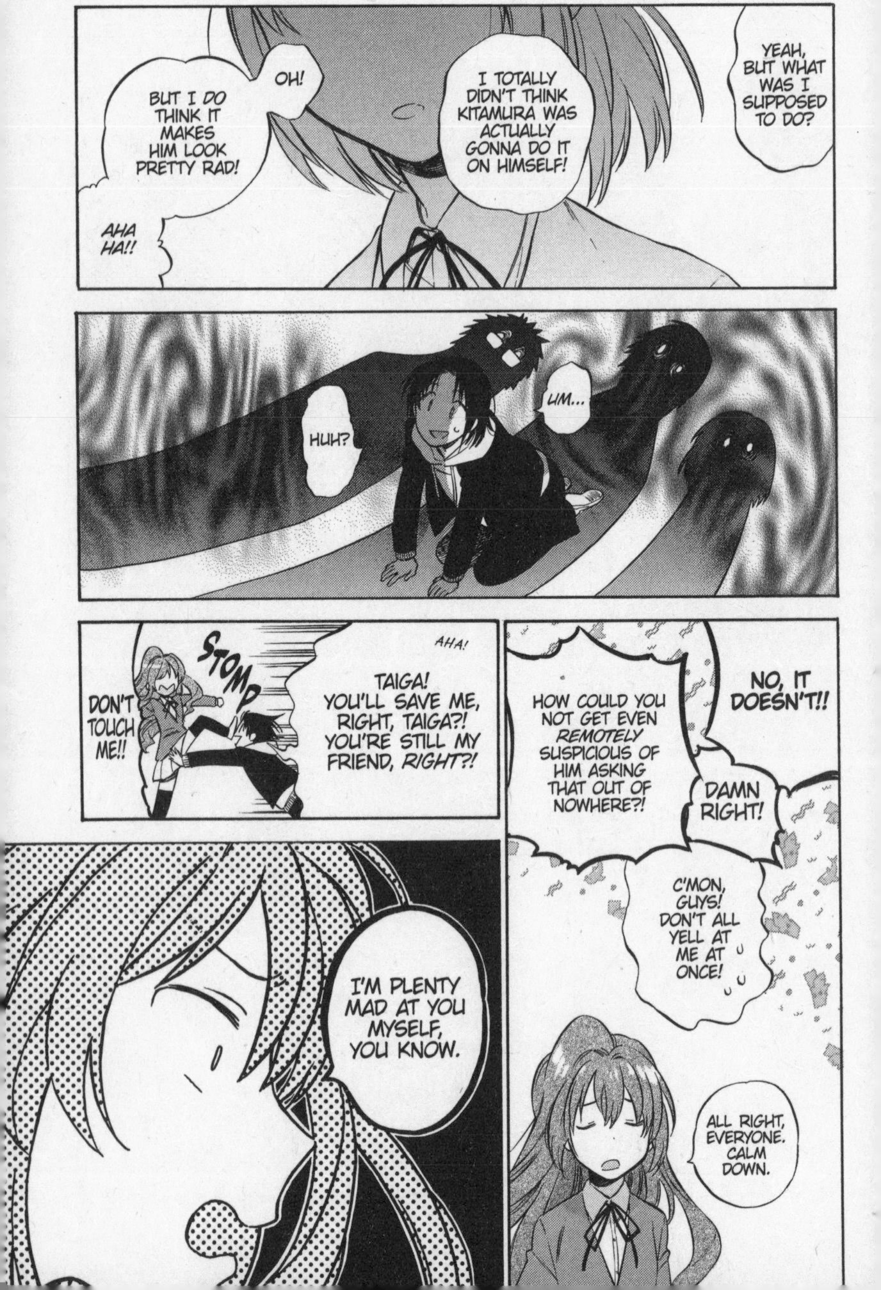
YEAH, BUT WHAT WAS I SUPPOSED TO DO?
I TOTALLY DIDN'T THINK KITAMURA WAS ACTUALLY GONNA DO IT ON HIMSELF!
OH!
BUT I *DO* THINK IT MAKES HIM LOOK PRETTY RAD!
AHA HA!!
UM...
HUH?
NO, IT DOESN'T!!
HOW COULD YOU NOT GET EVEN *REMOTELY* SUSPICIOUS OF HIM ASKING THAT OUT OF NOWHERE?!
DAMN RIGHT!
C'MON, GUYS! DON'T ALL YELL AT ME AT ONCE!
ALL RIGHT, EVERYONE. CALM DOWN.
AHA!
TAIGA! YOU'LL SAVE ME, RIGHT, TAIGA?! YOU'RE STILL MY FRIEND, *RIGHT*?!
STOMP
DON'T TOUCH ME!!
I'M PLENTY MAD AT YOU MYSELF, YOU KNOW.

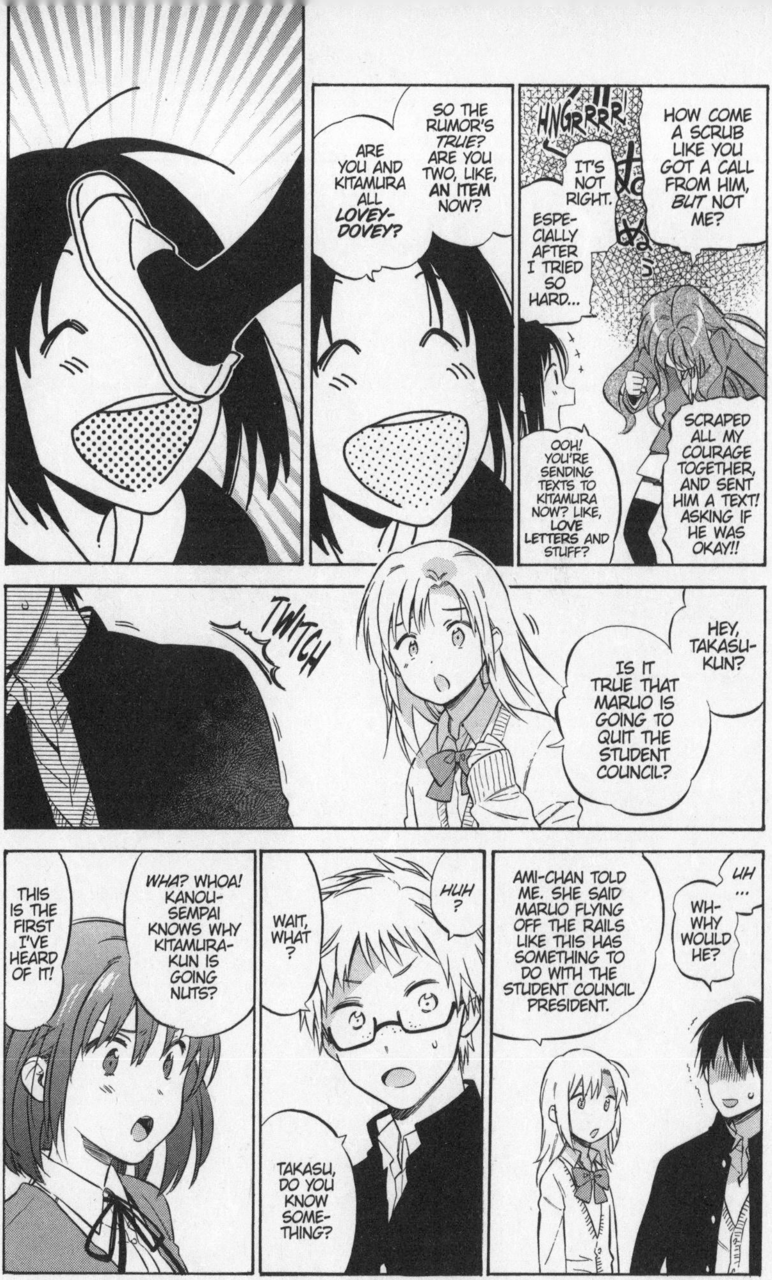
HNGRRRR
HOW COME A SCRUB LIKE YOU GOT A CALL FROM HIM, *BUT* NOT ME?
IT'S NOT RIGHT.
ESPECIALLY AFTER I TRIED SO HARD...
SCRAPED ALL MY COURAGE TOGETHER, AND SENT HIM A TEXT! ASKING IF HE WAS OKAY!!
OOH! YOU'RE SENDING TEXTS TO KITAMURA NOW? LIKE, LOVE LETTERS AND STUFF?
SO THE RUMOR'S *TRUE*? ARE YOU TWO, LIKE, AN ITEM NOW?
ARE YOU AND KITAMURA ALL ***LOVEY-DOVEY?***
HEY, TAKASU-KUN?
IS IT TRUE THAT MARUO IS GOING TO QUIT THE STUDENT COUNCIL?
TWITCH
UH ...
WH-WHY WOULD HE?
AMI-CHAN TOLD ME. SHE SAID MARUO FLYING OFF THE RAILS LIKE THIS HAS SOMETHING TO DO WITH THE STUDENT COUNCIL PRESIDENT.
HUH?
WAIT, WHAT?
TAKASU, DO YOU KNOW SOMETHING?
WHA? WHOA! KANOU-SEMPAI KNOWS WHY KITAMURA-KUN IS GOING NUTS?
THIS IS THE FIRST I'VE HEARD OF IT!

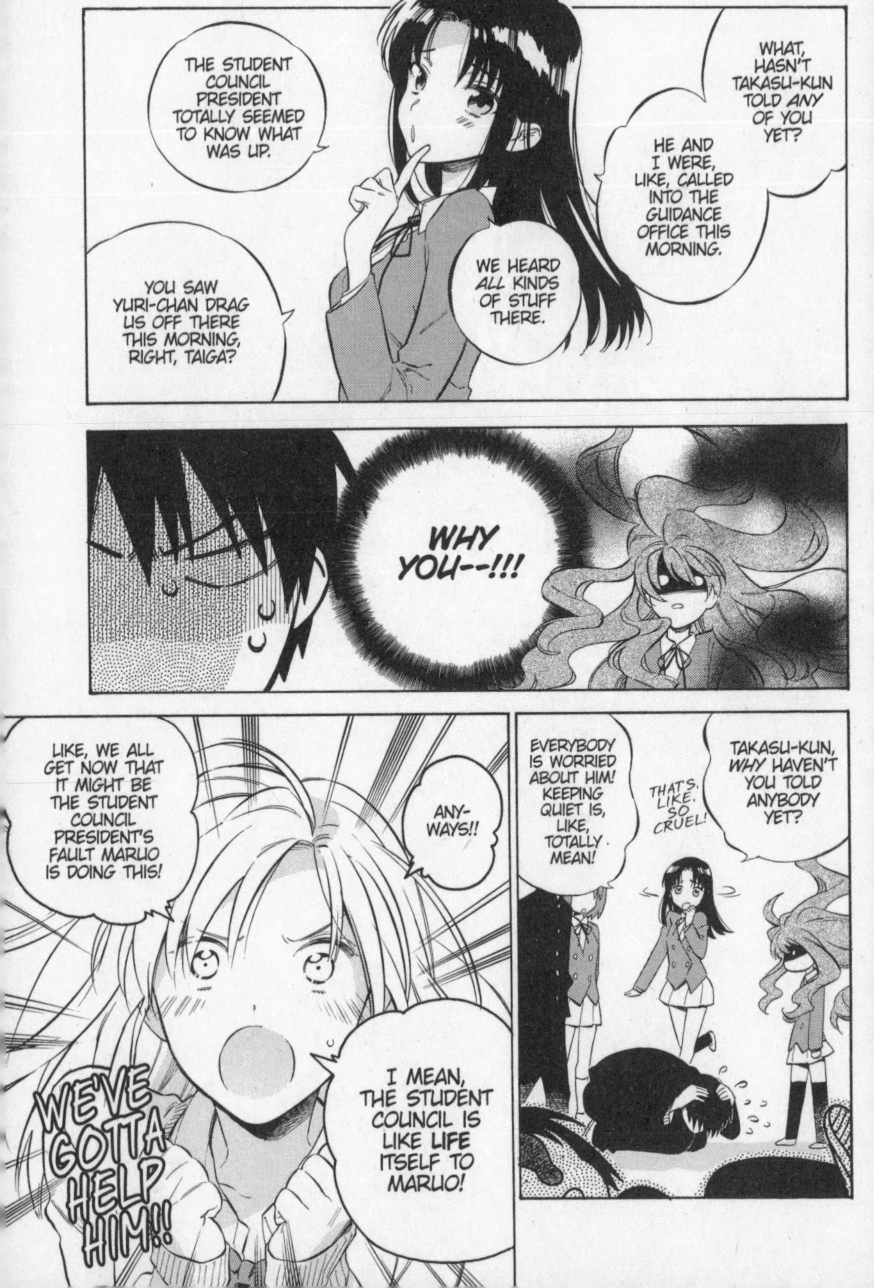
WHAT, HASN'T TAKASU-KUN TOLD *ANY* OF YOU YET?
HE AND I WERE, LIKE, CALLED INTO THE GUIDANCE OFFICE THIS MORNING.
WE HEARD *ALL* KINDS OF STUFF THERE.
THE STUDENT COUNCIL PRESIDENT TOTALLY SEEMED TO KNOW WHAT WAS UP.
YOU SAW YURI-CHAN DRAG US OFF THERE THIS MORNING, RIGHT, TAIGA?
WHY YOU--!!!
TAKASU-KUN, *WHY* HAVEN'T YOU TOLD ANYBODY YET?
THAT'S, LIKE, SO CRUEL!
EVERYBODY IS WORRIED ABOUT HIM! KEEPING QUIET IS, LIKE, TOTALLY MEAN!
ANY-WAYS!!
LIKE, WE ALL GET NOW THAT IT MIGHT BE THE STUDENT COUNCIL PRESIDENT'S FAULT MARUO IS DOING THIS!
I MEAN, THE STUDENT COUNCIL IS LIKE LIFE ITSELF TO MARUO!
WE'VE GOTTA HELP HIM!!

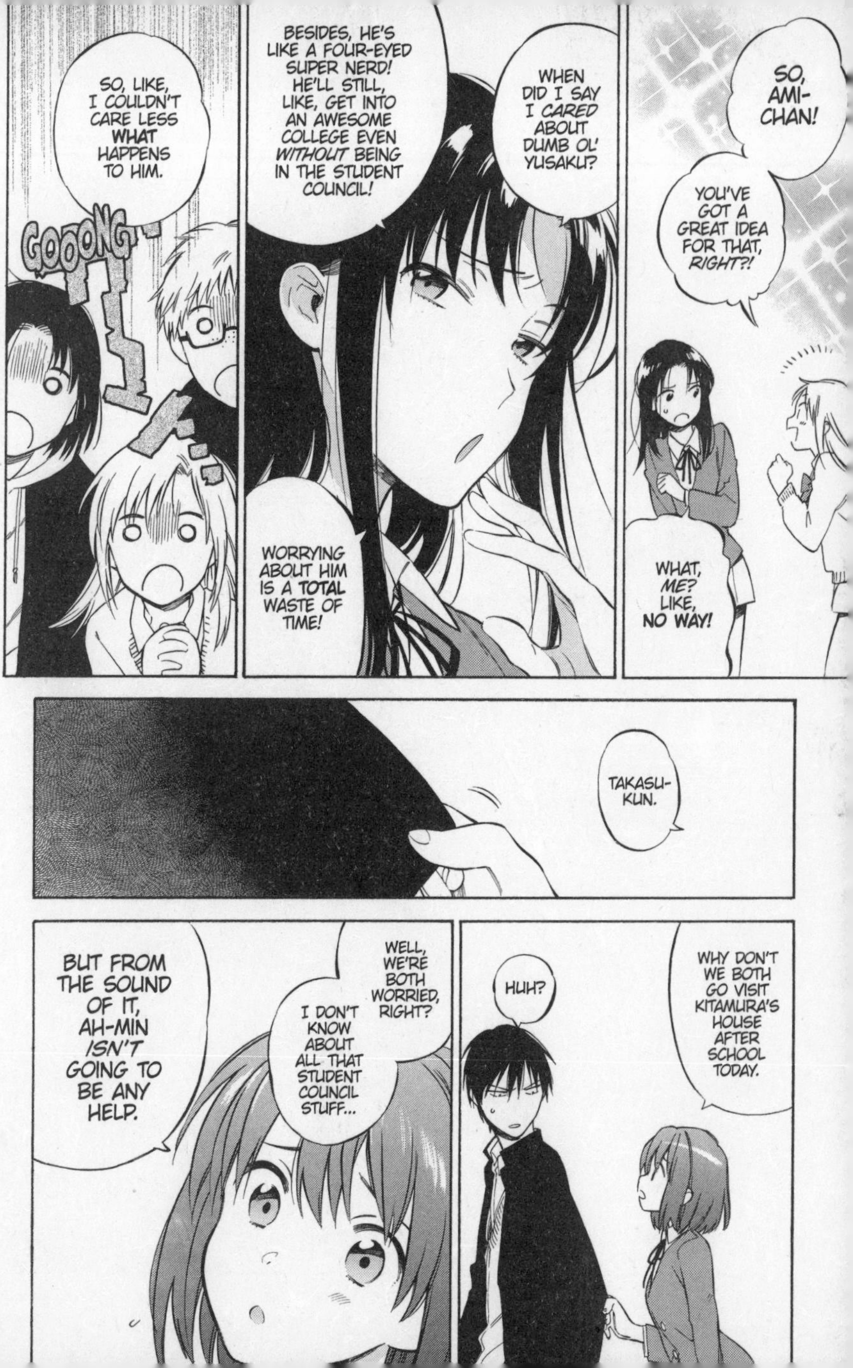
SO, AMI-CHAN!
YOU'VE GOT A GREAT IDEA FOR THAT, RIGHT?!
WHAT, ME? LIKE, NO WAY!
WHEN DID I SAY I CARED ABOUT DUMB OL' YUSAKU?
BESIDES, HE'S LIKE A FOUR-EYED SUPER NERD! HE'LL STILL, LIKE, GET INTO AN AWESOME COLLEGE EVEN WITHOUT BEING IN THE STUDENT COUNCIL!
WORRYING ABOUT HIM IS A TOTAL WASTE OF TIME!
SO, LIKE, I COULDN'T CARE LESS WHAT HAPPENS TO HIM.
GOOONG
TAKASU-KUN.
WHY DON'T WE BOTH GO VISIT KITAMURA'S HOUSE AFTER SCHOOL TODAY.
HUH?
WELL, WE'RE BOTH WORRIED, RIGHT?
I DON'T KNOW ABOUT ALL THAT STUDENT COUNCIL STUFF...
BUT FROM THE SOUND OF IT, AH-MIN ISN'T GOING TO BE ANY HELP.

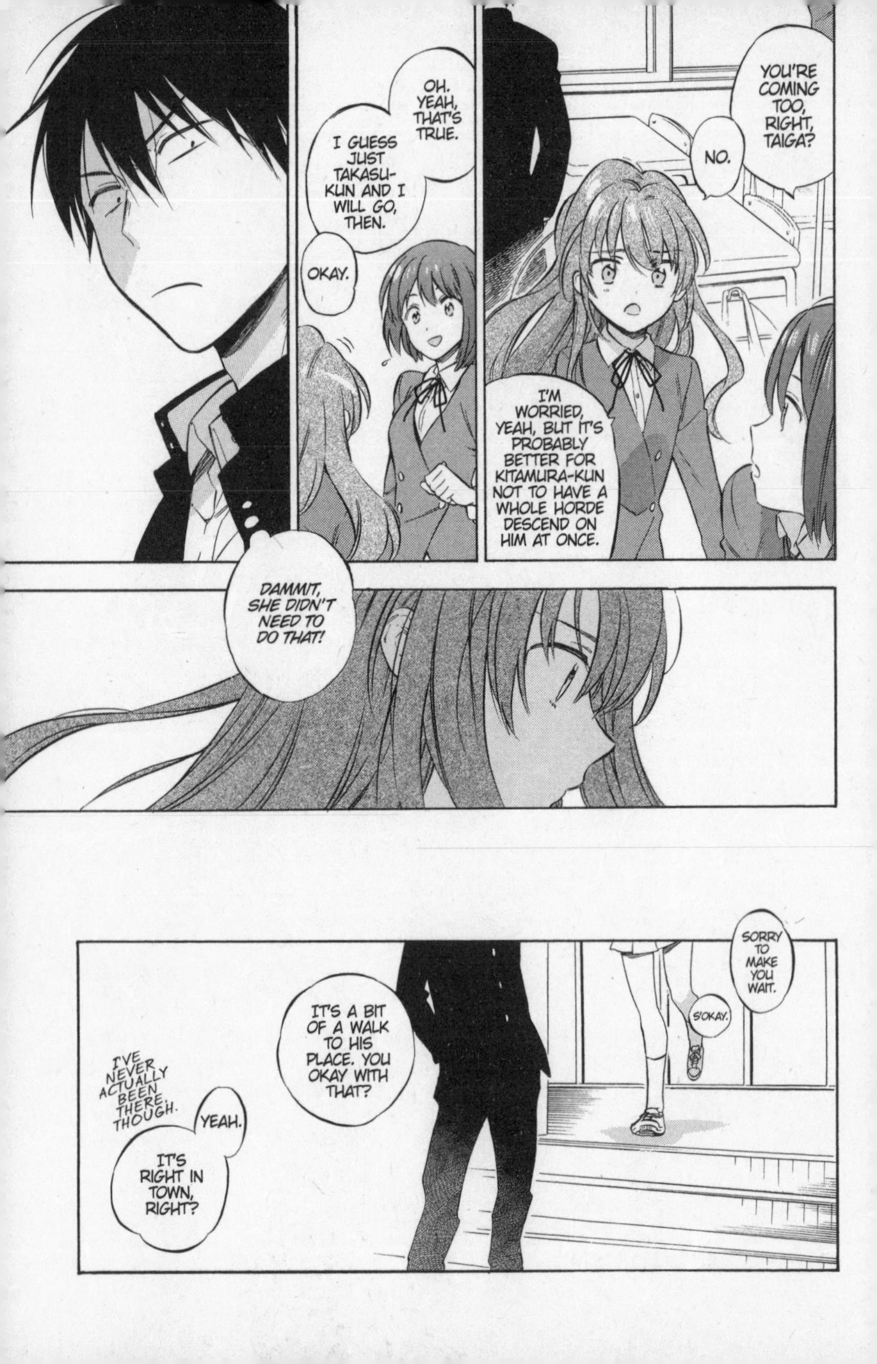
YOU'RE COMING TOO, RIGHT, TAIGA?
NO.
I'M WORRIED, YEAH, BUT IT'S PROBABLY BETTER FOR KITAMURA-KUN NOT TO HAVE A WHOLE HORDE DESCEND ON HIM AT ONCE.
OH. YEAH, THAT'S TRUE.
I GUESS JUST TAKASU-KUN AND I WILL GO, THEN.
OKAY.
DAMMIT, SHE DIDN'T NEED TO DO THAT!
SORRY TO MAKE YOU WAIT.
S'OKAY.
IT'S A BIT OF A WALK TO HIS PLACE. YOU OKAY WITH THAT?
YEAH.
I'VE NEVER ACTUALLY BEEN THERE THOUGH.
IT'S RIGHT IN TOWN, RIGHT?

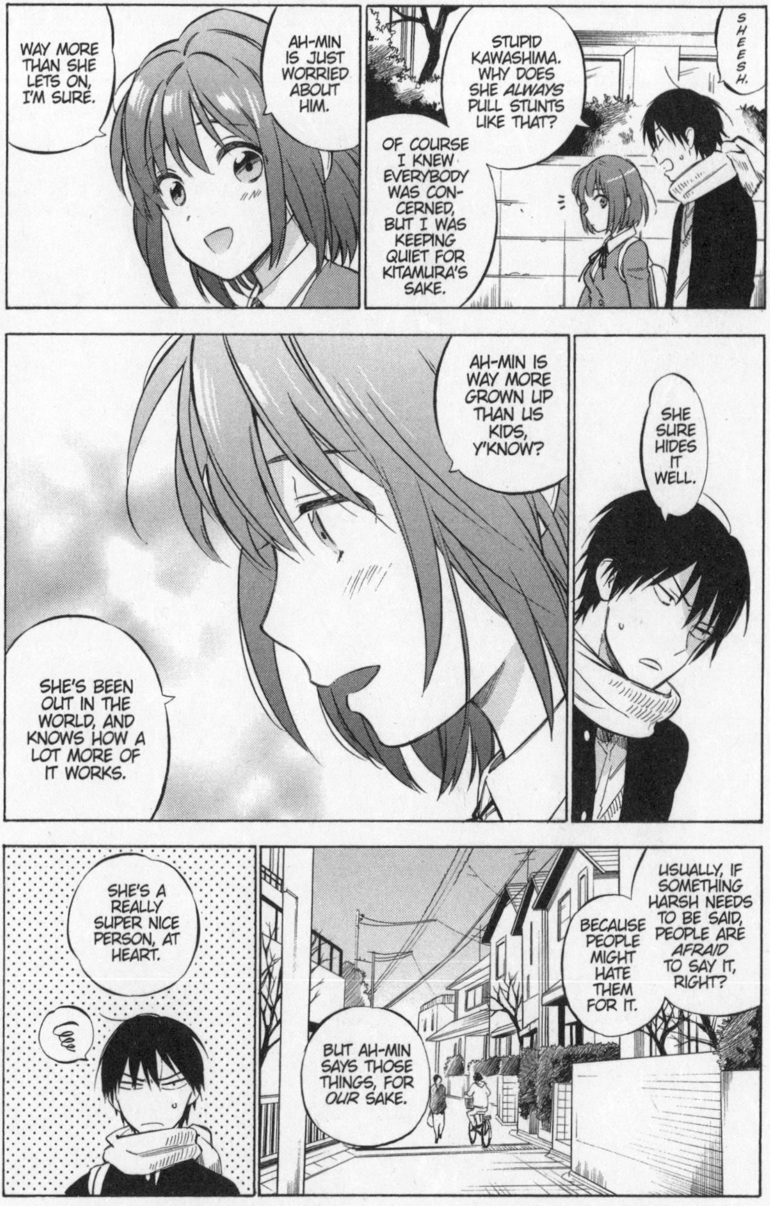
SHEESH.
STUPID KAWASHIMA. WHY DOES SHE *ALWAYS* PULL STUNTS LIKE THAT?
OF COURSE I KNEW EVERYBODY WAS CONCERNED, BUT I WAS KEEPING QUIET FOR KITAMURA'S SAKE.
AH-MIN IS JUST WORRIED ABOUT HIM.
WAY MORE THAN SHE LETS ON, I'M SURE.
SHE SURE HIDES IT WELL.
AH-MIN IS WAY MORE GROWN UP THAN US KIDS, Y'KNOW?
SHE'S BEEN OUT IN THE WORLD, AND KNOWS HOW A LOT MORE OF IT WORKS.
USUALLY, IF SOMETHING HARSH NEEDS TO BE SAID, PEOPLE ARE *AFRAID* TO SAY IT, RIGHT?
BECAUSE PEOPLE MIGHT HATE THEM FOR IT.
BUT AH-MIN SAYS THOSE THINGS, FOR *OUR* SAKE.
SHE'S A REALLY SUPER NICE PERSON, AT HEART.

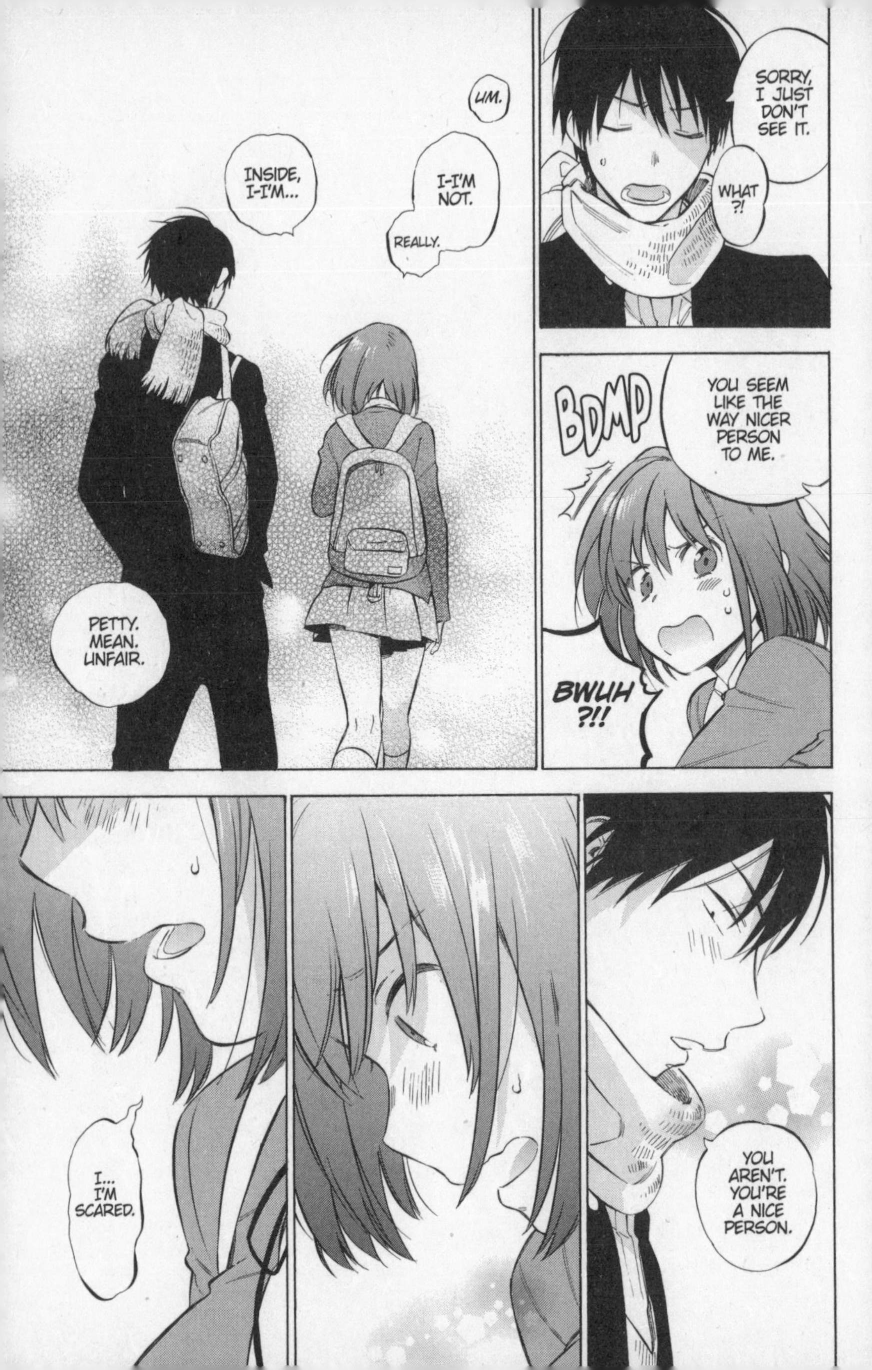
SORRY, I JUST DON'T SEE IT.
WHAT?!
YOU SEEM LIKE THE WAY NICER PERSON TO ME.
BDMP
BWUH?!!
UM.
I-I'M NOT.
REALLY.
INSIDE, I-I'M...
PETTY. MEAN. UNFAIR.
YOU AREN'T. YOU'RE A NICE PERSON.
I... I'M SCARED.

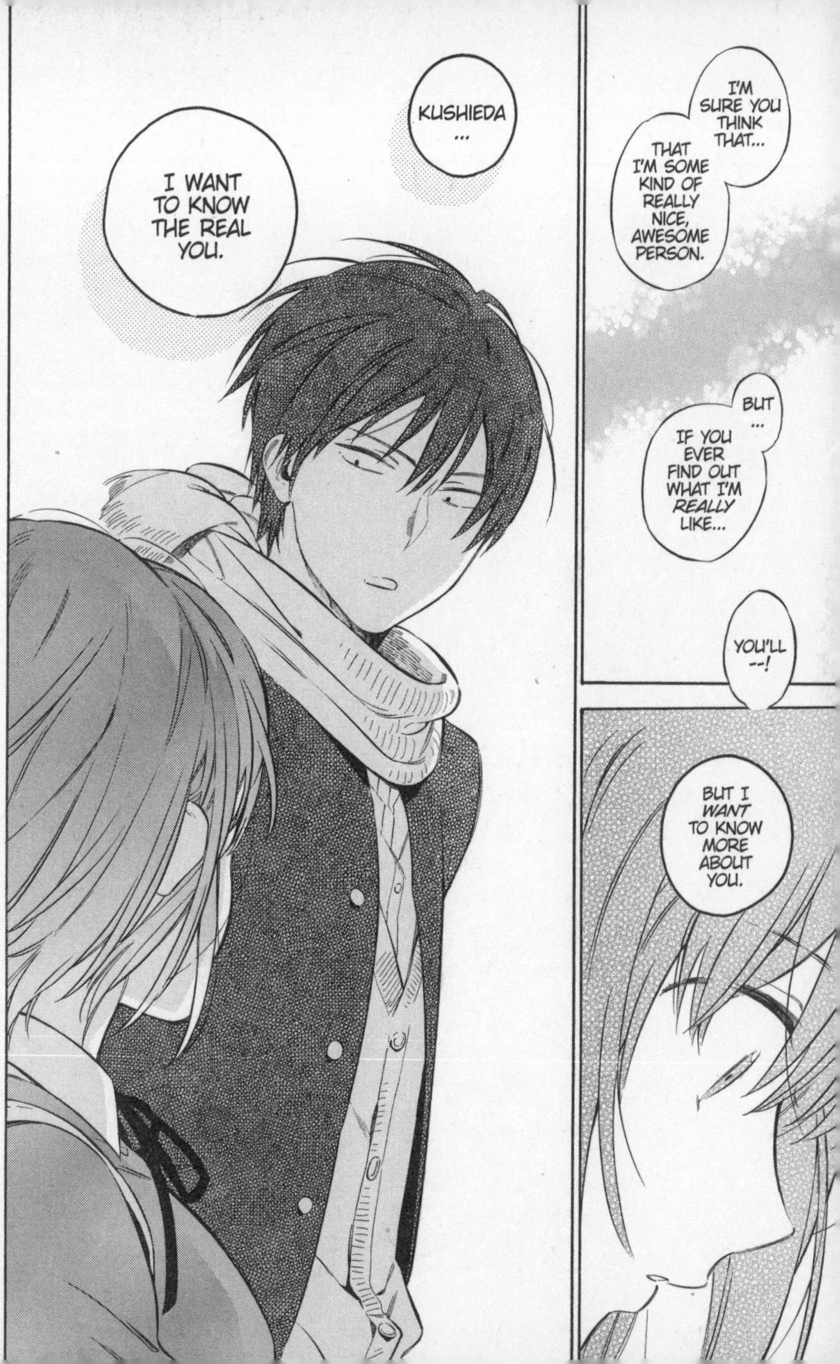
I'M SURE YOU THINK THAT...
THAT I'M SOME KIND OF REALLY NICE, AWESOME PERSON.
BUT...
IF YOU EVER FIND OUT WHAT I'M *REALLY* LIKE...
YOU'LL --!
BUT I *WANT* TO KNOW MORE ABOUT YOU.
KUSHIEDA...
I WANT TO KNOW THE REAL YOU.

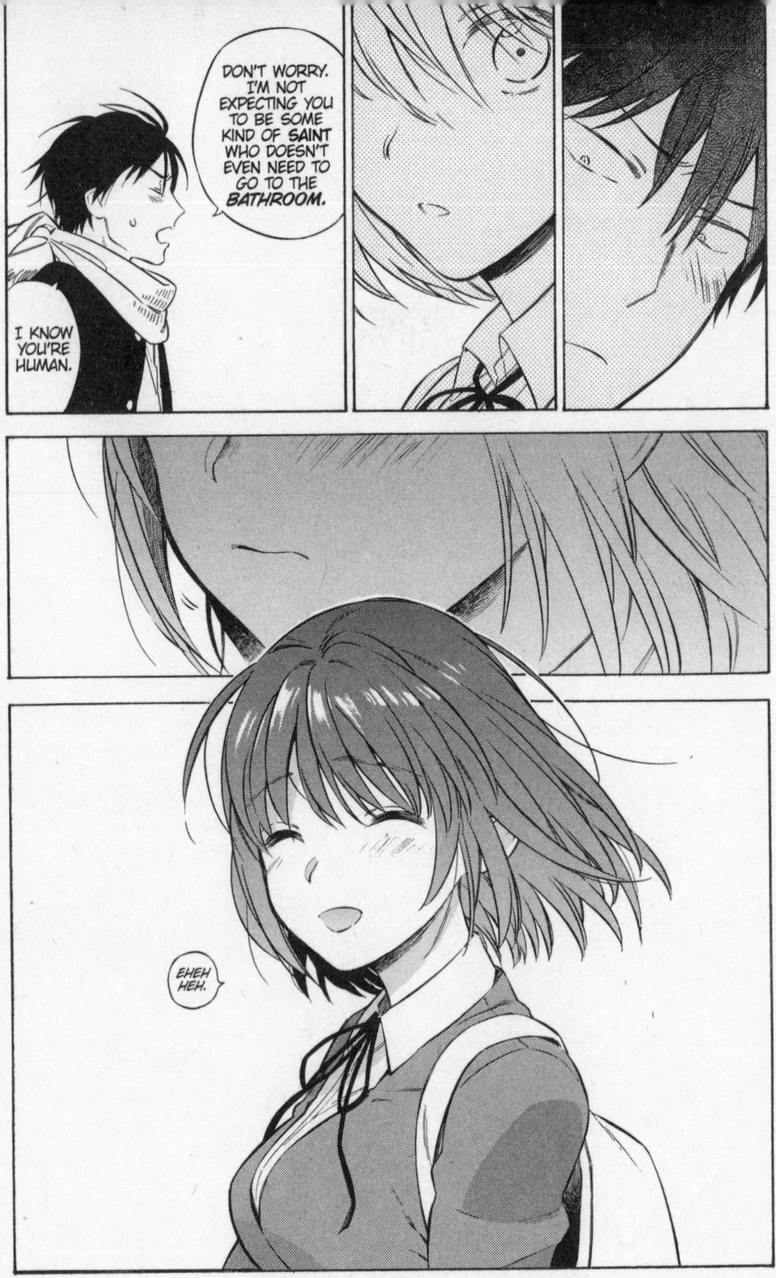
DON'T WORRY. I'M NOT EXPECTING YOU TO BE SOME KIND OF SAINT WHO DOESN'T EVEN NEED TO GO TO THE BATHROOM.
I KNOW YOU'RE HUMAN.
EHEH HEH.

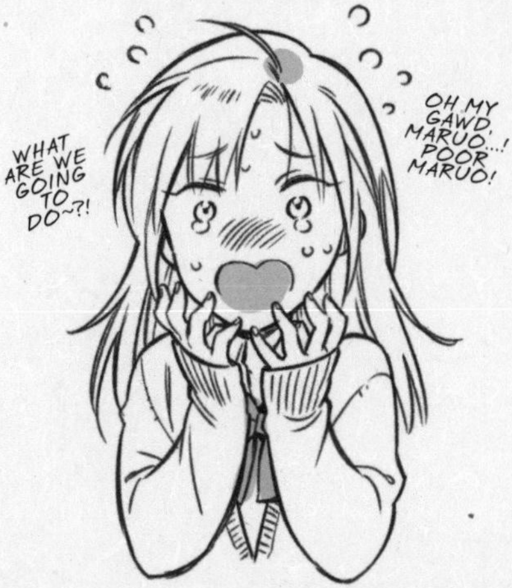
OH MY GAWD, MARUO...! POOR MARUO!
WHAT ARE WE GOING TO DO~?!

Chapter 62: ORION

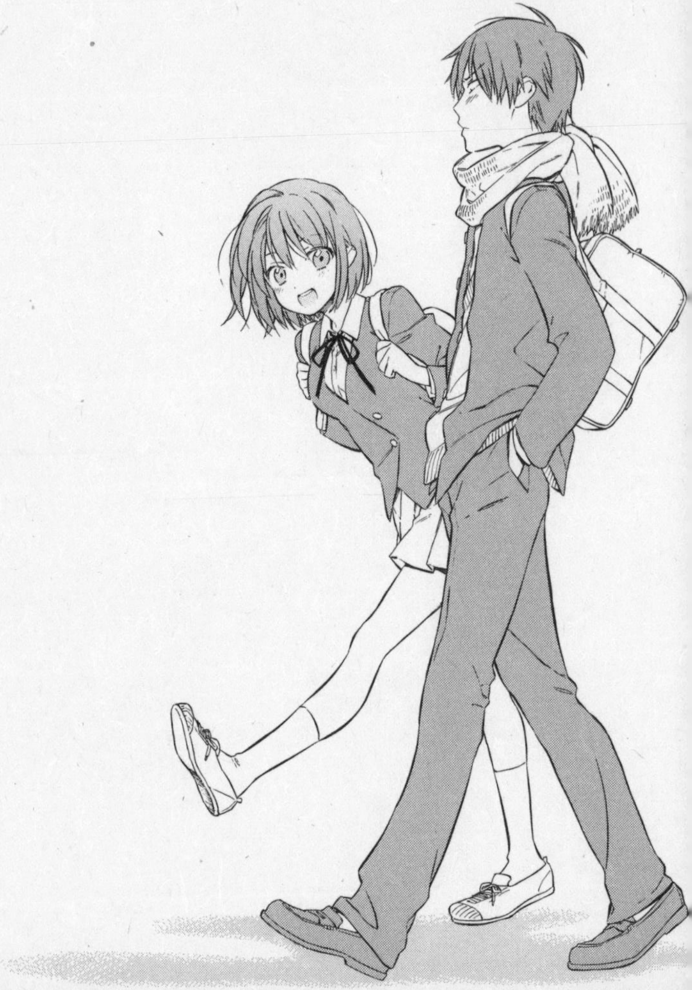

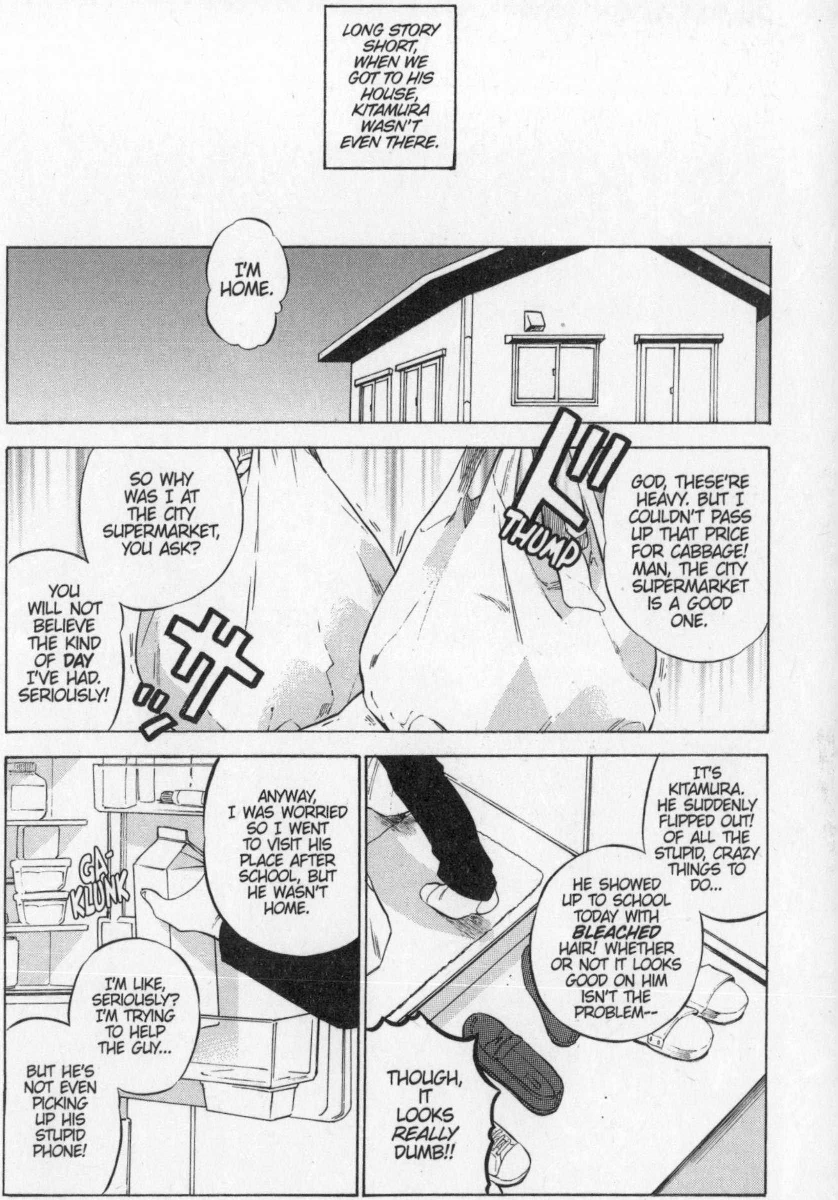
LONG STORY SHORT, WHEN WE GOT TO HIS HOUSE, KITAMURA WASN'T EVEN THERE.
I'M HOME.
GOD, THESE'RE HEAVY. BUT I COULDN'T PASS UP THAT PRICE FOR CABBAGE! MAN, THE CITY SUPERMARKET IS A GOOD ONE.
THUMP
SO WHY WAS I AT THE CITY SUPERMARKET, YOU ASK?
YOU WILL NOT BELIEVE THE KIND OF DAY I'VE HAD. SERIOUSLY!
IT'S KITAMURA. HE SUDDENLY FLIPPED OUT! OF ALL THE STUPID, CRAZY THINGS TO DO...
HE SHOWED UP TO SCHOOL TODAY WITH BLEACHED HAIR! WHETHER OR NOT IT LOOKS GOOD ON HIM ISN'T THE PROBLEM--
THOUGH, IT LOOKS REALLY DUMB!!
ANYWAY, I WAS WORRIED SO I WENT TO VISIT HIS PLACE AFTER SCHOOL, BUT HE WASN'T HOME.
GA-KLUNK
I'M LIKE, SERIOUSLY? I'M TRYING TO HELP THE GUY...
BUT HE'S NOT EVEN PICKING UP HIS STUPID PHONE!

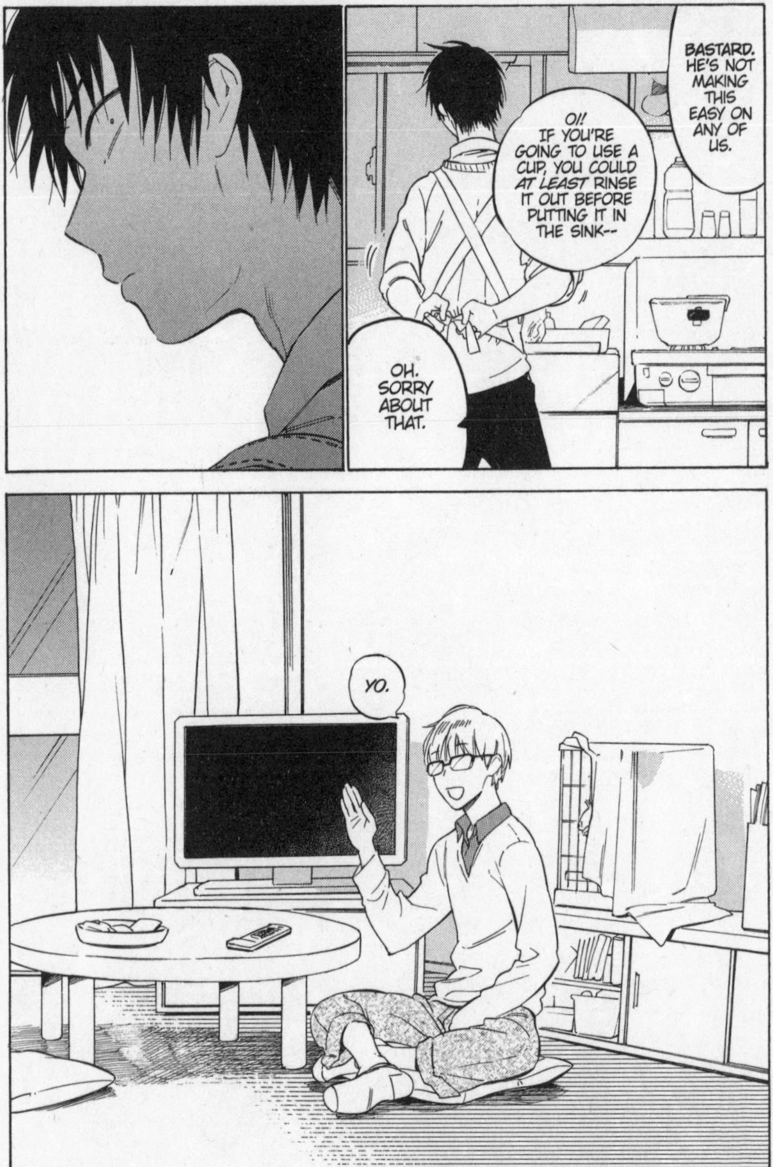
BASTARD. HE'S NOT MAKING THIS EASY ON ANY OF US.
OI! IF YOU'RE GOING TO USE A CUP, YOU COULD *AT LEAST* RINSE IT OUT BEFORE PUTTING IT IN THE SINK--
OH. SORRY ABOUT THAT.
YO.

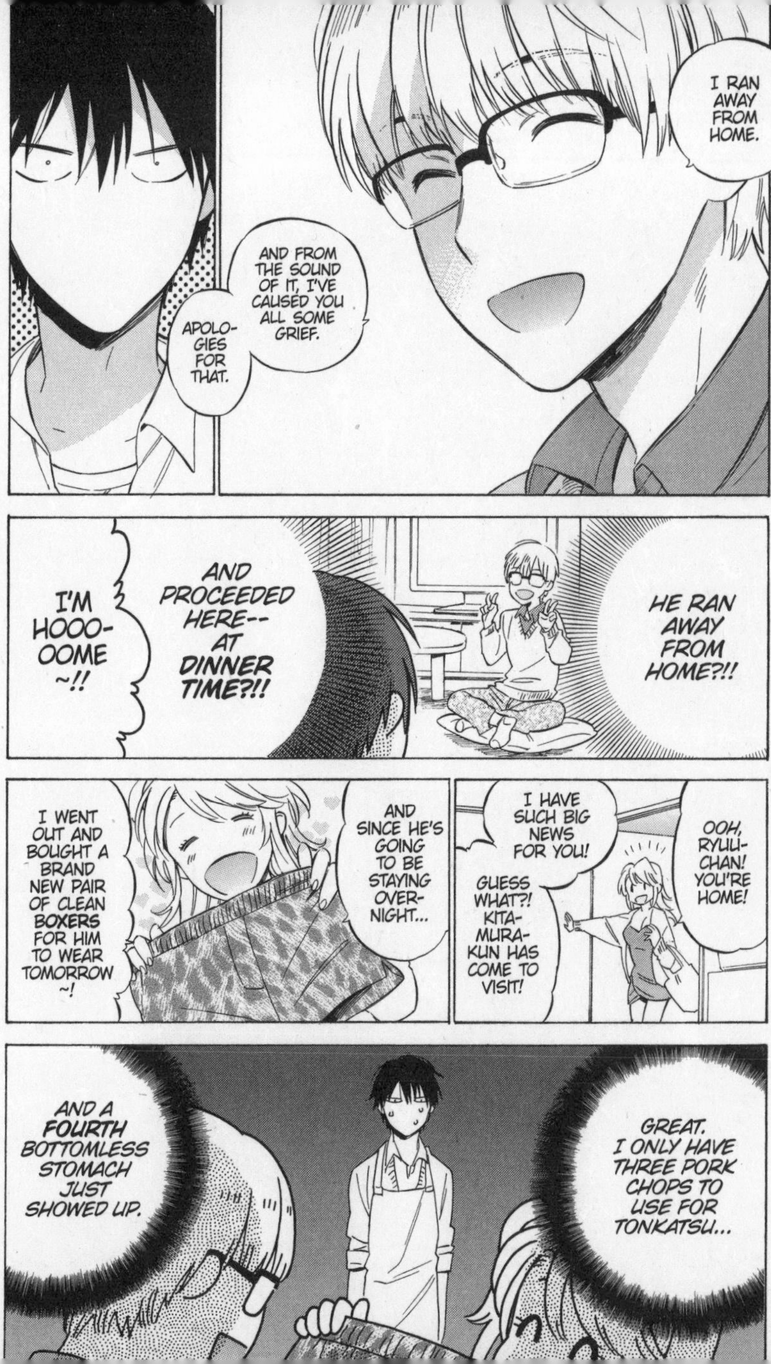
I RAN AWAY FROM HOME.
AND FROM THE SOUND OF IT, I'VE CAUSED YOU ALL SOME GRIEF.
APOLOGIES FOR THAT.
HE RAN AWAY FROM HOME?!!
AND PROCEEDED HERE--AT DINNER TIME?!!
I'M HOOOOOME~!!
OOH, RYUU-CHAN! YOU'RE HOME!
I HAVE SUCH BIG NEWS FOR YOU!
GUESS WHAT?! KITAMURA-KUN HAS COME TO VISIT!
AND SINCE HE'S GOING TO BE STAYING OVERNIGHT...
I WENT OUT AND BOUGHT A BRAND NEW PAIR OF CLEAN BOXERS FOR HIM TO WEAR TOMORROW~!
GREAT. I ONLY HAVE THREE PORK CHOPS TO USE FOR TONKATSU...
AND A FOURTH BOTTOMLESS STOMACH JUST SHOWED UP.

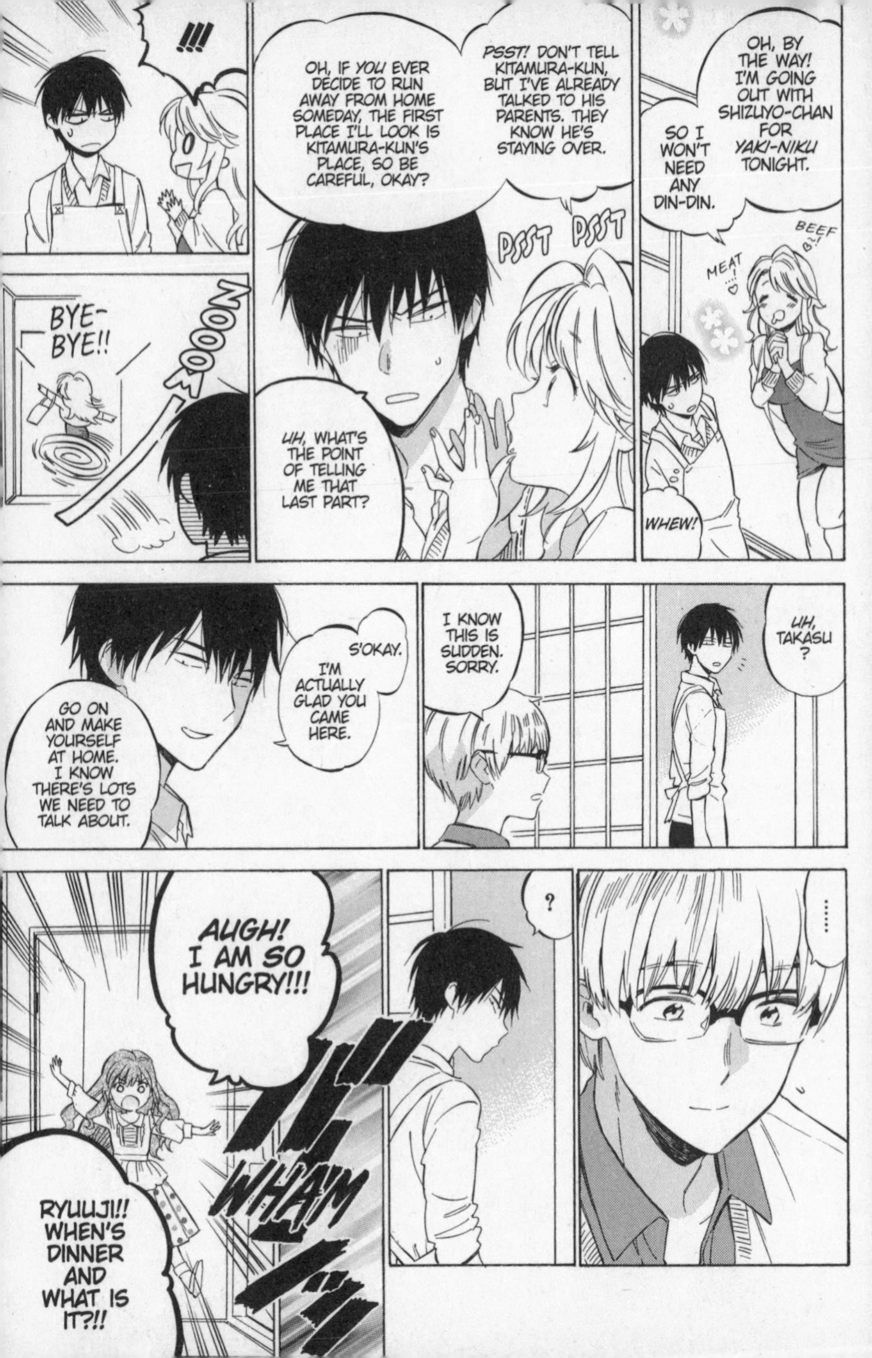
OH, BY THE WAY! I'M GOING OUT WITH SHIZUYO-CHAN FOR *YAKI-NIKU* TONIGHT.
SO I WON'T NEED ANY DIN-DIN.
BEEF ...!
MEAT ...!
WHEW!
PSST! DON'T TELL KITAMURA-KUN, BUT I'VE ALREADY TALKED TO HIS PARENTS. THEY KNOW HE'S STAYING OVER.
OH, IF *YOU* EVER DECIDE TO RUN AWAY FROM HOME SOMEDAY, THE FIRST PLACE I'LL LOOK IS KITAMURA-KUN'S PLACE, SO BE CAREFUL, OKAY?
PSST PSST
UH, WHAT'S THE POINT OF TELLING ME THAT LAST PART?
!!!
BYE-BYE!!
ZOOOOM
UH, TAKASU?
I KNOW THIS IS SUDDEN. SORRY.
S'OKAY.
I'M ACTUALLY GLAD YOU CAME HERE.
GO ON AND MAKE YOURSELF AT HOME. I KNOW THERE'S LOTS WE NEED TO TALK ABOUT.
......
?
AUGH! I AM SO HUNGRY!!!
WHAM
RYUUJI!! WHEN'S DINNER AND WHAT IS IT?!!

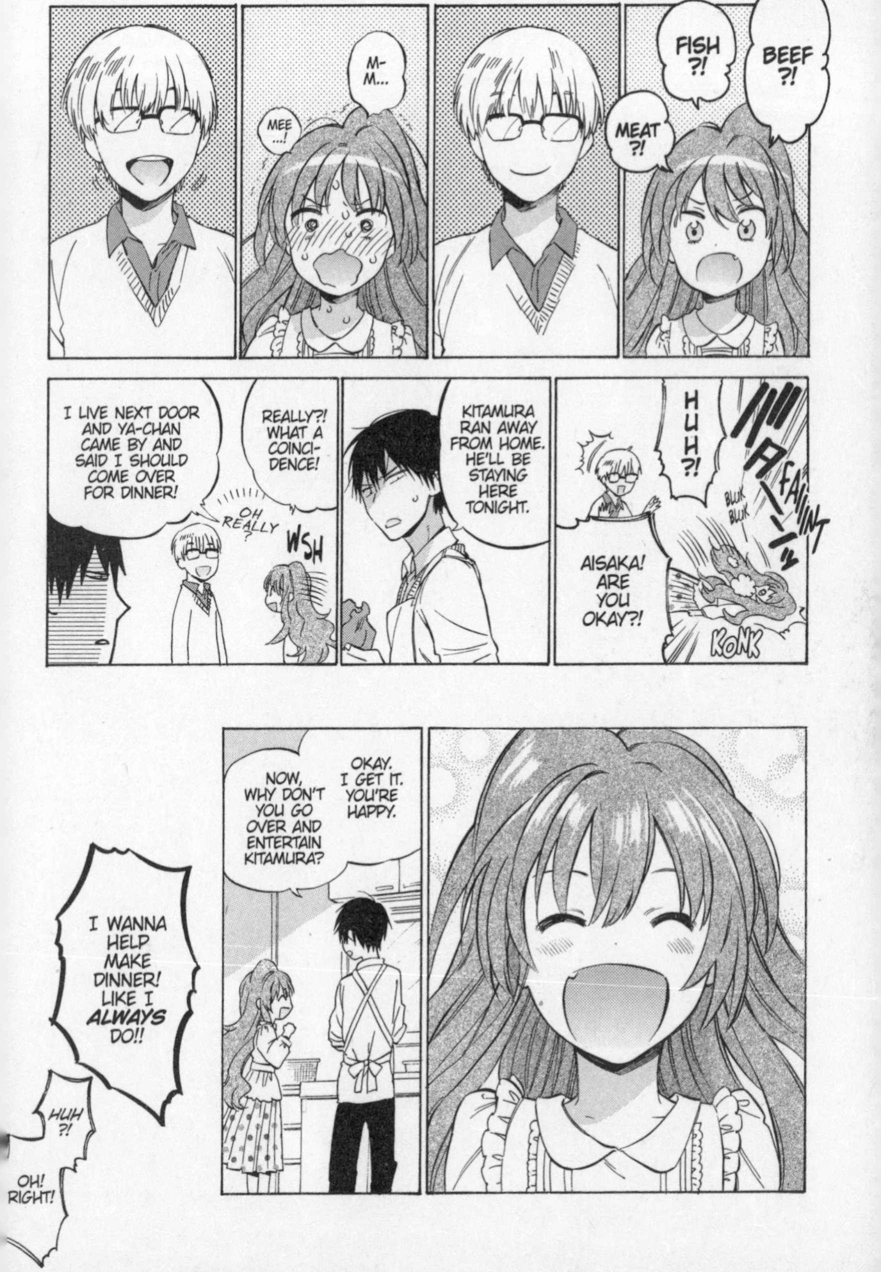
BEEF ?!
FISH ?!
MEAT ?!
M- M...
MEE ...!
HUH ?!
BLUK BLUK
FAIIINT
AISAKA! ARE YOU OKAY?!
KONK
KITAMURA RAN AWAY FROM HOME. HE'LL BE STAYING HERE TONIGHT.
REALLY?! WHAT A COINCI- DENCE!
I LIVE NEXT DOOR AND YA-CHAN CAME BY AND SAID I SHOULD COME OVER FOR DINNER!
OH REALLY
WSH
OKAY. I GET IT. YOU'RE HAPPY.
NOW, WHY DON'T YOU GO OVER AND ENTERTAIN KITAMURA?
I WANNA HELP MAKE DINNER! LIKE I ALWAYS DO!!
HUH ?!
OH! RIGHT!

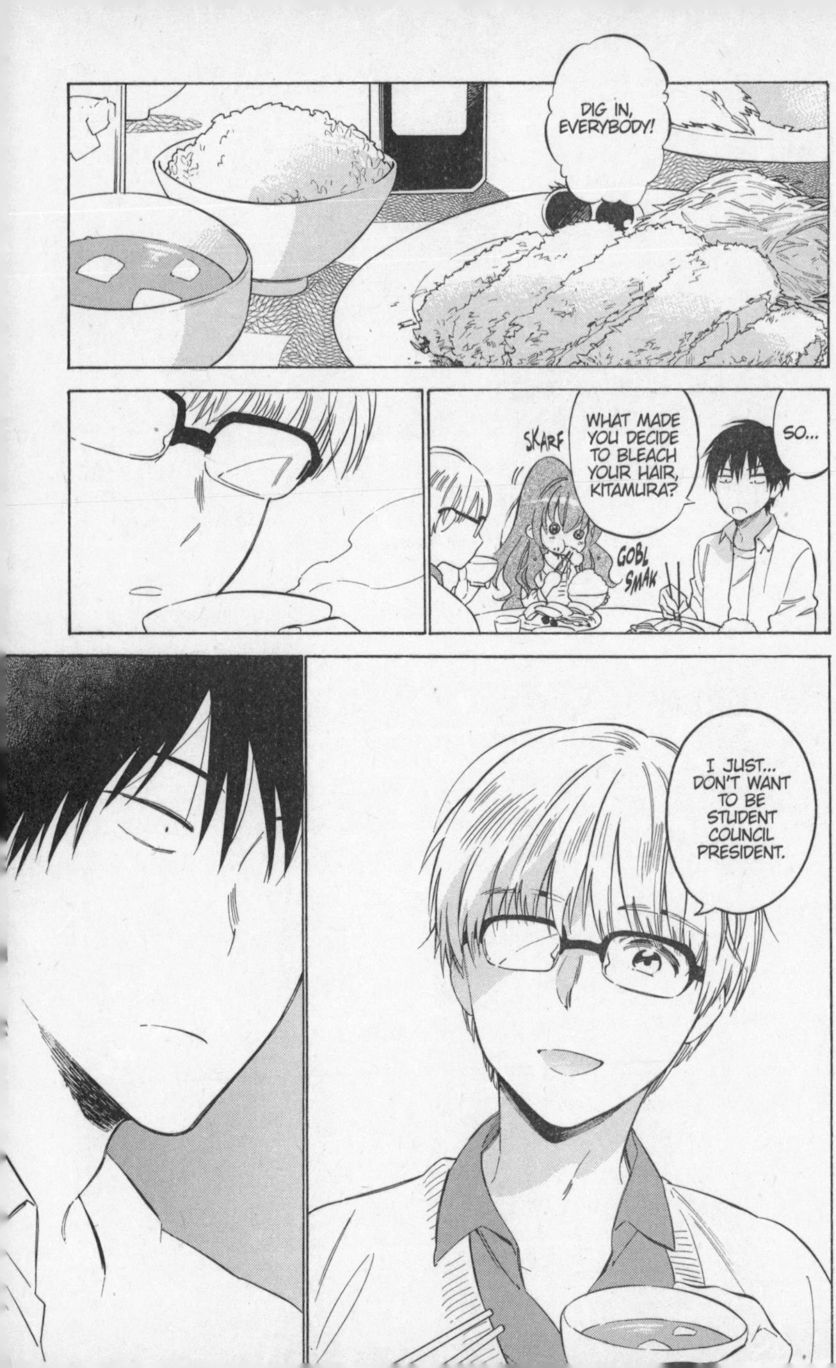
DIG IN, EVERYBODY!
SO...
WHAT MADE YOU DECIDE TO BLEACH YOUR HAIR, KITAMURA?
SKARF
GOBL SMAK
I JUST... DON'T WANT TO BE STUDENT COUNCIL PRESIDENT.

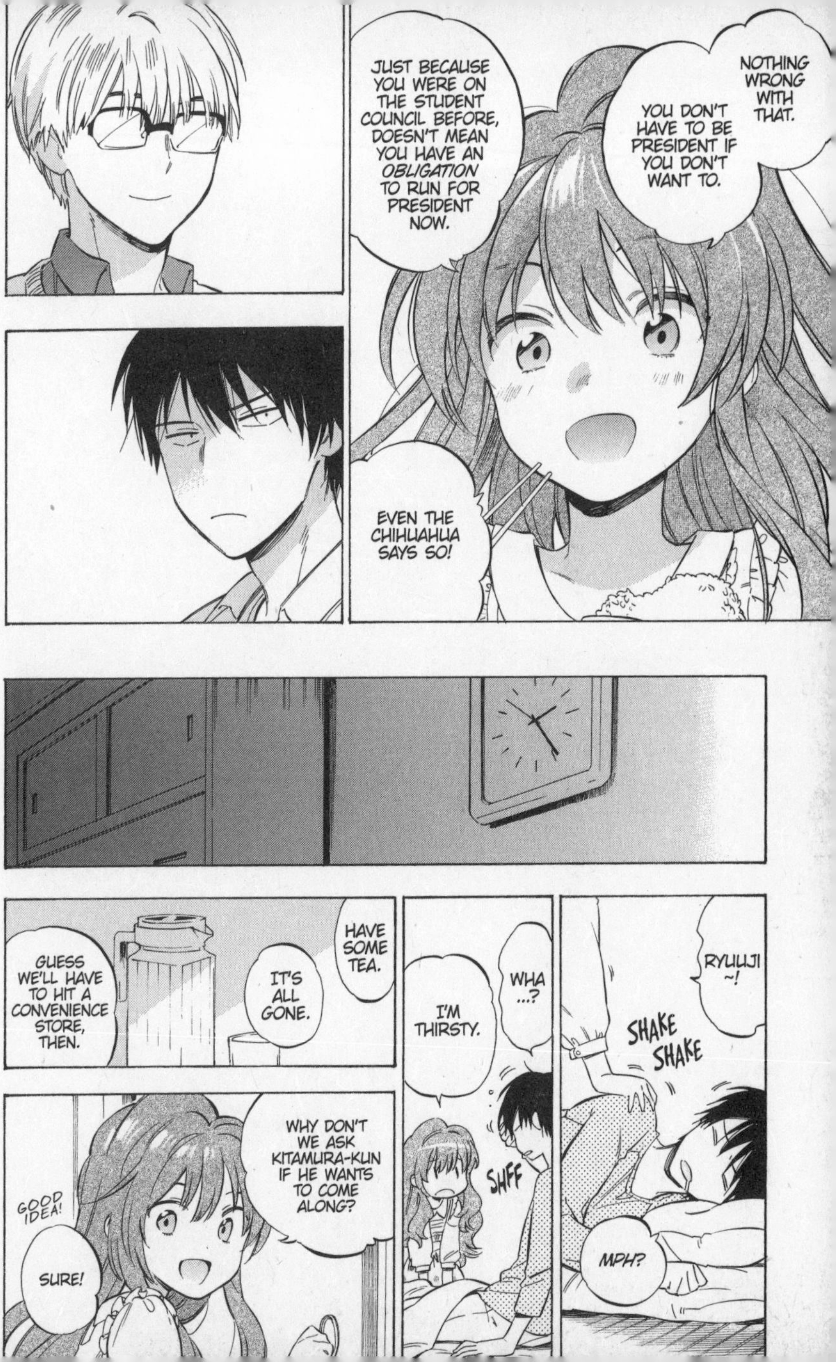
JUST BECAUSE YOU WERE ON THE STUDENT COUNCIL BEFORE, DOESN'T MEAN YOU HAVE AN *OBLIGATION* TO RUN FOR PRESIDENT NOW.
NOTHING WRONG WITH THAT.
YOU DON'T HAVE TO BE PRESIDENT IF YOU DON'T WANT TO.
EVEN THE CHIHUAHUA SAYS SO!
RYUUJI ~!
SHAKE SHAKE
MPH?
WHA ...?
I'M THIRSTY.
SHFF
HAVE SOME TEA.
IT'S ALL GONE.
GUESS WE'LL HAVE TO HIT A CONVENIENCE STORE, THEN.
WHY DON'T WE ASK KITAMURA-KUN IF HE WANTS TO COME ALONG?
GOOD IDEA!
SURE!

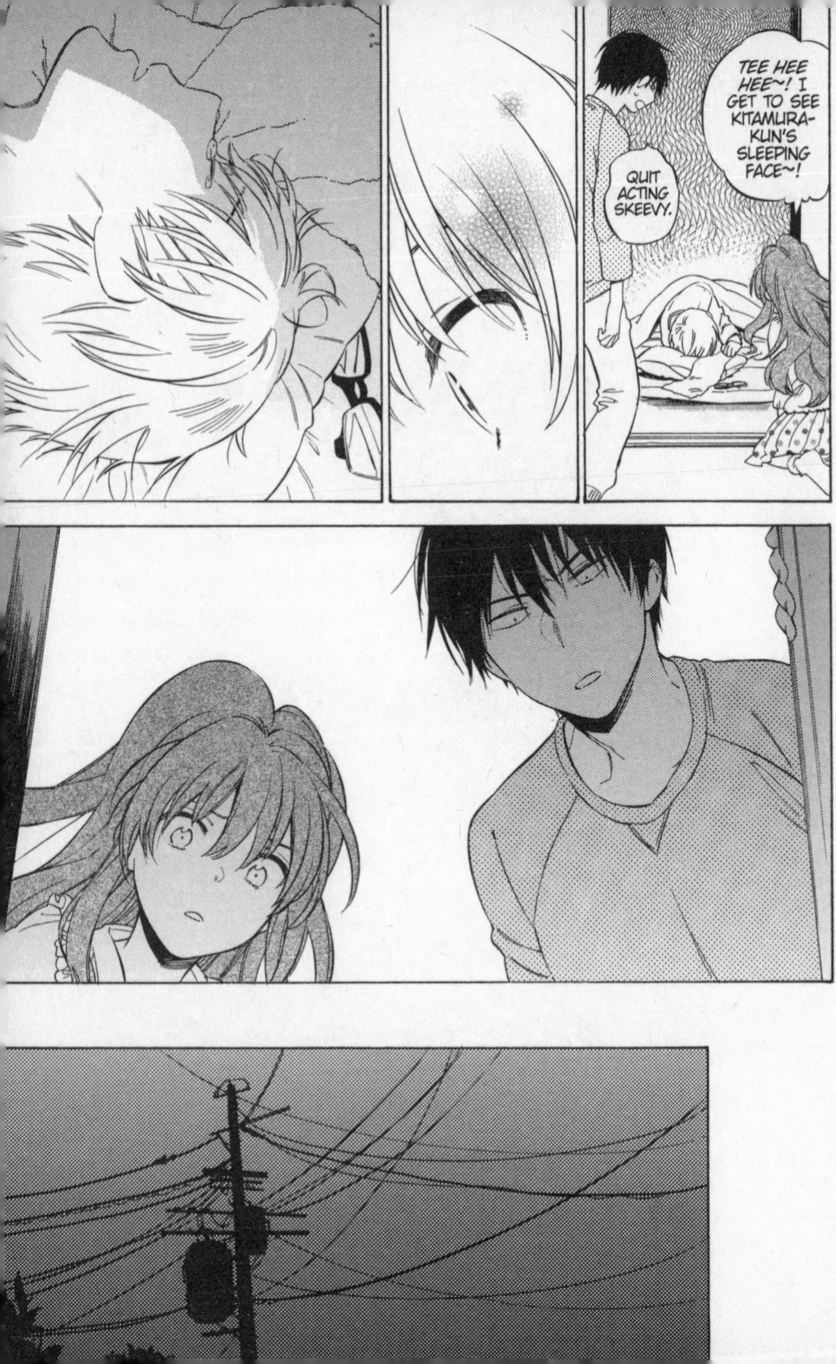
TEE HEE HEE~! I GET TO SEE KITAMURA-KUN'S SLEEPING FACE~!
QUIT ACTING SKEEVY.

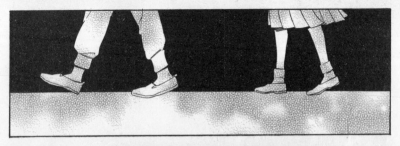

RYUUJI ?

OI, DON'T GET TOO FAR BEHIND. IT'S DANGEROUS OUT AT NIGHT.

WHY WAS I SO HAPPY?

HOW COULD I ACT LIKE THIS WAS A PARTY?

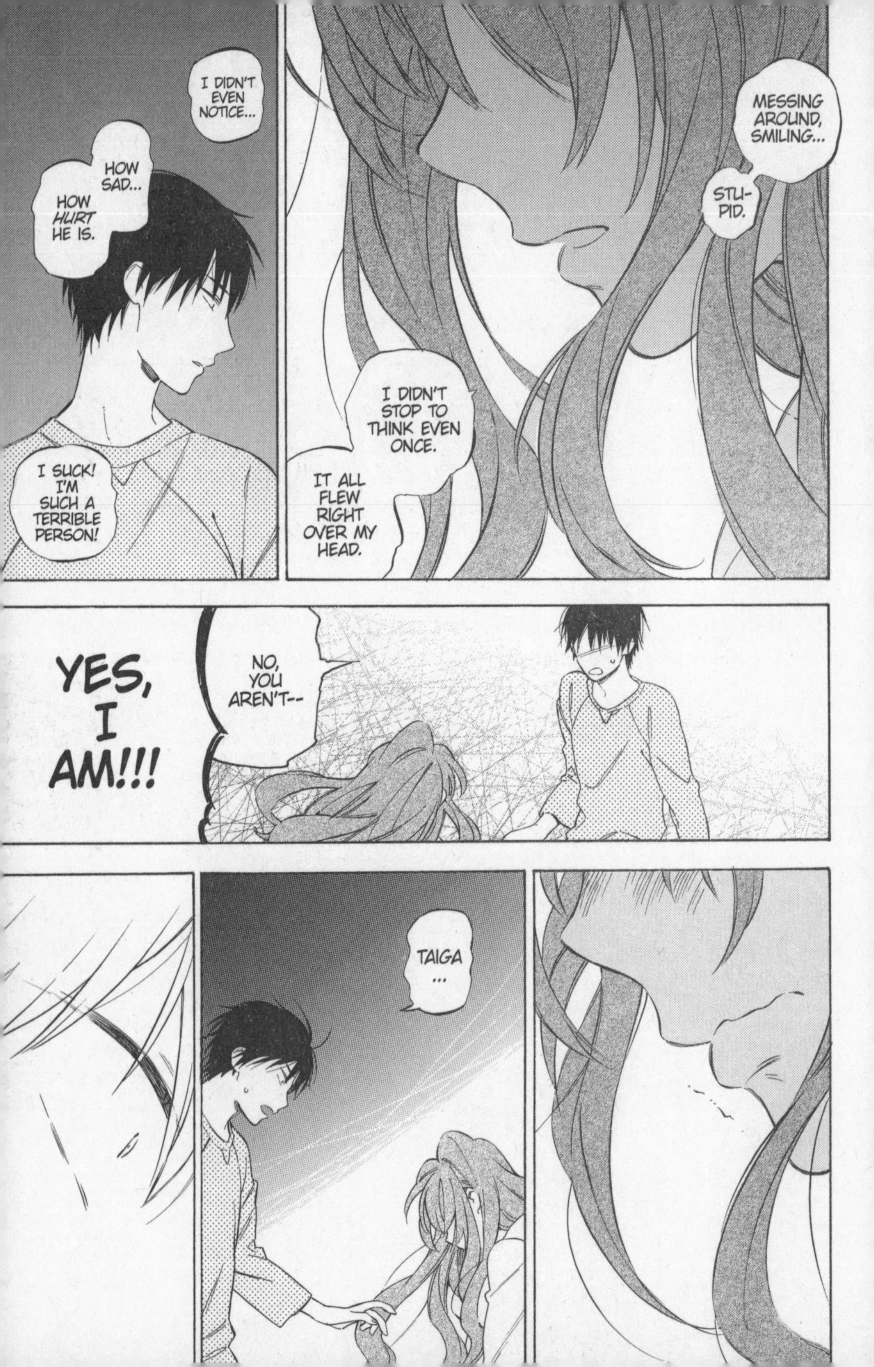
MESSING AROUND, SMILING...
STU-PID.
I DIDN'T STOP TO THINK EVEN ONCE.
IT ALL FLEW RIGHT OVER MY HEAD.
I DIDN'T EVEN NOTICE...
HOW SAD... HOW *HURT* HE IS.
I SUCK! I'M SUCH A TERRIBLE PERSON!
NO, YOU AREN'T--
YES, I AM!!!
...
TAIGA ...

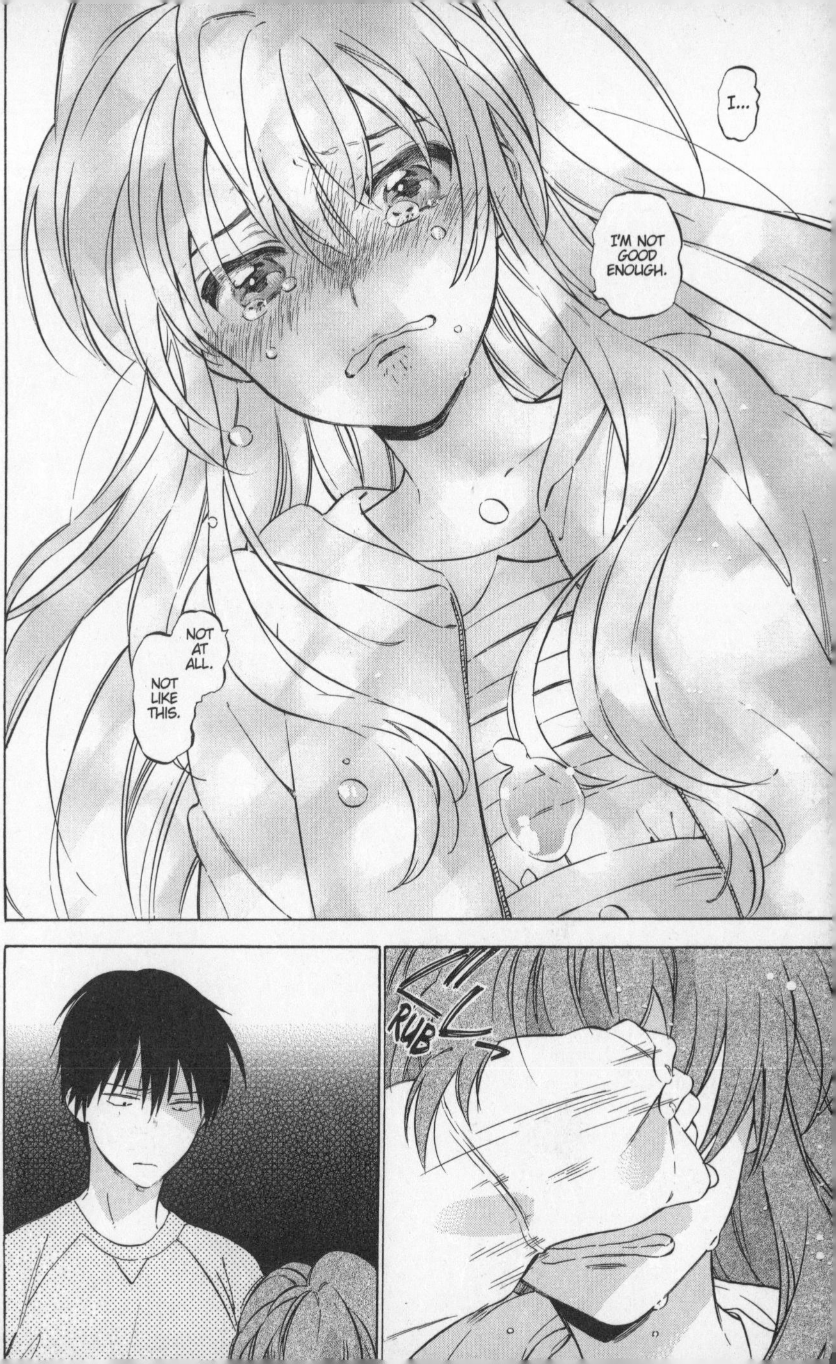
I...
I'M NOT GOOD ENOUGH.
NOT AT ALL.
NOT LIKE THIS.
RUB

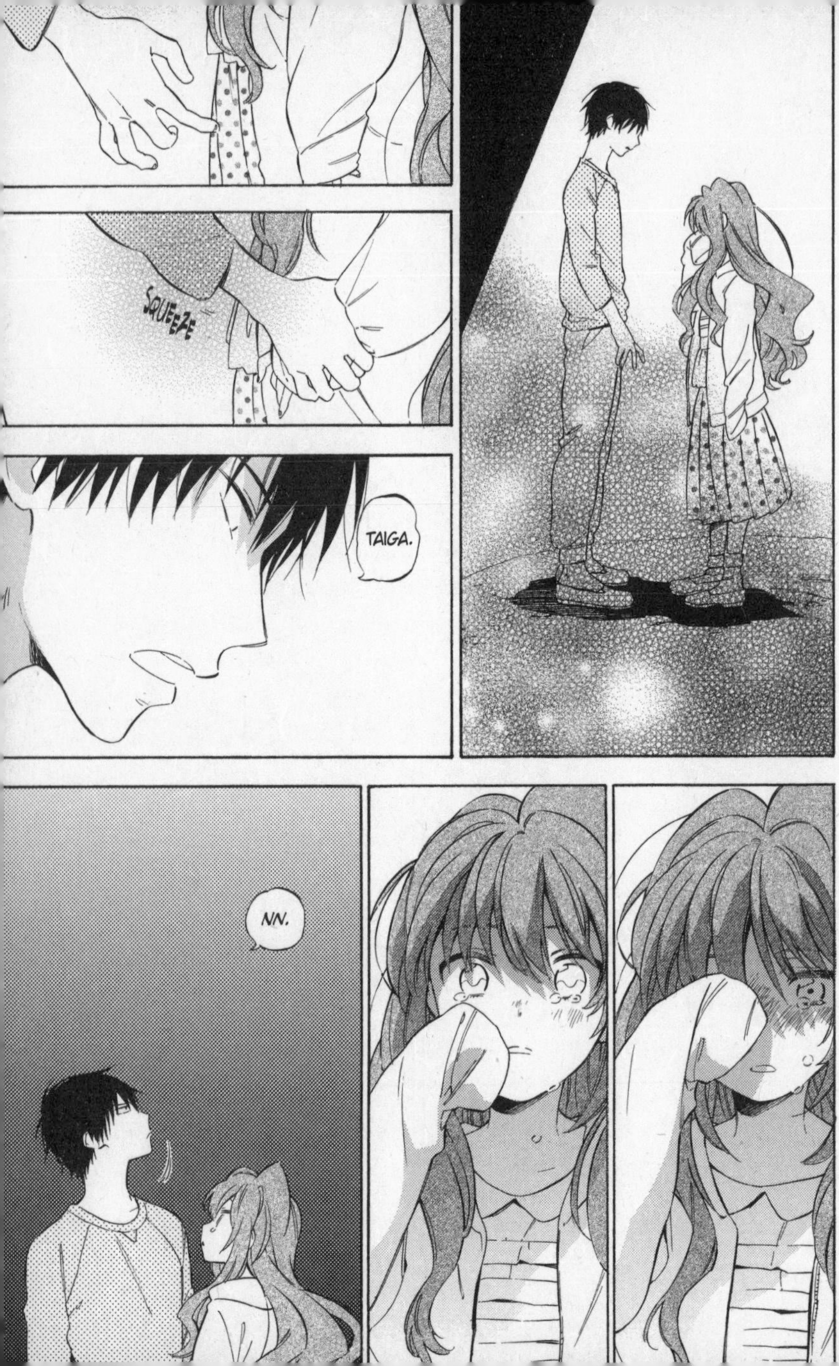
SQUEEZE
TAIGA.
NN.

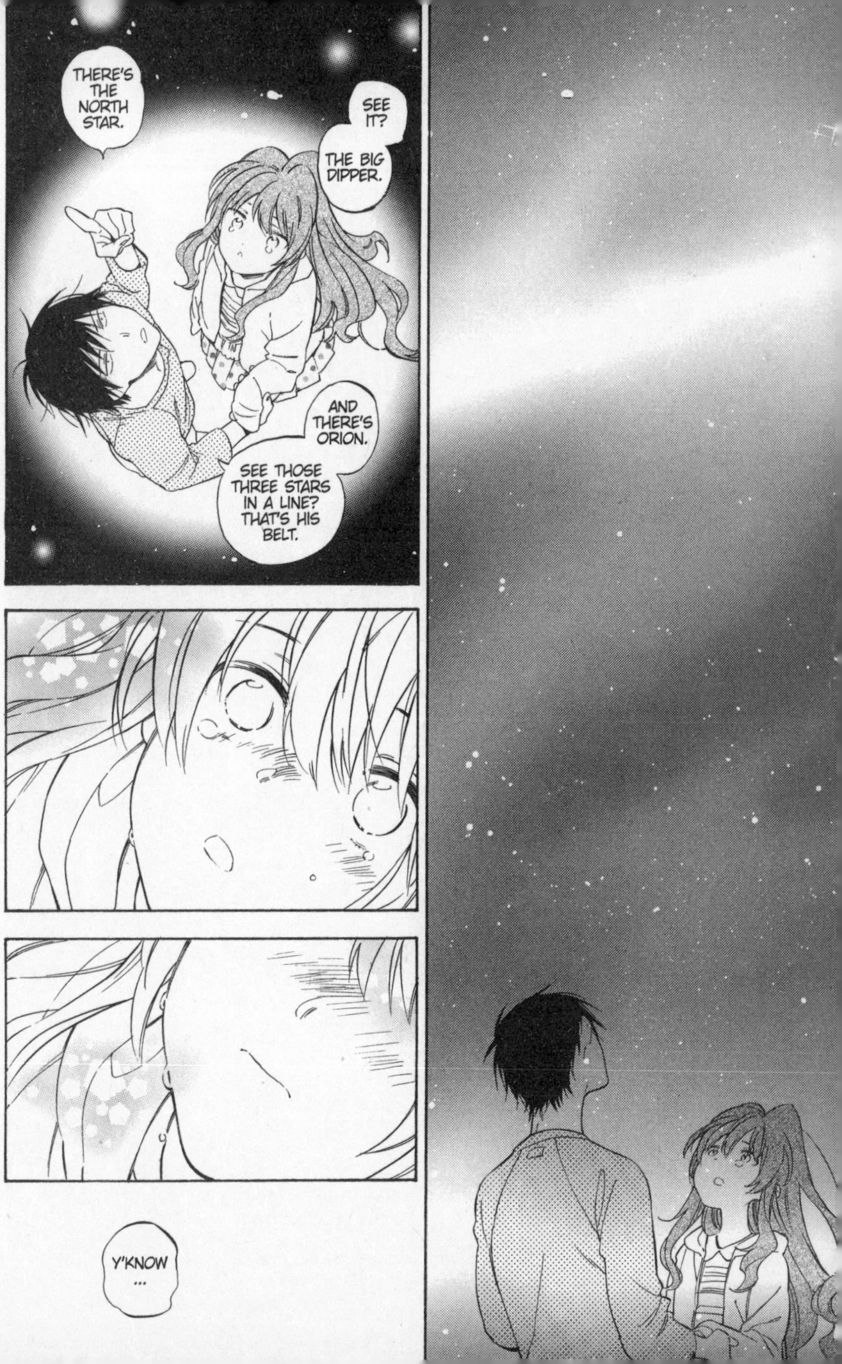
THERE'S THE NORTH STAR.
SEE IT?
THE BIG DIPPER.
AND THERE'S ORION.
SEE THOSE THREE STARS IN A LINE? THAT'S HIS BELT.
Y'KNOW ...

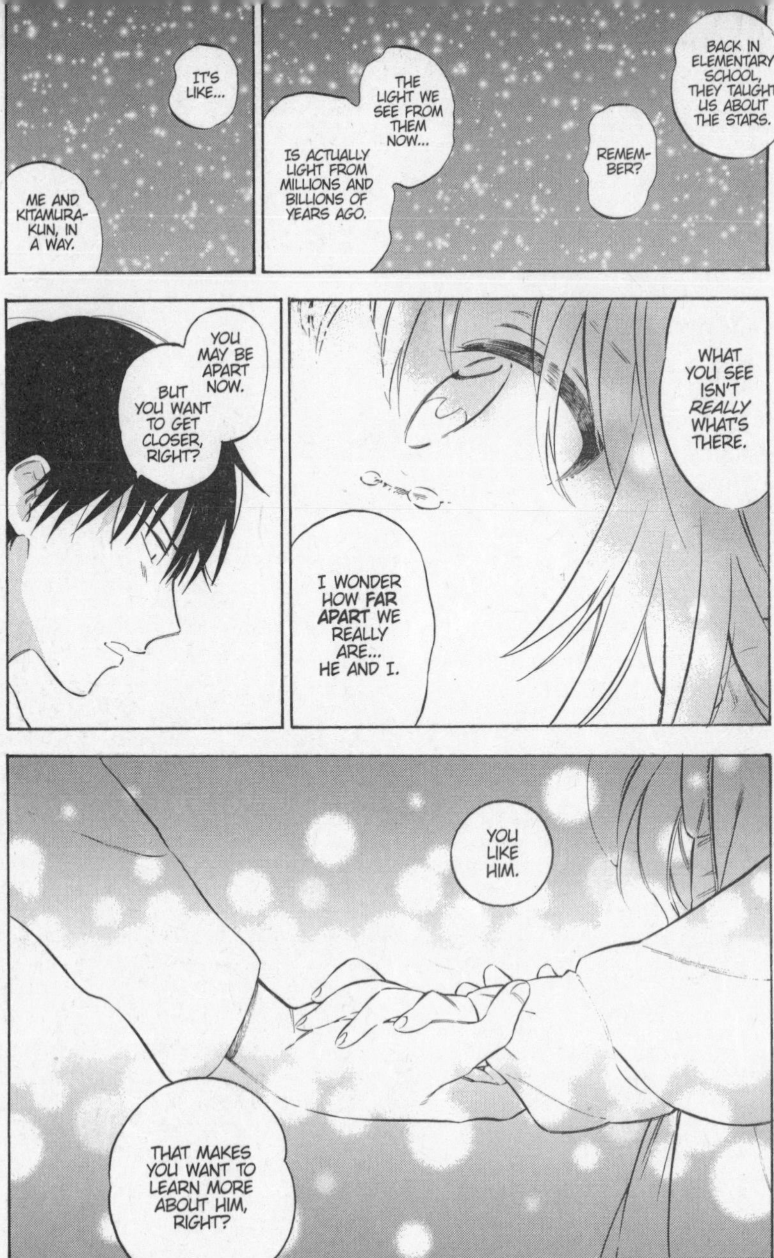
BACK IN ELEMENTARY SCHOOL, THEY TAUGHT US ABOUT THE STARS.
REMEMBER?
THE LIGHT WE SEE FROM THEM NOW...
IS ACTUALLY LIGHT FROM MILLIONS AND BILLIONS OF YEARS AGO.
IT'S LIKE...
ME AND KITAMURA-KUN, IN A WAY.
WHAT YOU SEE ISN'T *REALLY* WHAT'S THERE.
I WONDER HOW **FAR APART** WE REALLY ARE... HE AND I.
YOU MAY BE APART NOW.
BUT YOU WANT TO GET CLOSER, RIGHT?
YOU LIKE HIM.
THAT MAKES YOU WANT TO LEARN MORE ABOUT HIM, RIGHT?

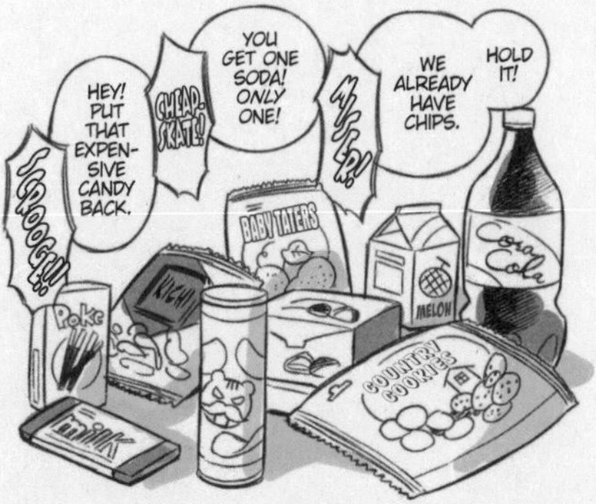
HOLD IT!
WE ALREADY HAVE CHIPS.
MISER!
YOU GET ONE SODA! ONLY ONE!
CHEAPSKATE!
HEY! PUT THAT EXPEN- SIVE CANDY BACK.
SCROOGE!!
BABY TATERS
RICH
Poke
MELON
Coron Cola
COUNTRY COOKIES

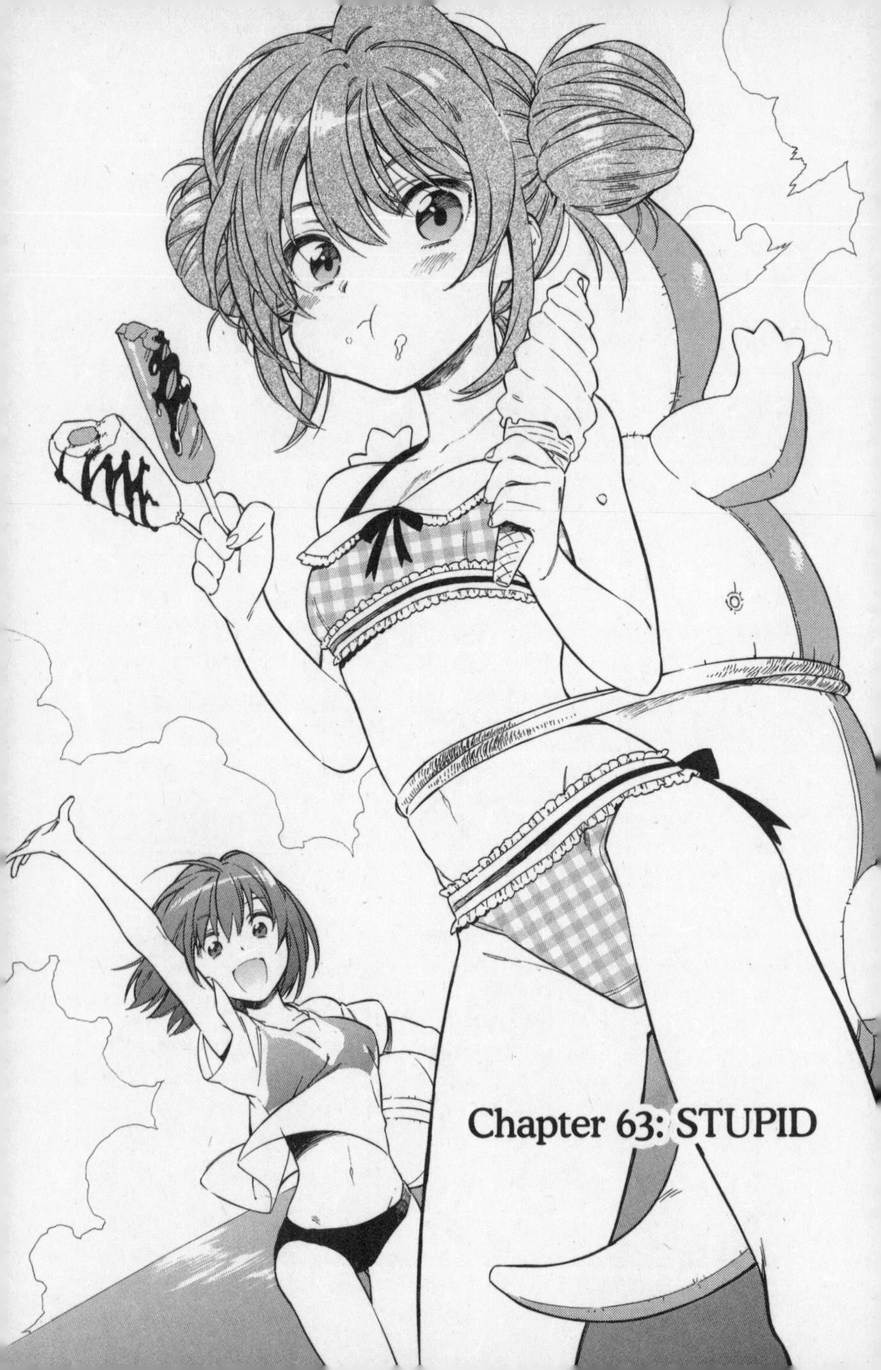

Chapter 63: STUPID

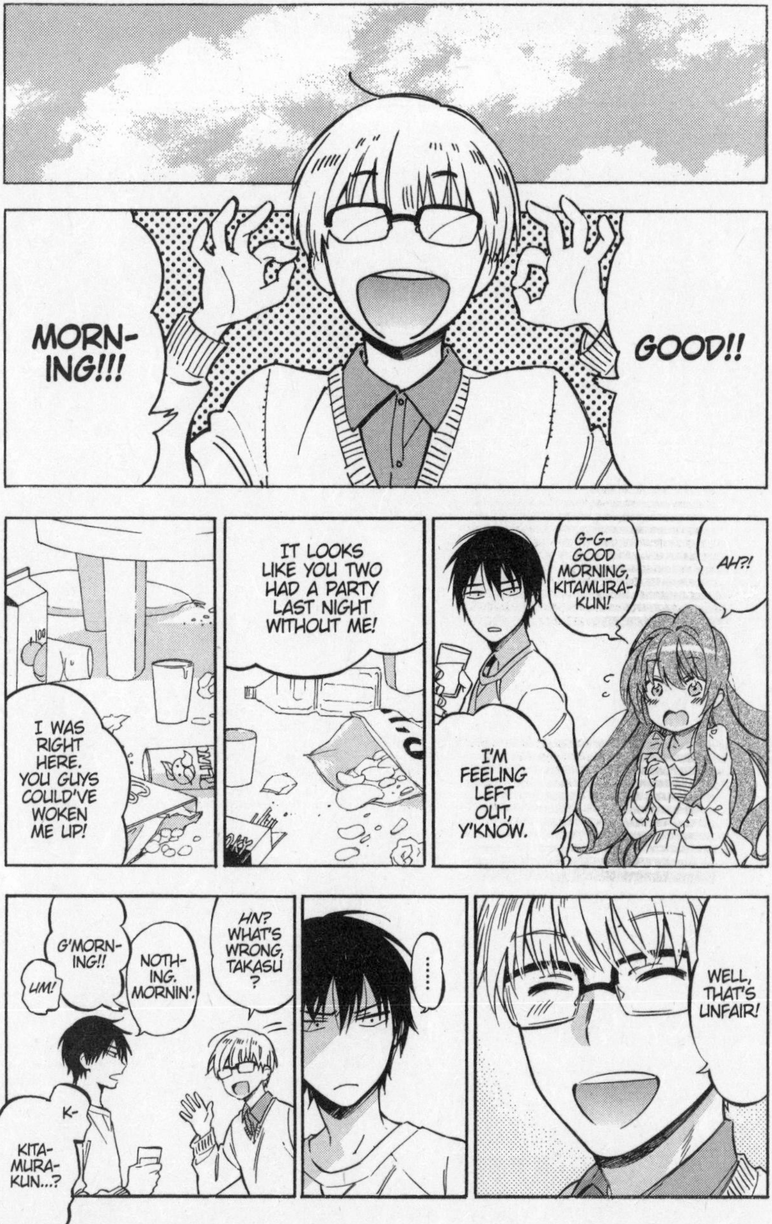
GOOD!!
MORN-ING!!!
AH?!
G-G-GOOD MORNING, KITAMURA-KUN!
I'M FEELING LEFT OUT, Y'KNOW.
IT LOOKS LIKE YOU TWO HAD A PARTY LAST NIGHT WITHOUT ME!
I WAS RIGHT HERE. YOU GUYS COULD'VE WOKEN ME UP!
WELL, THAT'S UNFAIR!
......
HN? WHAT'S WRONG, TAKASU?
NOTHING. MORNIN'.
G'MORN-ING!!
UM!
K- KITAMURA-KUN...?

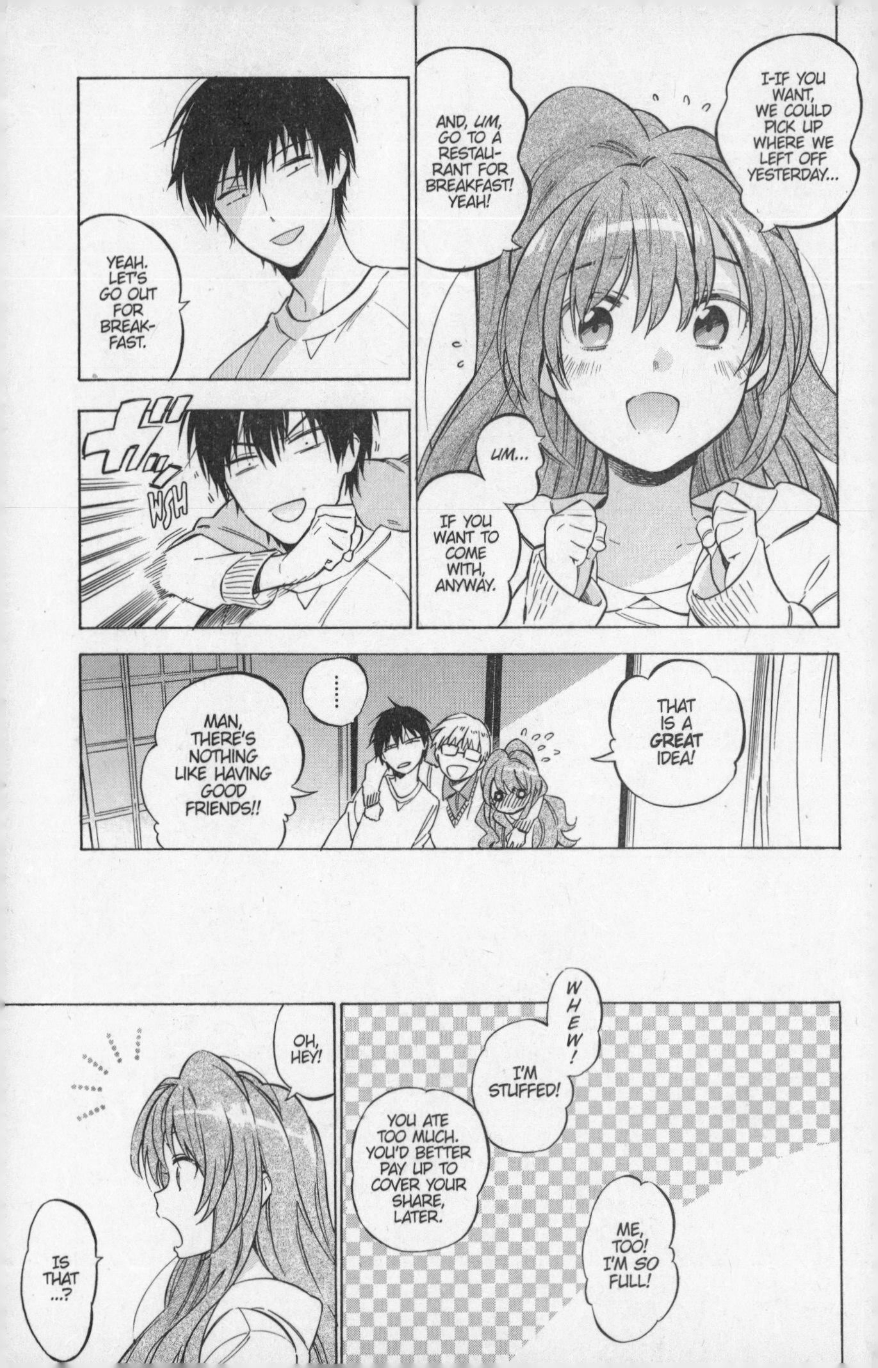
I-IF YOU WANT, WE COULD PICK UP WHERE WE LEFT OFF YESTERDAY...
AND, UM, GO TO A RESTAURANT FOR BREAKFAST! YEAH!
UM...
IF YOU WANT TO COME WITH, ANYWAY.
YEAH. LET'S GO OUT FOR BREAKFAST.
WSH
THAT IS A GREAT IDEA!
......
MAN, THERE'S NOTHING LIKE HAVING GOOD FRIENDS!!
WHEW!
I'M STUFFED!
YOU ATE TOO MUCH. YOU'D BETTER PAY UP TO COVER YOUR SHARE, LATER.
ME, TOO! I'M SO FULL!
OH, HEY!
IS THAT ...?

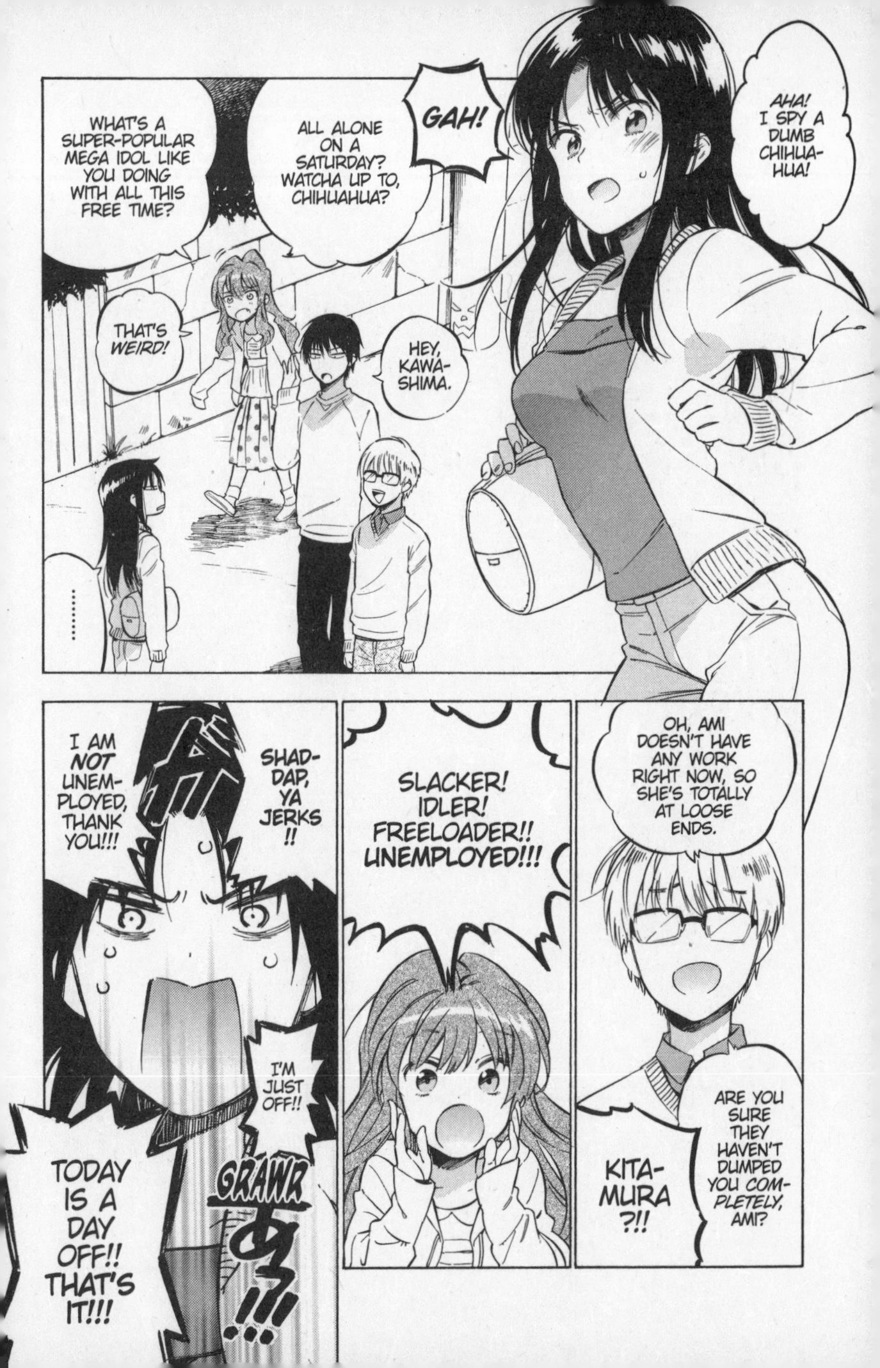
AHA! I SPY A DUMB CHIHUAHUA!
GAH!
ALL ALONE ON A SATURDAY? WATCHA UP TO, CHIHUAHUA?
WHAT'S A SUPER-POPULAR MEGA IDOL LIKE YOU DOING WITH ALL THIS FREE TIME?
HEY, KAWA-SHIMA.
THAT'S *WEIRD!*
……
OH, AMI DOESN'T HAVE ANY WORK RIGHT NOW, SO SHE'S TOTALLY AT LOOSE ENDS.
ARE YOU SURE THEY HAVEN'T DUMPED YOU COM-PLETELY, AMI?
KITA-MURA ?!!
SLACKER! IDLER! FREELOADER!! UNEMPLOYED!!!
SHAD-DAP, YA JERKS !!
I AM *NOT* UNEM-PLOYED, THANK YOU!!!
I'M JUST OFF!!
GRAWR
TODAY IS A DAY OFF!! THAT'S IT!!!

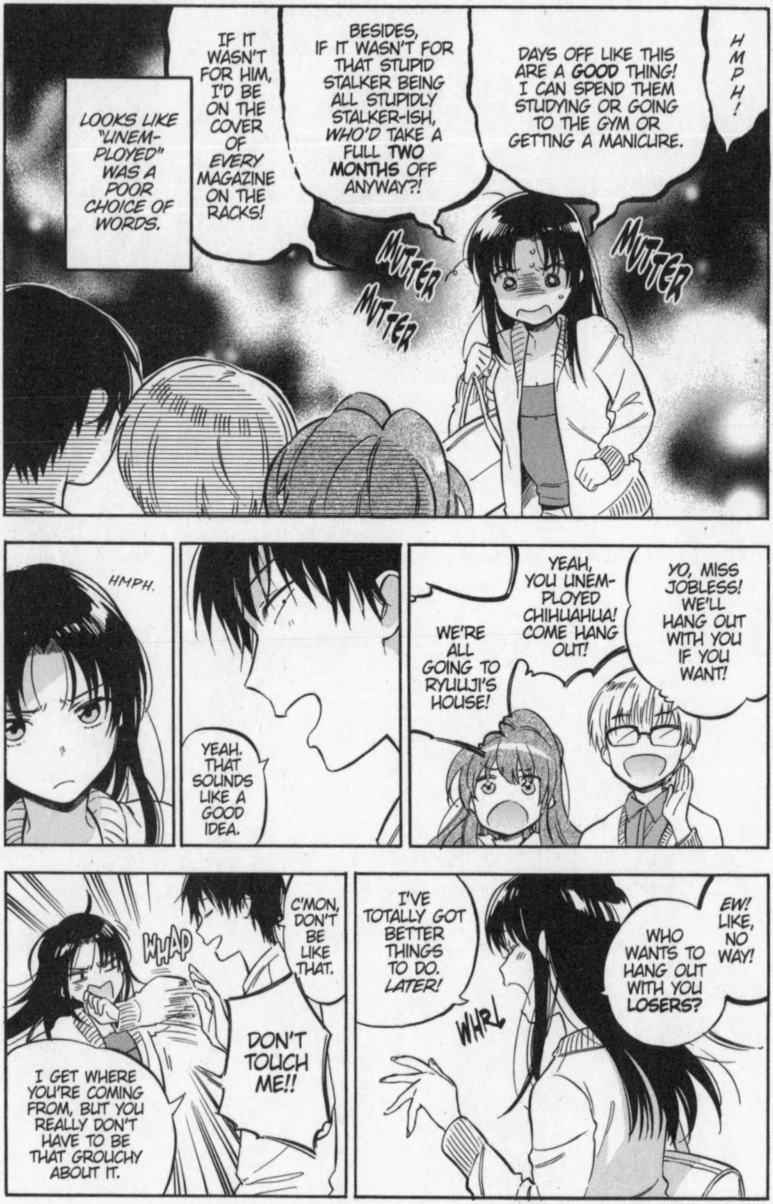
HMPH!
DAYS OFF LIKE THIS ARE A **GOOD** THING! I CAN SPEND THEM STUDYING OR GOING TO THE GYM OR GETTING A MANICURE.
BESIDES, IF IT WASN'T FOR THAT STUPID STALKER BEING ALL STUPIDLY STALKER-ISH, *WHO'D TAKE A* FULL **TWO MONTHS** OFF ANYWAY?!
IF IT WASN'T FOR HIM, I'D BE ON THE COVER OF *EVERY* MAGAZINE ON THE RACKS!
LOOKS LIKE "UNEMPLOYED" WAS A POOR CHOICE OF WORDS.
MUTTER
MUTTER
MUTTER
YO, MISS JOBLESS! WE'LL HANG OUT WITH YOU IF YOU WANT!
YEAH, YOU UNEMPLOYED CHIHUAHUA! COME HANG OUT!
WE'RE ALL GOING TO RYUUJI'S HOUSE!
YEAH. THAT SOUNDS LIKE A GOOD IDEA.
HMPH.
EW! LIKE, NO WAY!
WHO WANTS TO HANG OUT WITH YOU **LOSERS?**
I'VE TOTALLY GOT BETTER THINGS TO DO. *LATER!*
WHRL
C'MON, DON'T BE LIKE THAT.
WHAP
DON'T TOUCH ME!!
I GET WHERE YOU'RE COMING FROM, BUT YOU REALLY DON'T HAVE TO BE THAT GROUCHY ABOUT IT.

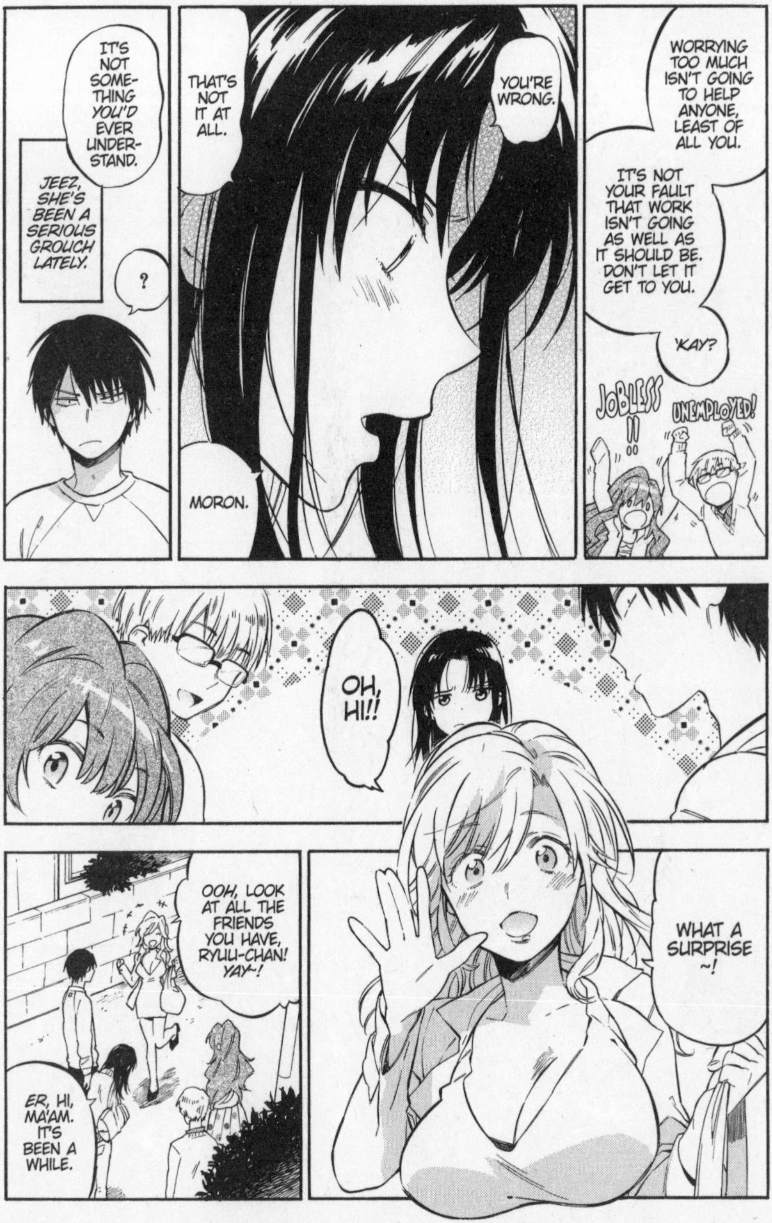
WORRYING TOO MUCH ISN'T GOING TO HELP ANYONE, LEAST OF ALL YOU.
IT'S NOT YOUR FAULT THAT WORK ISN'T GOING AS WELL AS IT SHOULD BE. DON'T LET IT GET TO YOU.
'KAY?
UNEMPLOYED!
JOBLESS!!
YOU'RE WRONG.
THAT'S NOT IT AT ALL.
MORON.
IT'S NOT SOME-THING YOU'D EVER UNDER-STAND.
JEEZ, SHE'S BEEN A SERIOUS GROUCH LATELY.
?
OH, HI!!
WHAT A SURPRISE ~!
OOH, LOOK AT ALL THE FRIENDS YOU HAVE, RYUU-CHAN! YAY~!
ER, HI, MA'AM. IT'S BEEN A WHILE.

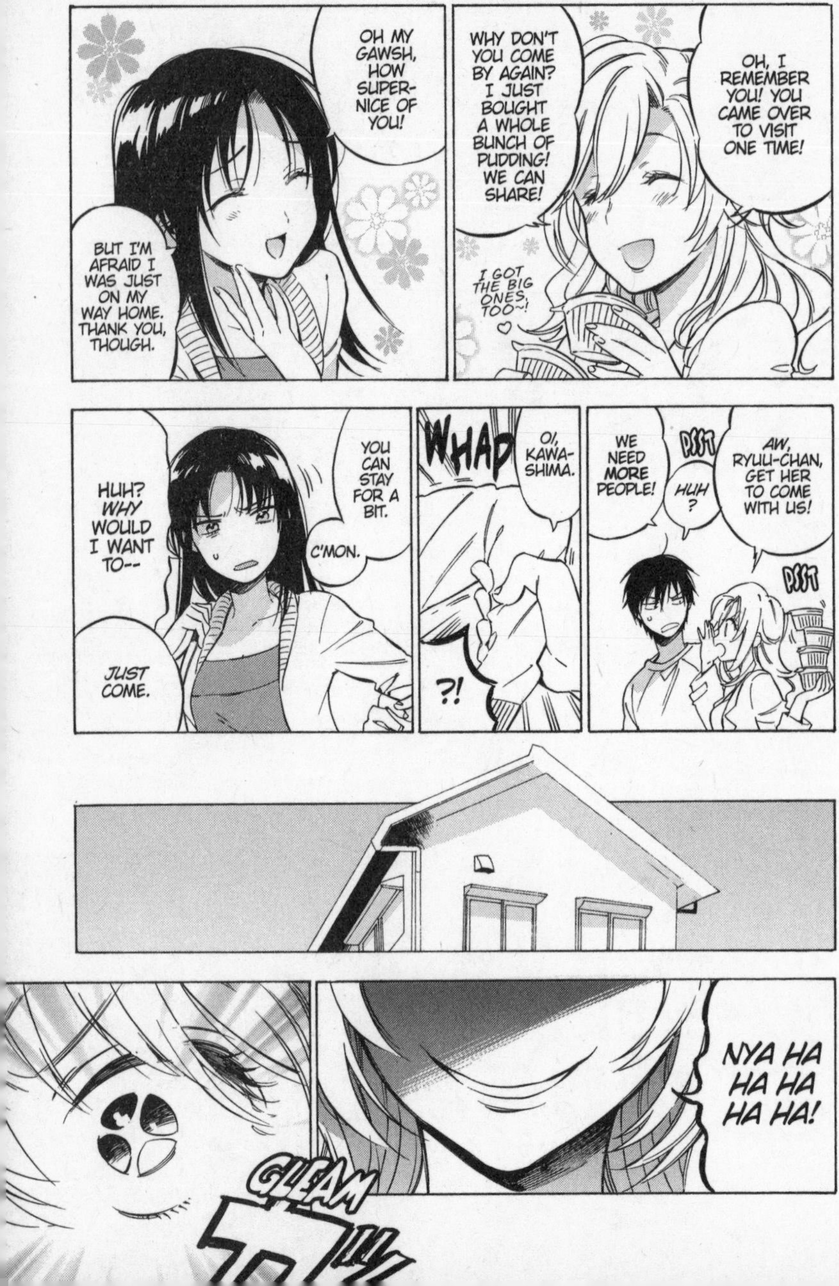
OH, I REMEMBER YOU! YOU CAME OVER TO VISIT ONE TIME!
WHY DON'T YOU COME BY AGAIN? I JUST BOUGHT A WHOLE BUNCH OF PUDDING! WE CAN SHARE!
I GOT THE BIG ONES, TOO~! ♡
OH MY GAWSH, HOW SUPER-NICE OF YOU!
BUT I'M AFRAID I WAS JUST ON MY WAY HOME. THANK YOU, THOUGH.
AW, RYUU-CHAN, GET HER TO COME WITH US!
PSST
HUH?
PSST
WE NEED MORE PEOPLE!
WHAP
OI, KAWASHIMA.
?!
YOU CAN STAY FOR A BIT.
C'MON.
HUH? *WHY* WOULD I WANT TO--
JUST COME.
NYA HA HA HA HA HA!
GLEAM

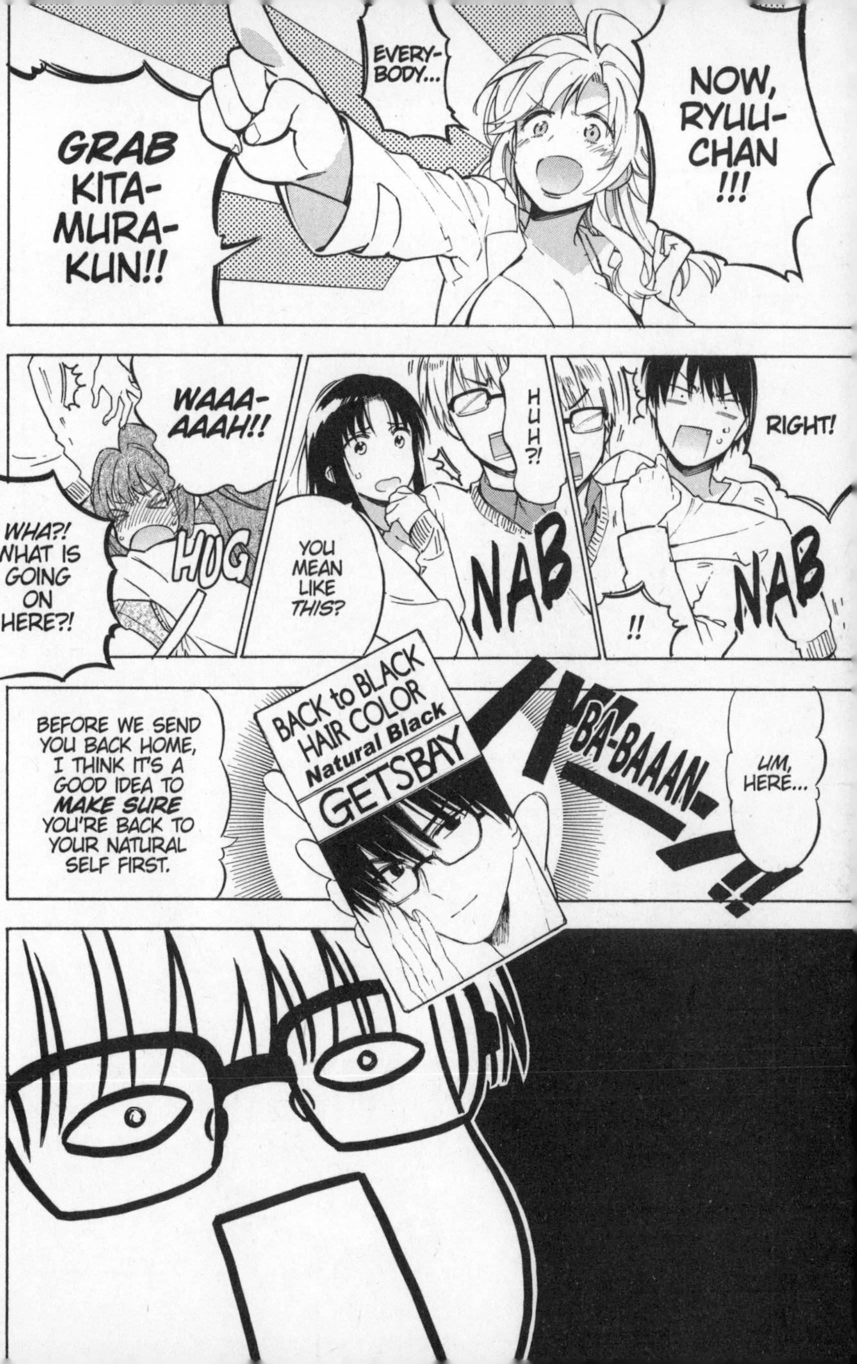
NOW, RYUU-CHAN!!!
EVERY-BODY...
GRAB KITA-MURA-KUN!!
RIGHT!
NAB
!!
HUH?!
NAB
YOU MEAN LIKE THIS?
WAAA-AAAH!!
HUG
WHA?! WHAT IS GOING ON HERE?!
UM, HERE...
BA-BAAAN
BACK to BLACK HAIR COLOR Natural Black
GETSBAY
BEFORE WE SEND YOU BACK HOME, I THINK IT'S A GOOD IDEA TO MAKE SURE YOU'RE BACK TO YOUR NATURAL SELF FIRST.

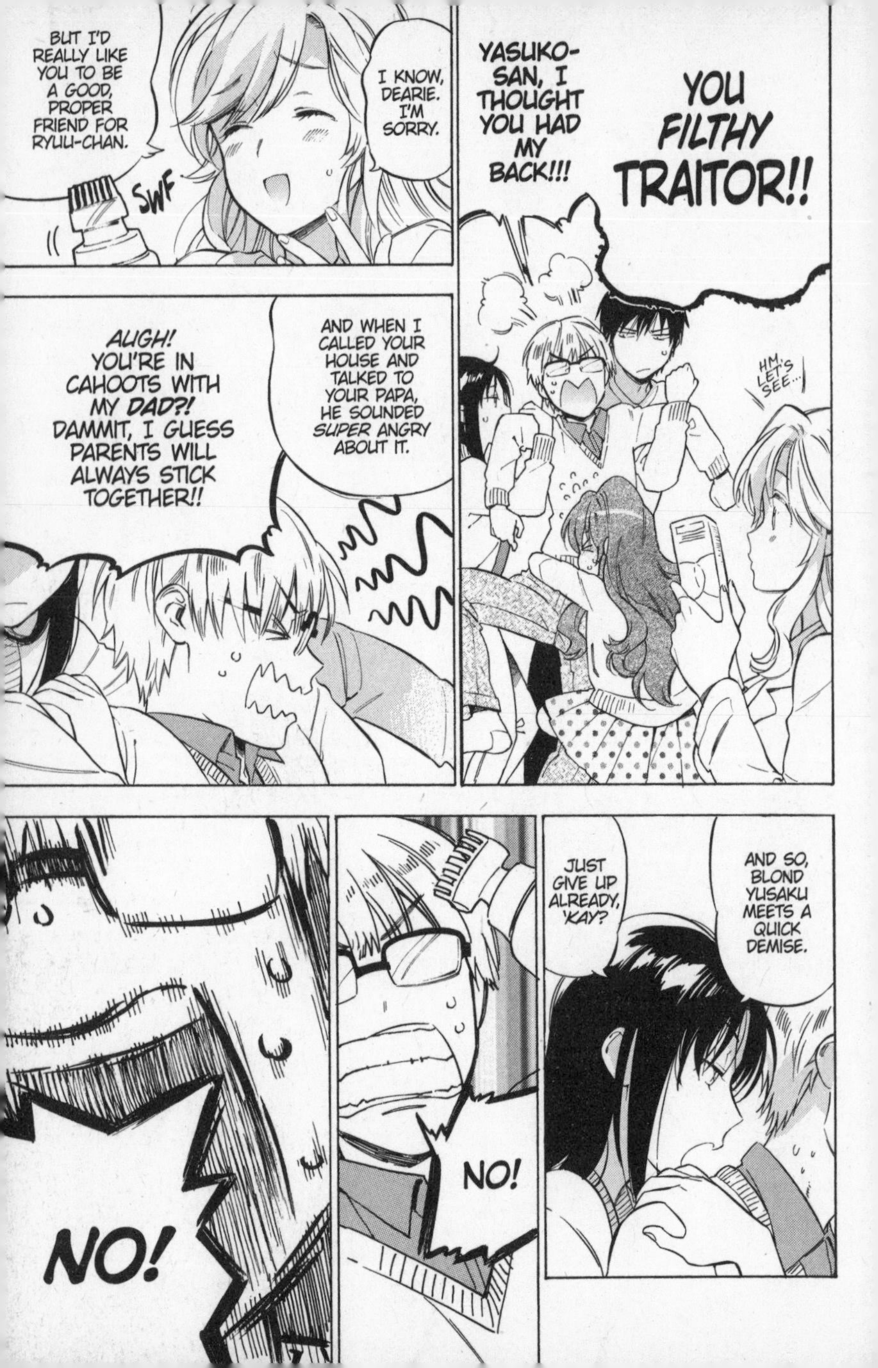
YASUKO-SAN, I THOUGHT YOU HAD MY BACK!!!
YOU FILTHY TRAITOR!!
HM, LET'S SEE...
I KNOW, DEARIE. I'M SORRY.
BUT I'D REALLY LIKE YOU TO BE A GOOD, PROPER FRIEND FOR RYUU-CHAN.
SWF
AND WHEN I CALLED YOUR HOUSE AND TALKED TO YOUR PAPA, HE SOUNDED *SUPER* ANGRY ABOUT IT.
AUGH! YOU'RE IN CAHOOTS WITH MY *DAD?!* DAMMIT, I GUESS PARENTS WILL ALWAYS STICK TOGETHER!!
AND SO, BLOND YUSAKU MEETS A QUICK DEMISE.
JUST GIVE UP ALREADY, 'KAY?
NO!
NO!

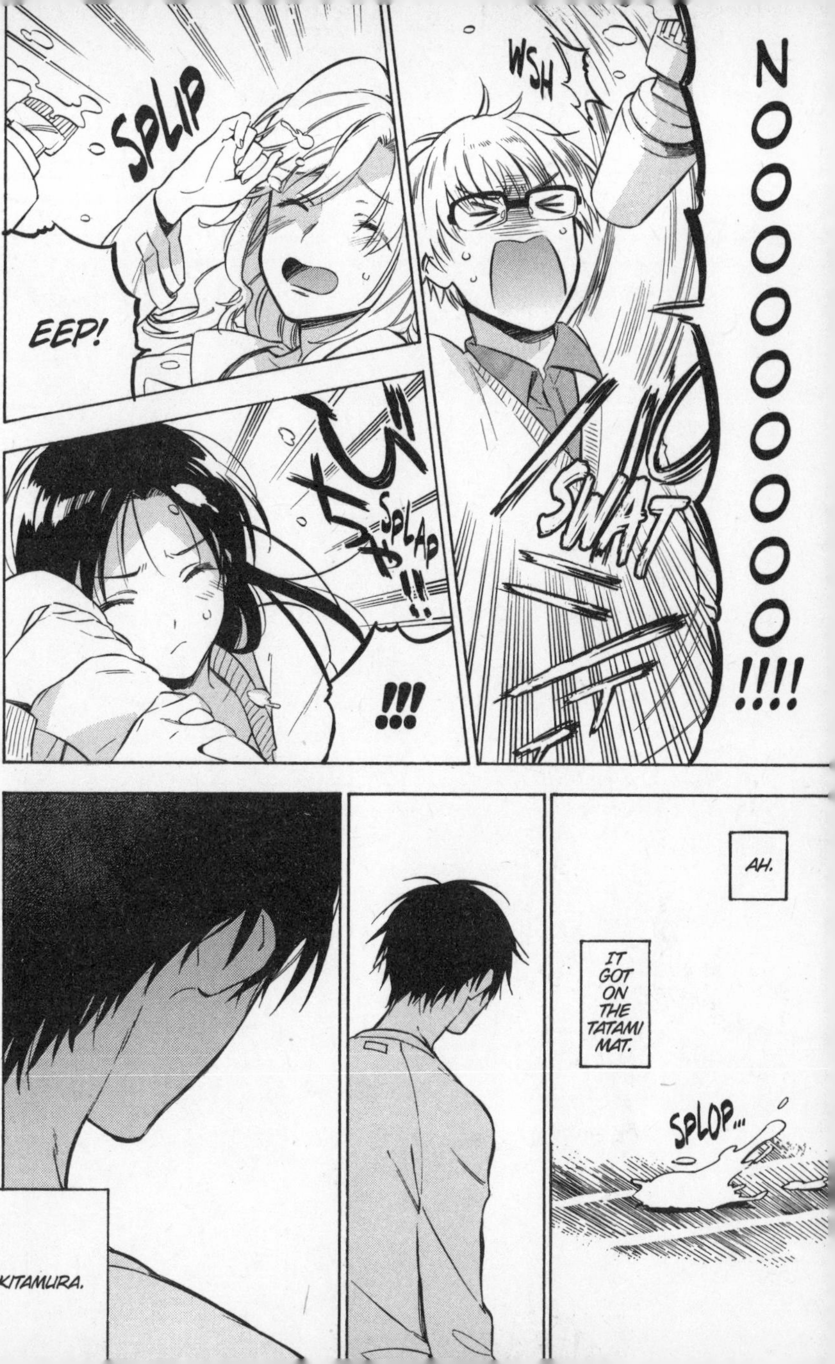
WSH
NOOOOOOOOOO!!!!
SWAT
SPLIP
EEP!
SPLAP!!
!!!
AH.
IT GOT ON THE TATAMI MAT.
SPLOP...
KITAMURA.

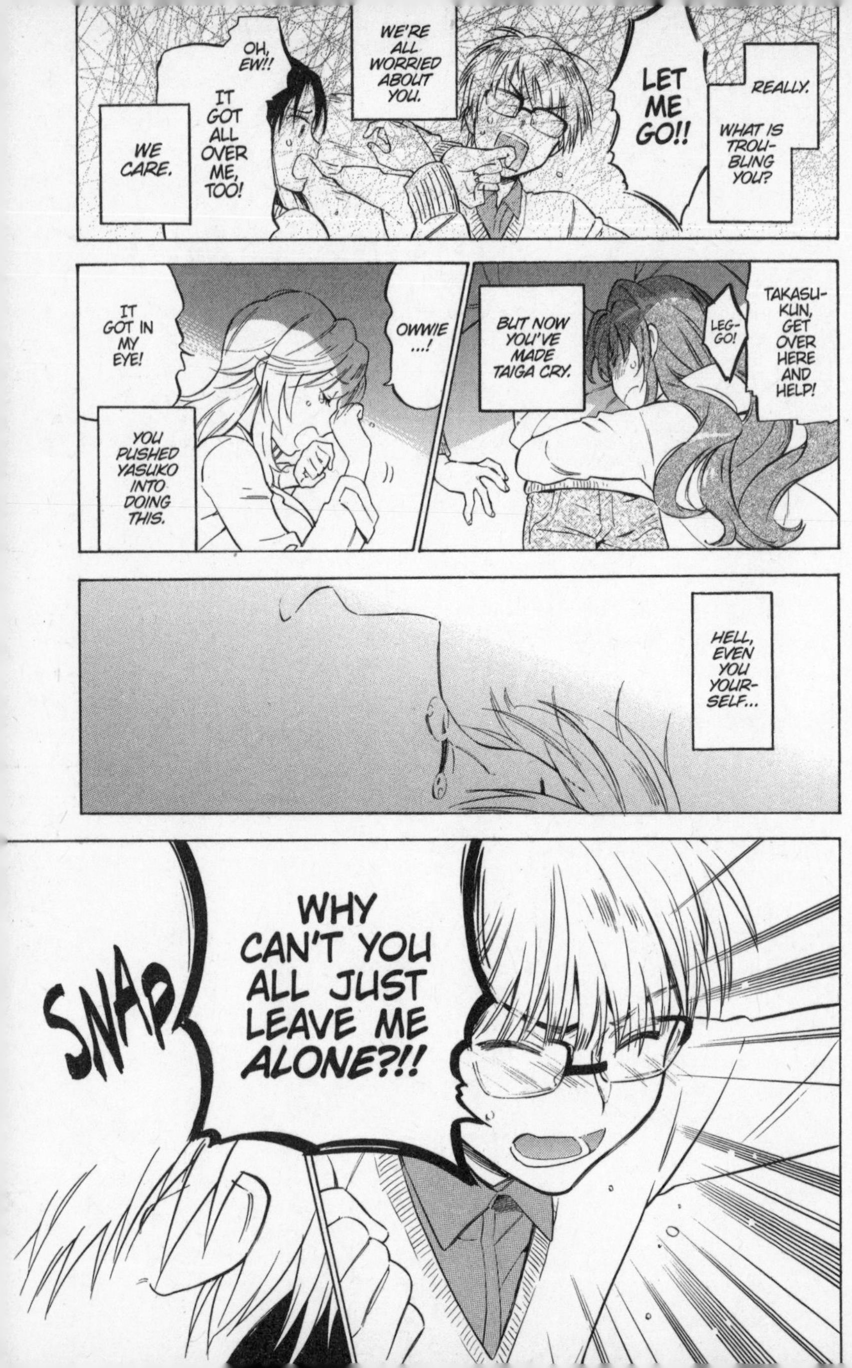
REALLY.
WHAT IS TROUBLING YOU?
LET ME GO!!
WE'RE ALL WORRIED ABOUT YOU.
OH, EW!!
IT GOT ALL OVER ME, TOO!
WE CARE.
TAKASU-KUN, GET OVER HERE AND HELP!
LEG-GO!
BUT NOW YOU'VE MADE TAIGA CRY.
OWWIE ...!
IT GOT IN MY EYE!
YOU PUSHED YASUKO INTO DOING THIS.
HELL, EVEN YOU YOURSELF...
WHY CAN'T YOU ALL JUST LEAVE ME ALONE?!!
SNAP

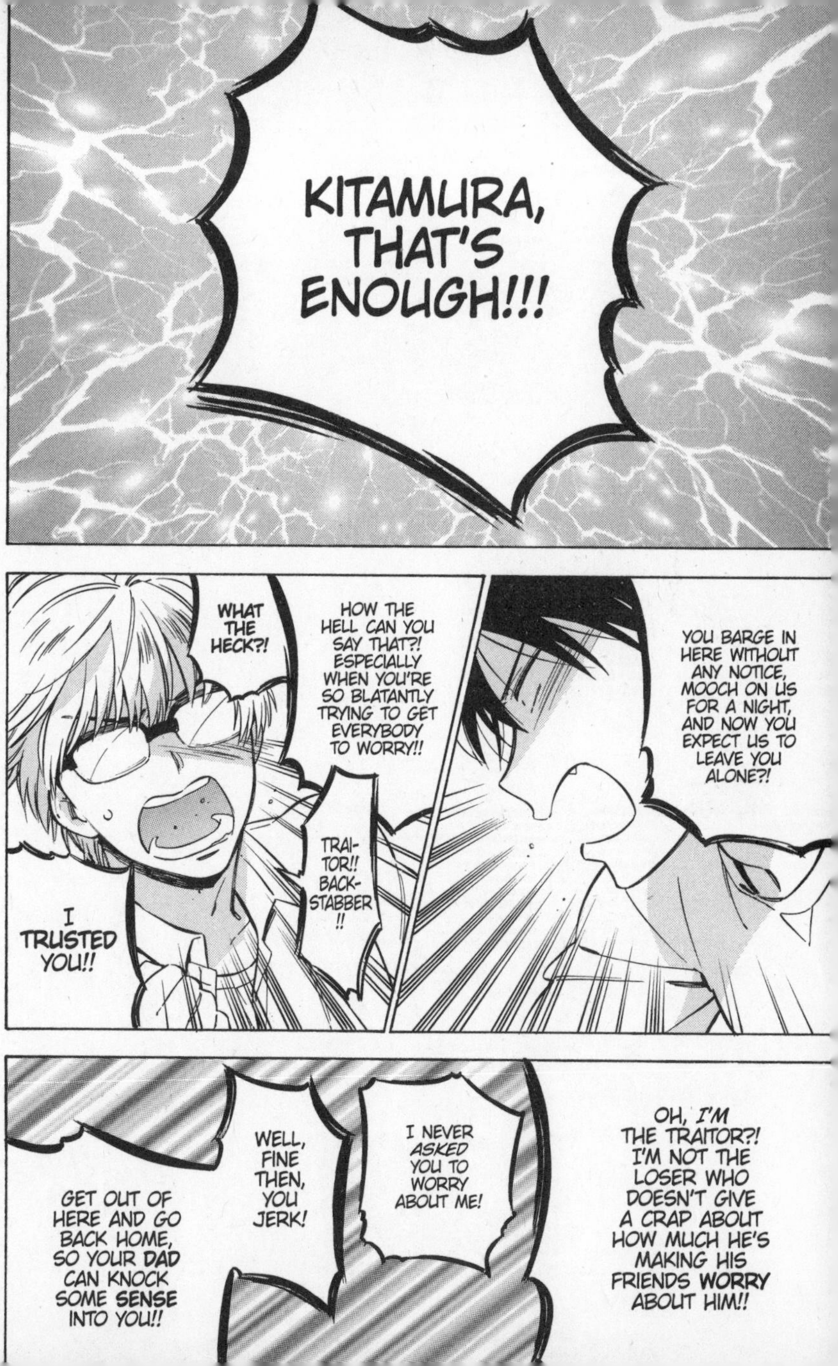
KITAMURA, THAT'S ENOUGH!!!
YOU BARGE IN HERE WITHOUT ANY NOTICE, MOOCH ON US FOR A NIGHT, AND NOW YOU EXPECT US TO LEAVE YOU ALONE?!
HOW THE HELL CAN YOU SAY THAT?! ESPECIALLY WHEN YOU'RE SO BLATANTLY TRYING TO GET EVERYBODY TO WORRY!!
WHAT THE HECK?!
TRAITOR!! BACK-STABBER!!
I TRUSTED YOU!!
OH, *I'M* THE TRAITOR?! I'M NOT THE LOSER WHO DOESN'T GIVE A CRAP ABOUT HOW MUCH HE'S MAKING HIS FRIENDS **WORRY** ABOUT HIM!!
I NEVER *ASKED* YOU TO WORRY ABOUT ME!
WELL, FINE THEN, YOU JERK!
GET OUT OF HERE AND GO BACK HOME, SO YOUR **DAD** CAN KNOCK SOME **SENSE** INTO YOU!!

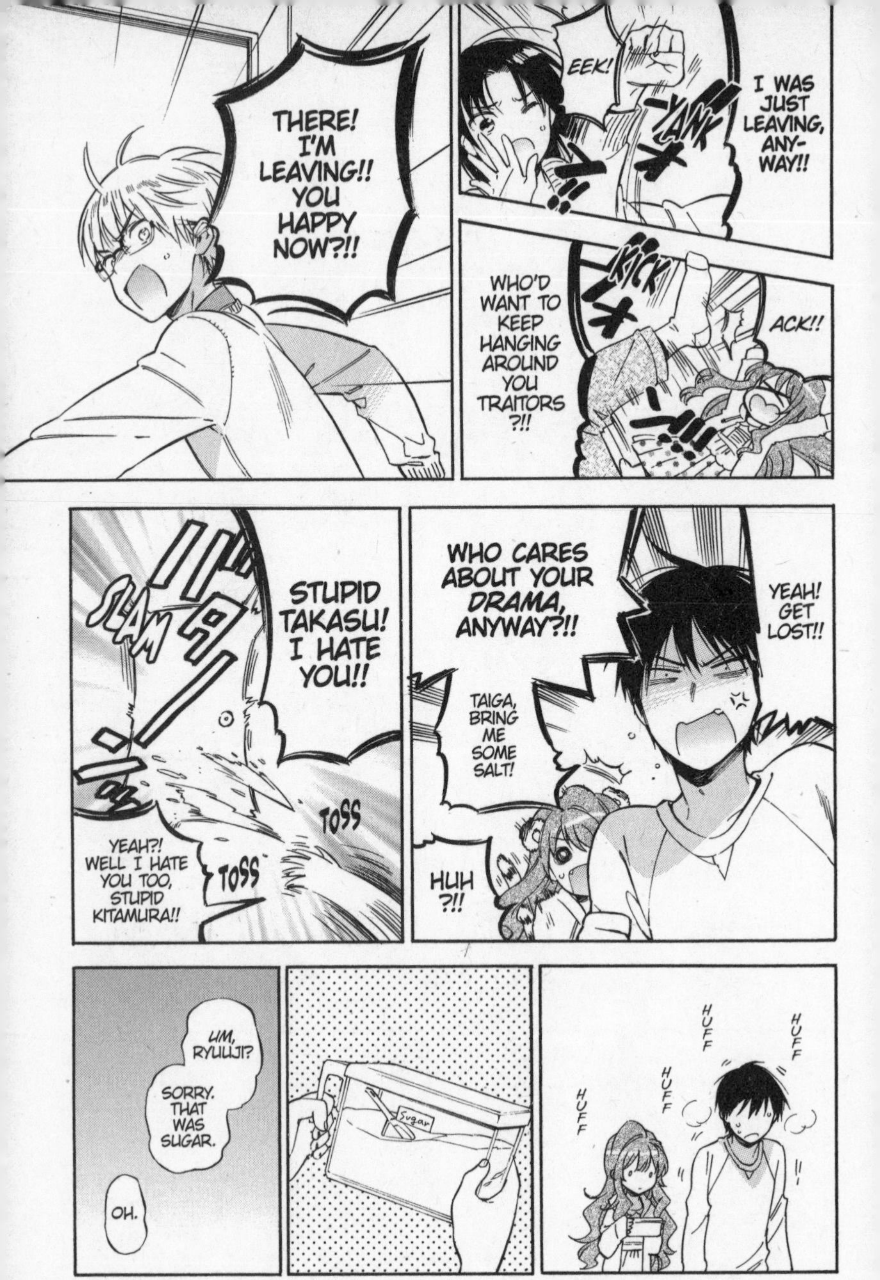
I WAS JUST LEAVING, ANYWAY!!
EEK!
YANK
KICK
ACK!!
WHO'D WANT TO KEEP HANGING AROUND YOU TRAITORS ?!!
THERE! I'M LEAVING!! YOU HAPPY NOW?!!
YEAH! GET LOST!!
WHO CARES ABOUT YOUR DRAMA, ANYWAY?!!
TAIGA, BRING ME SOME SALT!
HUH ?!!
STUPID TAKASU! I HATE YOU!!
SLAM
TOSS
YEAH?! WELL I HATE YOU TOO, STUPID KITAMURA!!
TOSS
HUFF
HUFF
HUFF
HUFF
Sugar
UM, RYUUJI?
SORRY. THAT WAS SUGAR.
OH.

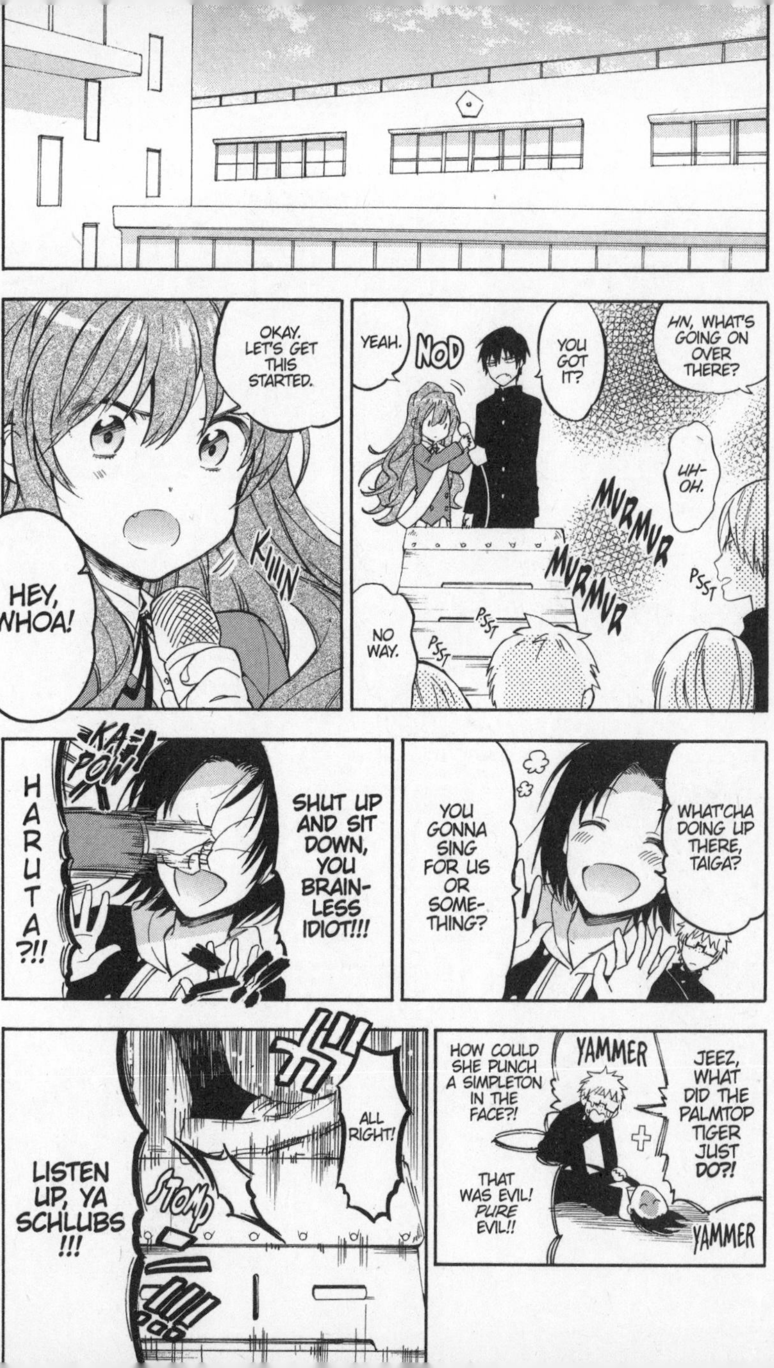
HN, WHAT'S GOING ON OVER THERE?
UH-OH.
MURMUR
MURMUR
PSST
YOU GOT IT?
NOD
YEAH.
NO WAY.
PSST
PSST
OKAY. LET'S GET THIS STARTED.
KIIIN
HEY, WHOA!
WHAT'CHA DOING UP THERE, TAIGA?
YOU GONNA SING FOR US OR SOMETHING?
POW
SHUT UP AND SIT DOWN, YOU BRAIN-LESS IDIOT!!!
HARUTA?!!
JEEZ, WHAT DID THE PALMTOP TIGER JUST DO?!
YAMMER
HOW COULD SHE PUNCH A SIMPLETON IN THE FACE?!
THAT WAS EVIL! PURE EVIL!!
YAMMER
ALL RIGHT!
STOMP
LISTEN UP, YA SCHLUBS!!!

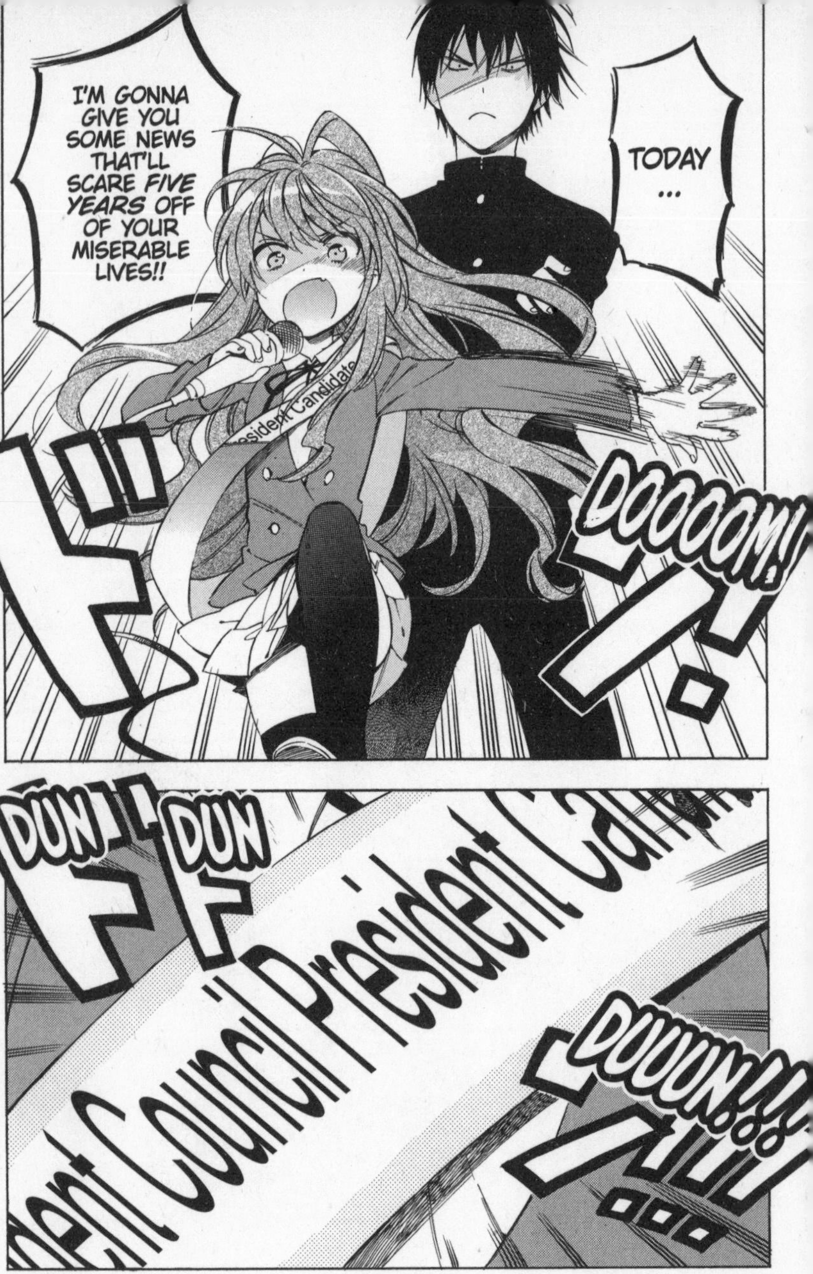

TODAY ...
I'M GONNA GIVE YOU SOME NEWS THAT'LL SCARE *FIVE YEARS* OFF OF YOUR MISERABLE LIVES!!
resident Candidate
DOOOOM!
DUN DUN
dent Council President Ca
DUUUN!!!

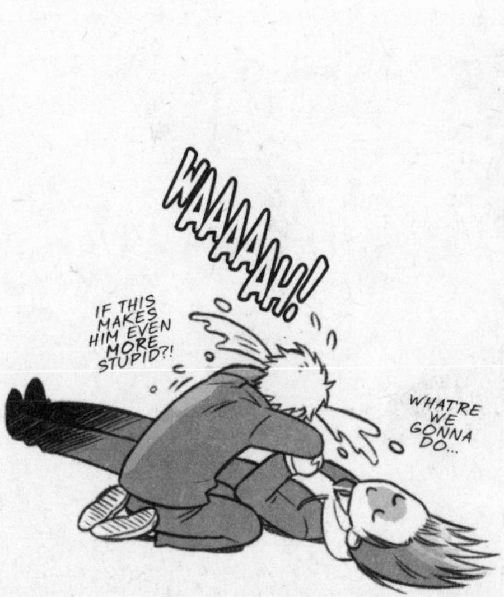
WAAAAAH!
WHAT'RE WE GONNA DO...
IF THIS MAKES HIM EVEN MORE STUPID?!

Chapter 64: NOT STUPID

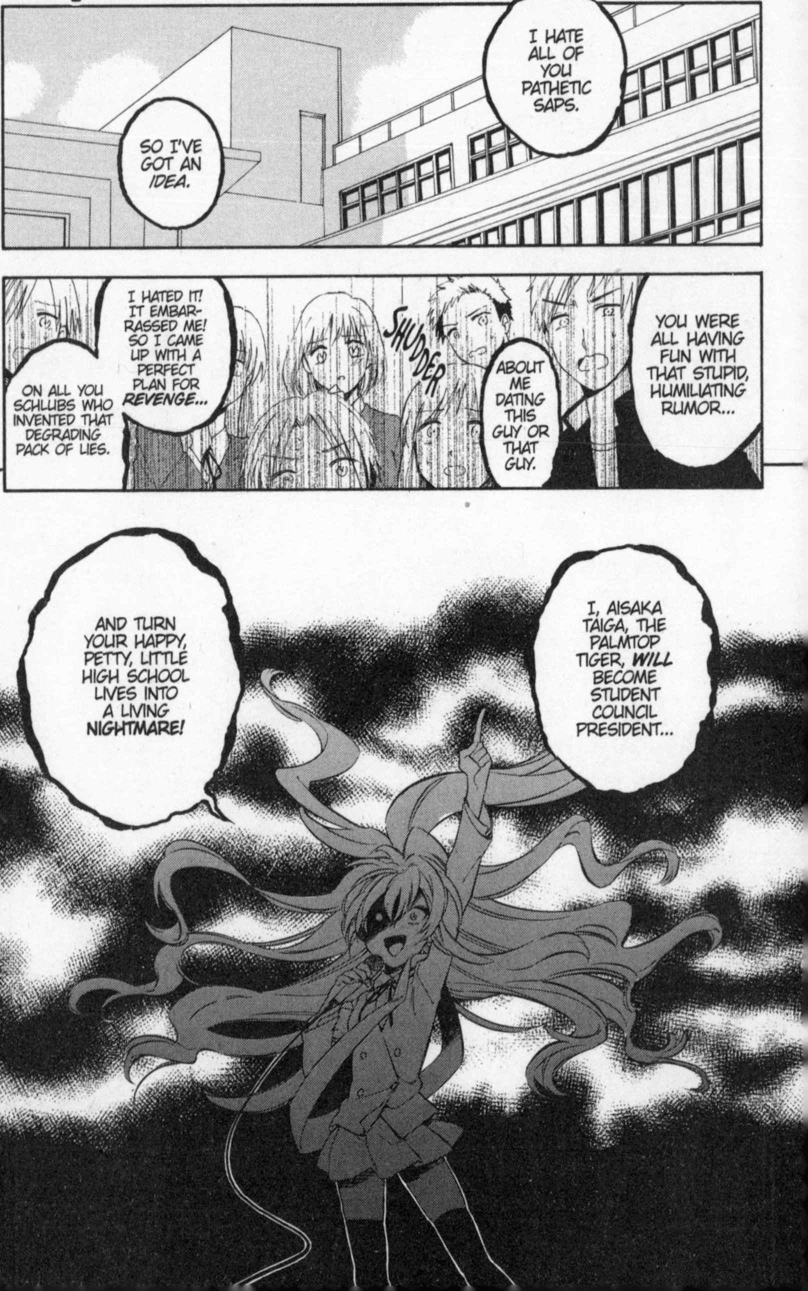
I HATE ALL OF YOU PATHETIC SAPS.
SO I'VE GOT AN *IDEA.*
YOU WERE ALL HAVING FUN WITH THAT STUPID, HUMILIATING RUMOR...
ABOUT ME DATING THIS GUY OR THAT GUY.
SHUDDER
I HATED IT! IT EMBARRASSED ME! SO I CAME UP WITH A PERFECT PLAN FOR ***REVENGE...***
ON ALL YOU SCHLUBS WHO INVENTED THAT DEGRADING PACK OF LIES.
I, AISAKA TAIGA, THE PALMTOP TIGER, ***WILL*** BECOME STUDENT COUNCIL PRESIDENT...
AND TURN YOUR HAPPY, PETTY, LITTLE HIGH SCHOOL LIVES INTO A LIVING **NIGHTMARE!**

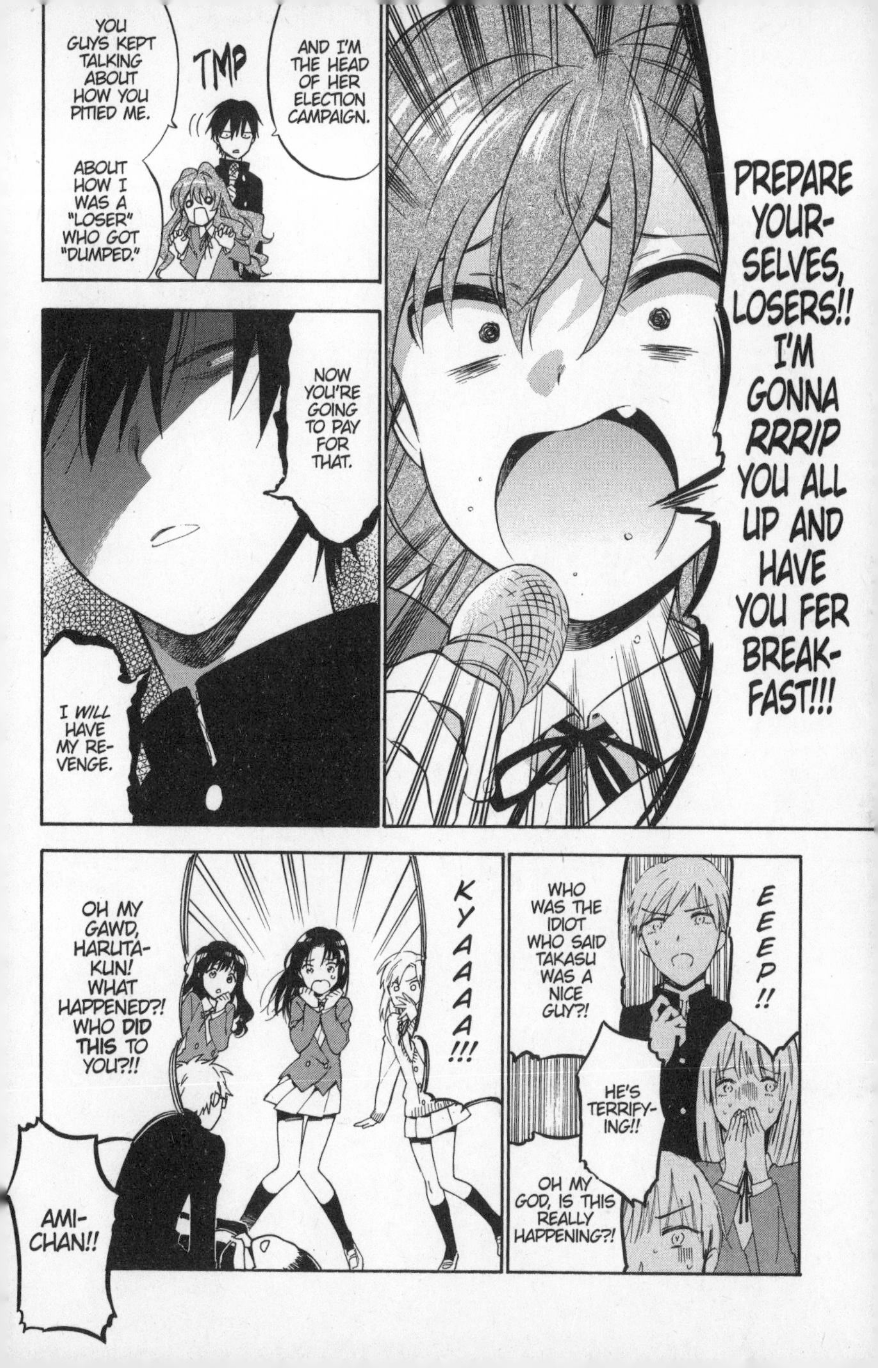
PREPARE YOURSELVES, LOSERS!! I'M GONNA *RRRIP* YOU ALL UP AND HAVE YOU FER BREAKFAST!!!
AND I'M THE HEAD OF HER ELECTION CAMPAIGN.
TMP
YOU GUYS KEPT TALKING ABOUT HOW YOU PITIED ME.
ABOUT HOW I WAS A "LOSER" WHO GOT "DUMPED."
NOW YOU'RE GOING TO PAY FOR THAT.
I *WILL* HAVE MY REVENGE.
EEEEP!!
WHO WAS THE IDIOT WHO SAID TAKASU WAS A NICE GUY?!
HE'S TERRIFYING!!
OH MY GOD, IS THIS REALLY HAPPENING?!
KYAAAAA!!!
OH MY GAWD, HARUTA-KUN! WHAT HAPPENED?! WHO DID THIS TO YOU?!!
AMI-CHAN!!

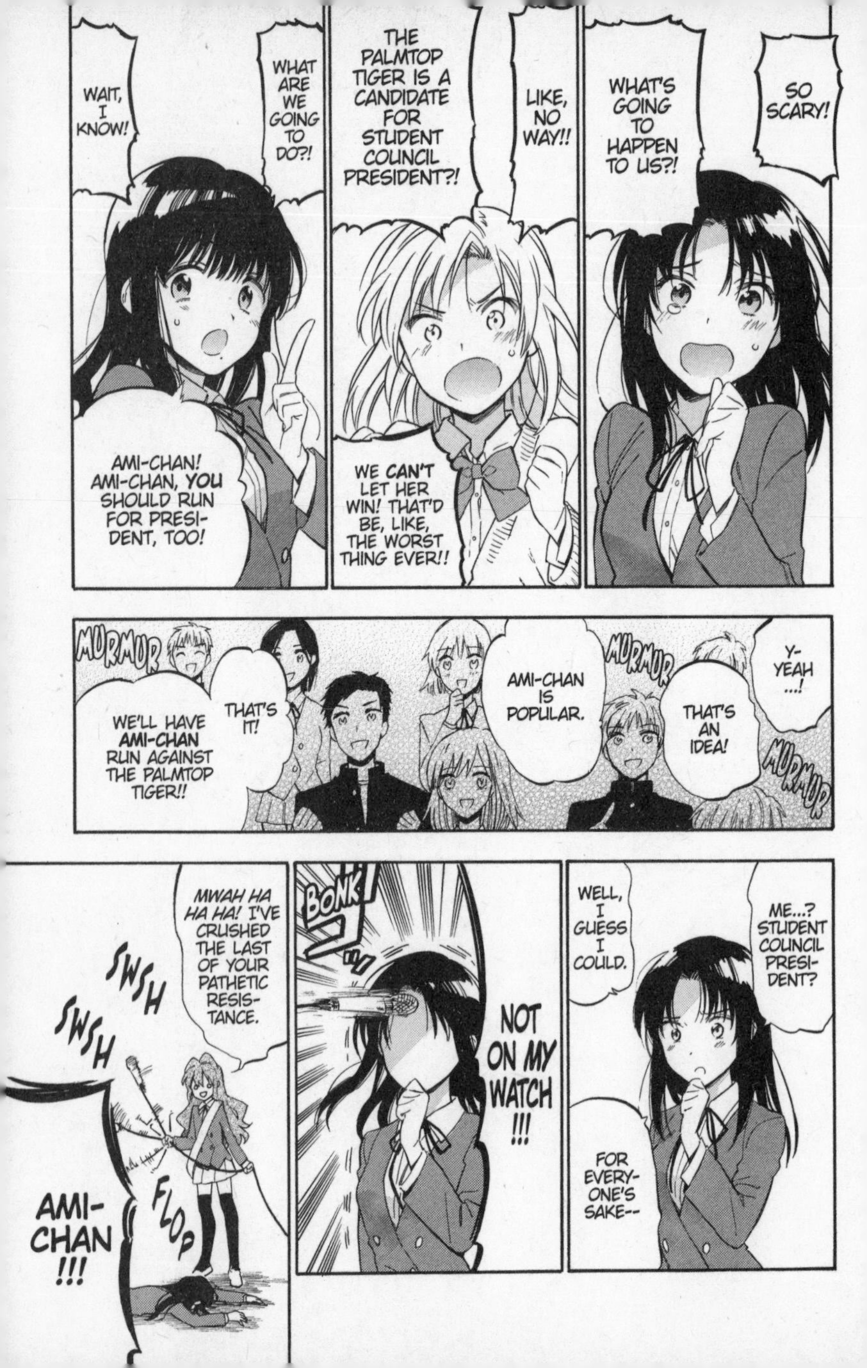
SO SCARY!
WHAT'S GOING TO HAPPEN TO US?!
LIKE, NO WAY!!
THE PALMTOP TIGER IS A CANDIDATE FOR STUDENT COUNCIL PRESIDENT?!
WE CAN'T LET HER WIN! THAT'D BE, LIKE, THE WORST THING EVER!!
WHAT ARE WE GOING TO DO?!
WAIT, I KNOW!
AMI-CHAN! AMI-CHAN, YOU SHOULD RUN FOR PRESI-DENT, TOO!
Y-YEAH...!
MURMUR
THAT'S AN IDEA!
MURMUR
AMI-CHAN IS POPULAR.
THAT'S IT!
WE'LL HAVE AMI-CHAN RUN AGAINST THE PALMTOP TIGER!!
MURMUR
ME...? STUDENT COUNCIL PRESI-DENT?
WELL, I GUESS I COULD.
FOR EVERY-ONE'S SAKE--
BONK
NOT ON MY WATCH!!!
MWAH HA HA HA! I'VE CRUSHED THE LAST OF YOUR PATHETIC RESIS-TANCE.
SWSH
SWSH
FLOP
AMI-CHAN!!!

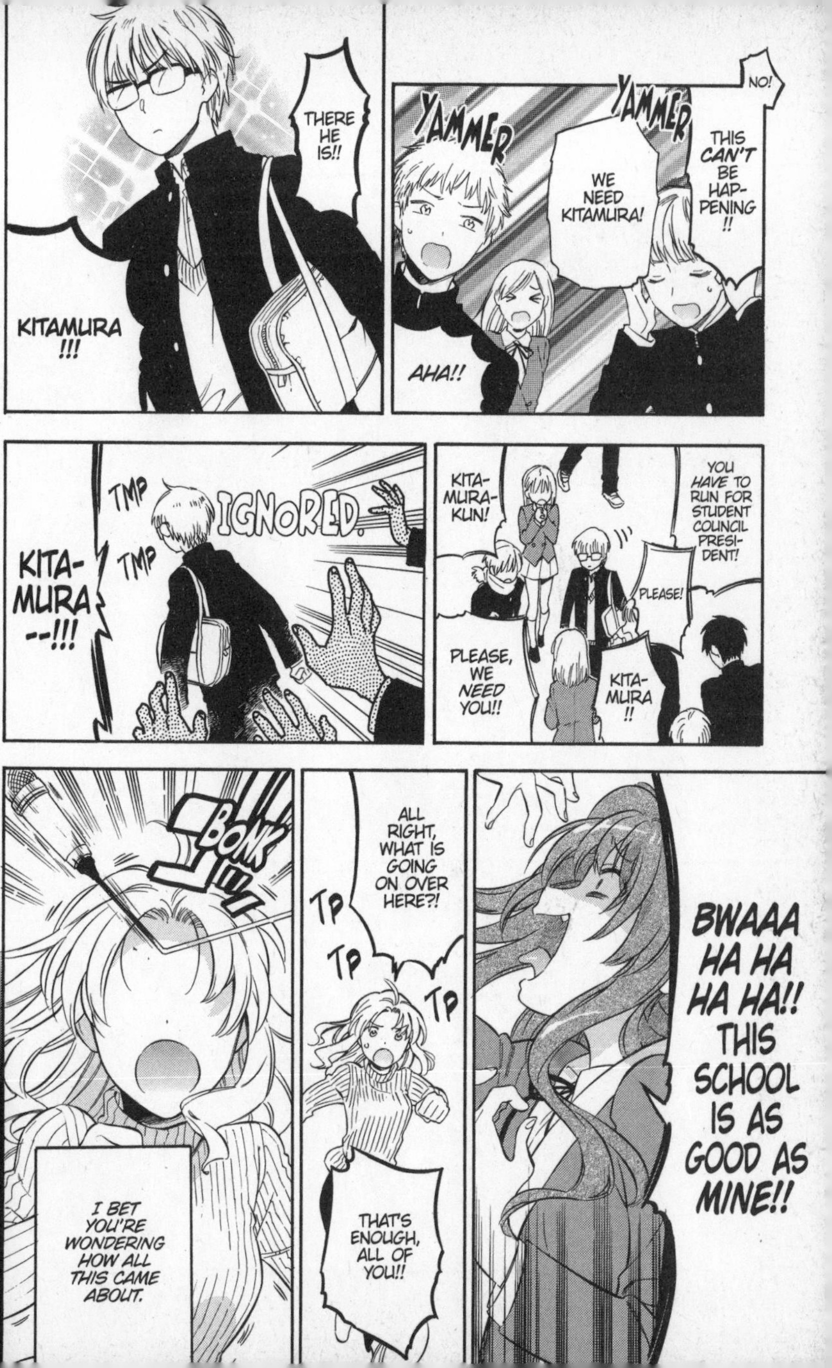
NO!
THIS CAN'T BE HAP-PENING!!
YAMMER
YAMMER
WE NEED KITAMURA!
AHA!!
THERE HE IS!!
KITAMURA!!!
YOU HAVE TO RUN FOR STUDENT COUNCIL PRESI-DENT!
PLEASE!
KITA-MURA-KUN!
KITA-MURA!!
PLEASE, WE NEED YOU!!
IGNORED.
TMP
TMP
KITA-MURA--!!!
BWAAA HA HA HA HA!! THIS SCHOOL IS AS GOOD AS MINE!!
ALL RIGHT, WHAT IS GOING ON OVER HERE?!
Tp
Tp
Tp
THAT'S ENOUGH, ALL OF YOU!!
BONK
I BET YOU'RE WONDERING HOW ALL THIS CAME ABOUT.

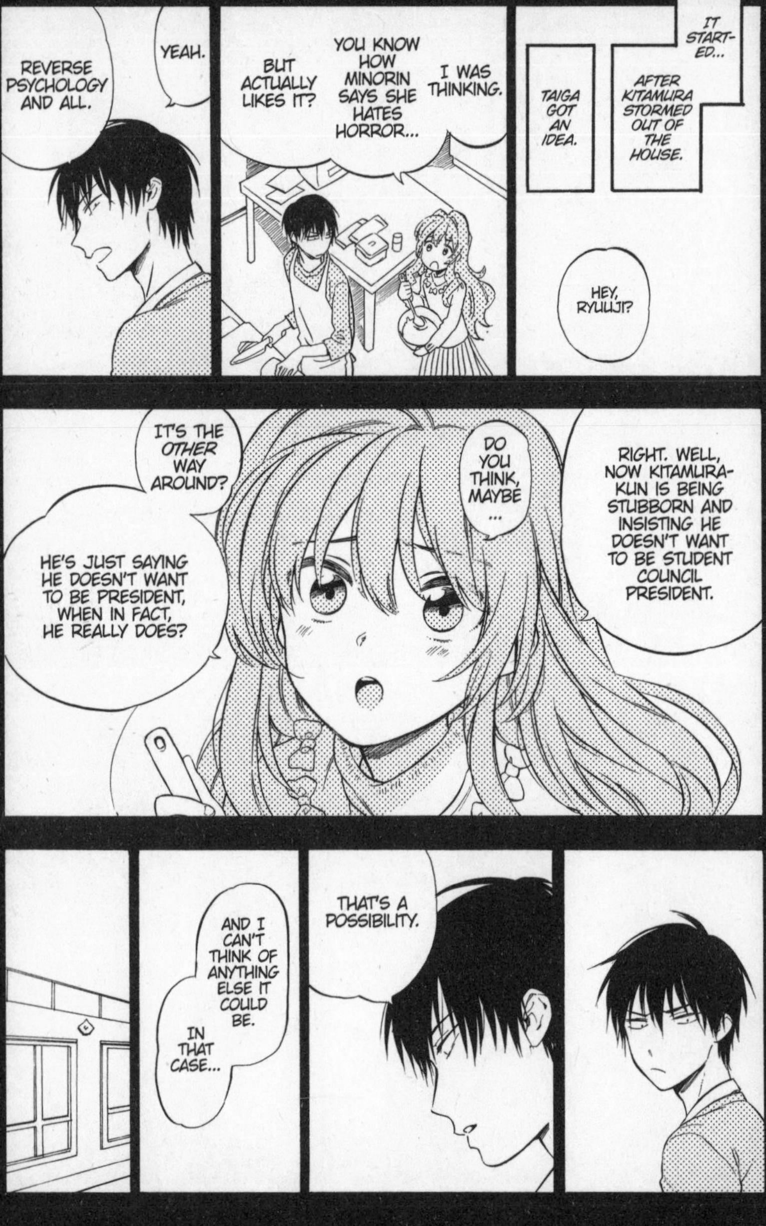
IT START-ED...
AFTER KITAMURA STORMED OUT OF THE HOUSE.
TAIGA GOT AN IDEA.
HEY, RYUUJI?
I WAS THINKING.
YOU KNOW HOW MINORIN SAYS SHE HATES HORROR...
BUT ACTUALLY LIKES IT?
YEAH.
REVERSE PSYCHOLOGY AND ALL.
RIGHT. WELL, NOW KITAMURA-KUN IS BEING STUBBORN AND INSISTING HE DOESN'T WANT TO BE STUDENT COUNCIL PRESIDENT.
DO YOU THINK, MAYBE...
IT'S THE *OTHER* WAY AROUND?
HE'S JUST SAYING HE DOESN'T WANT TO BE PRESIDENT, WHEN IN FACT, HE REALLY DOES?
THAT'S A POSSIBILITY.
AND I CAN'T THINK OF ANYTHING ELSE IT COULD BE.
IN THAT CASE...

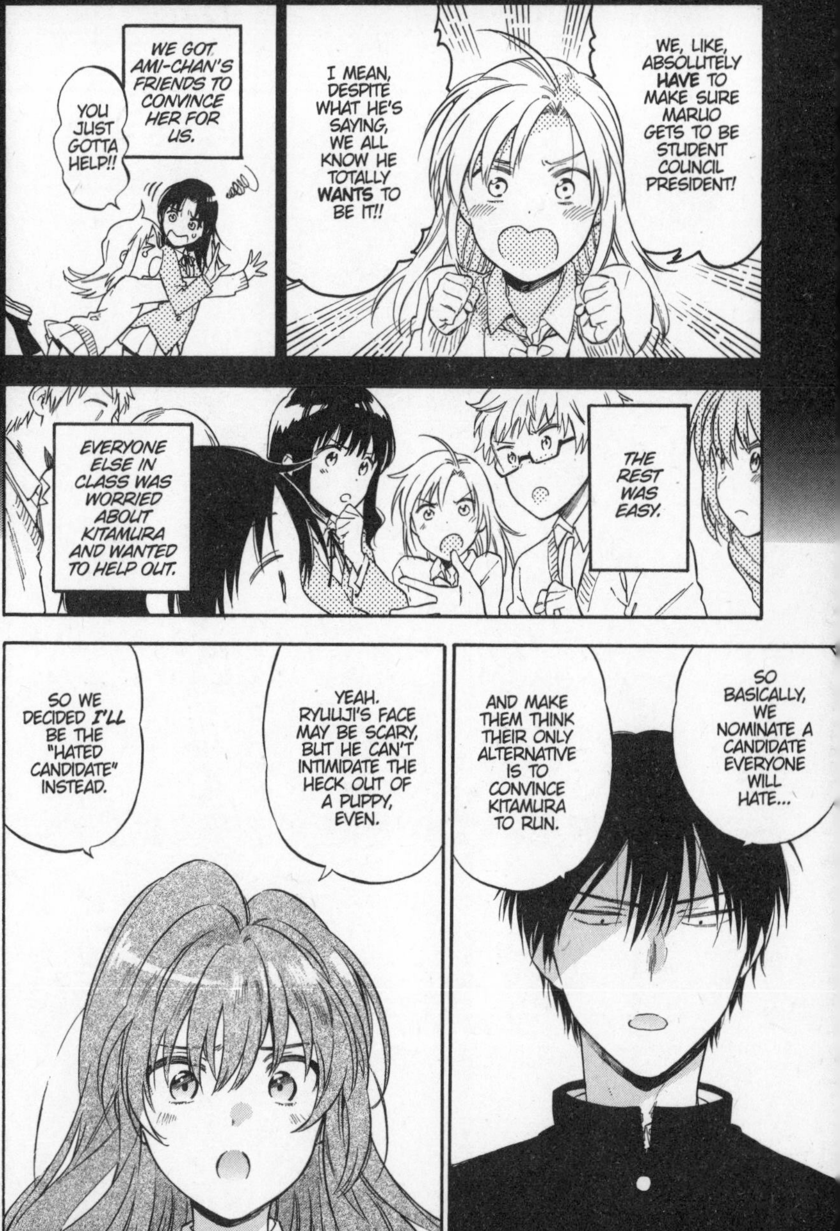
WE, LIKE, ABSOLUTELY HAVE TO MAKE SURE MARUO GETS TO BE STUDENT COUNCIL PRESIDENT!
I MEAN, DESPITE WHAT HE'S SAYING, WE ALL KNOW HE TOTALLY WANTS TO BE IT!!
WE GOT AMI-CHAN'S FRIENDS TO CONVINCE HER FOR US.
YOU JUST GOTTA HELP!!
THE REST WAS EASY.
EVERYONE ELSE IN CLASS WAS WORRIED ABOUT KITAMURA AND WANTED TO HELP OUT.
SO BASICALLY, WE NOMINATE A CANDIDATE EVERYONE WILL HATE...
AND MAKE THEM THINK THEIR ONLY ALTERNATIVE IS TO CONVINCE KITAMURA TO RUN.
YEAH. RYUUJI'S FACE MAY BE SCARY, BUT HE CAN'T INTIMIDATE THE HECK OUT OF A PUPPY, EVEN.
SO WE DECIDED I'LL BE THE "HATED CANDIDATE" INSTEAD.

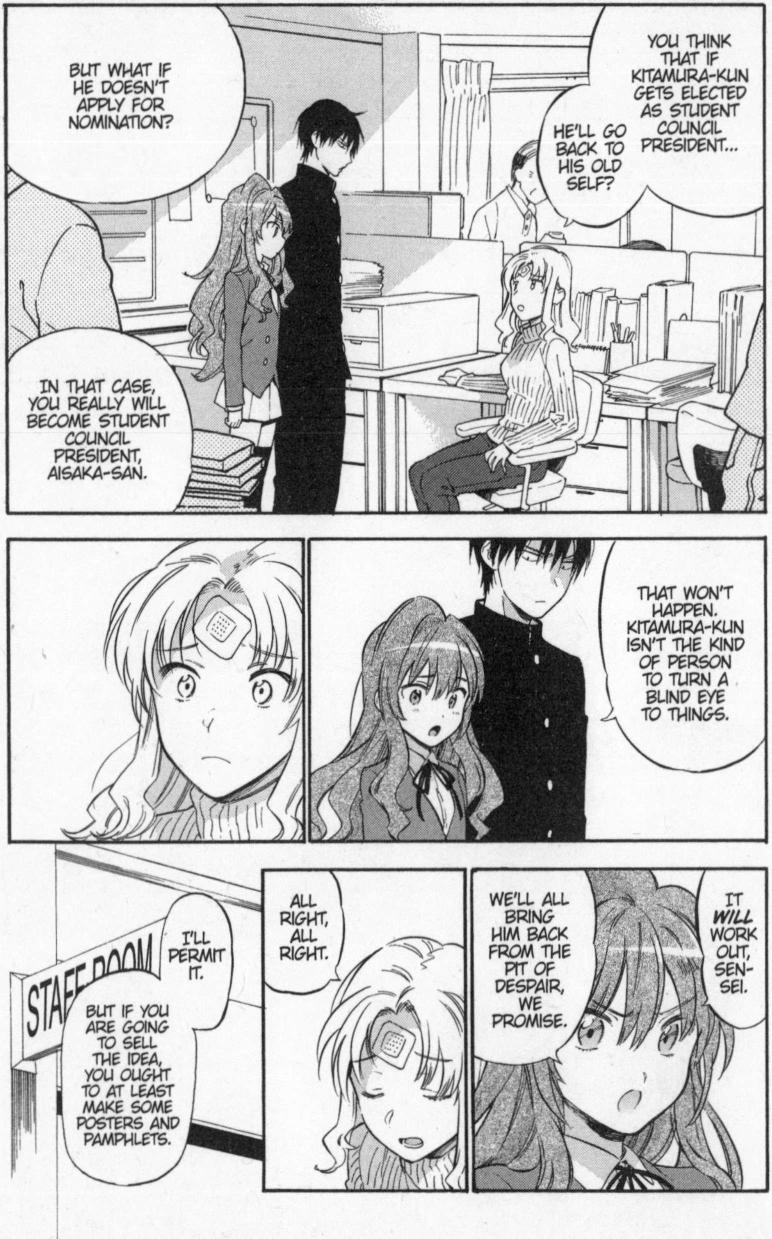
YOU THINK THAT IF KITAMURA-KUN GETS ELECTED AS STUDENT COUNCIL PRESIDENT...
HE'LL GO BACK TO HIS OLD SELF?
BUT WHAT IF HE DOESN'T APPLY FOR NOMINATION?
IN THAT CASE, YOU REALLY WILL BECOME STUDENT COUNCIL PRESIDENT, AISAKA-SAN.
THAT WON'T HAPPEN. KITAMURA-KUN ISN'T THE KIND OF PERSON TO TURN A BLIND EYE TO THINGS.
IT *WILL* WORK OUT, SEN-SEI.
WE'LL ALL BRING HIM BACK FROM THE PIT OF DESPAIR, WE PROMISE.
ALL RIGHT, ALL RIGHT.
I'LL PERMIT IT.
BUT IF YOU ARE GOING TO SELL THE IDEA, YOU OUGHT TO AT LEAST MAKE SOME POSTERS AND PAMPHLETS.

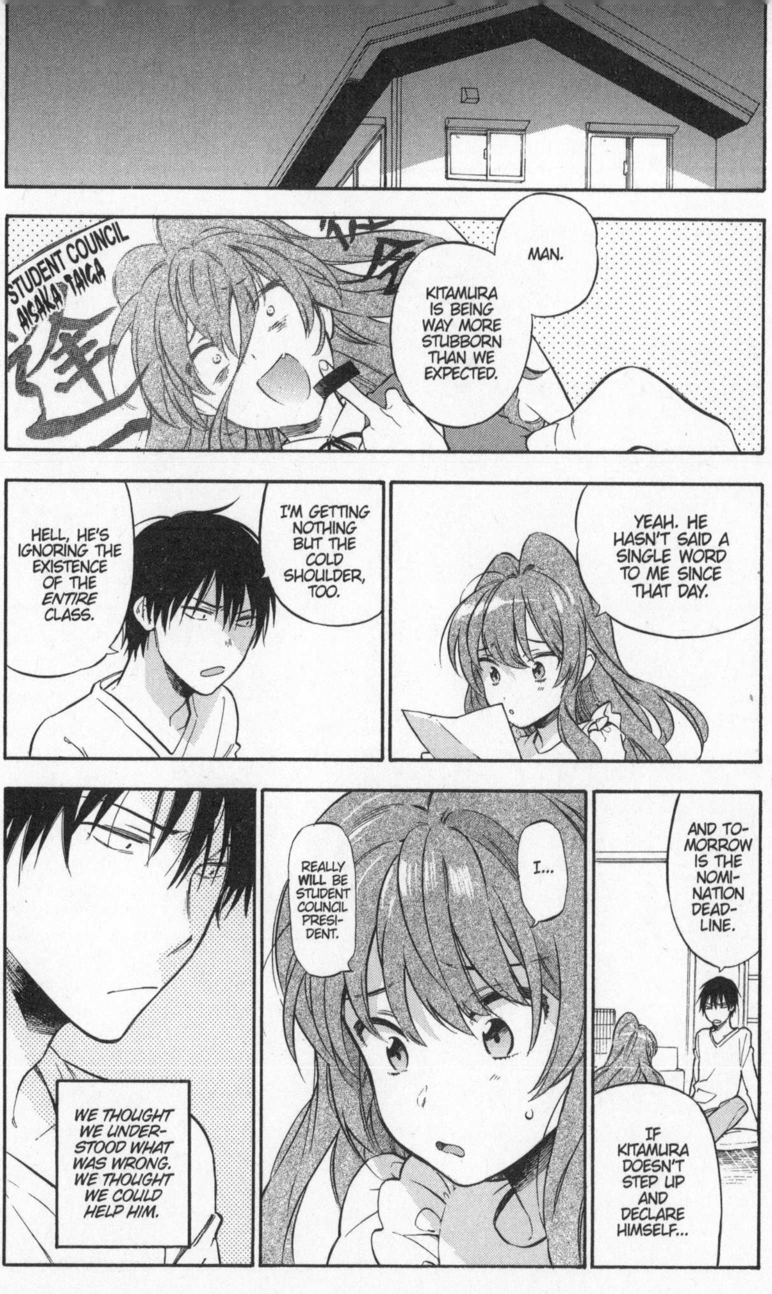
MAN.
KITAMURA IS BEING WAY MORE STUBBORN THAN WE EXPECTED.
STUDENT COUNCIL AISAKA TAIGA
YEAH. HE HASN'T SAID A SINGLE WORD TO ME SINCE THAT DAY.
I'M GETTING NOTHING BUT THE COLD SHOULDER, TOO.
HELL, HE'S IGNORING THE EXISTENCE OF THE *ENTIRE* CLASS.
AND TOMORROW IS THE NOMINATION DEADLINE.
IF KITAMURA DOESN'T STEP UP AND DECLARE HIMSELF...
I...
REALLY WILL BE STUDENT COUNCIL PRESIDENT.
WE THOUGHT WE UNDERSTOOD WHAT WAS WRONG. WE THOUGHT WE COULD HELP HIM.

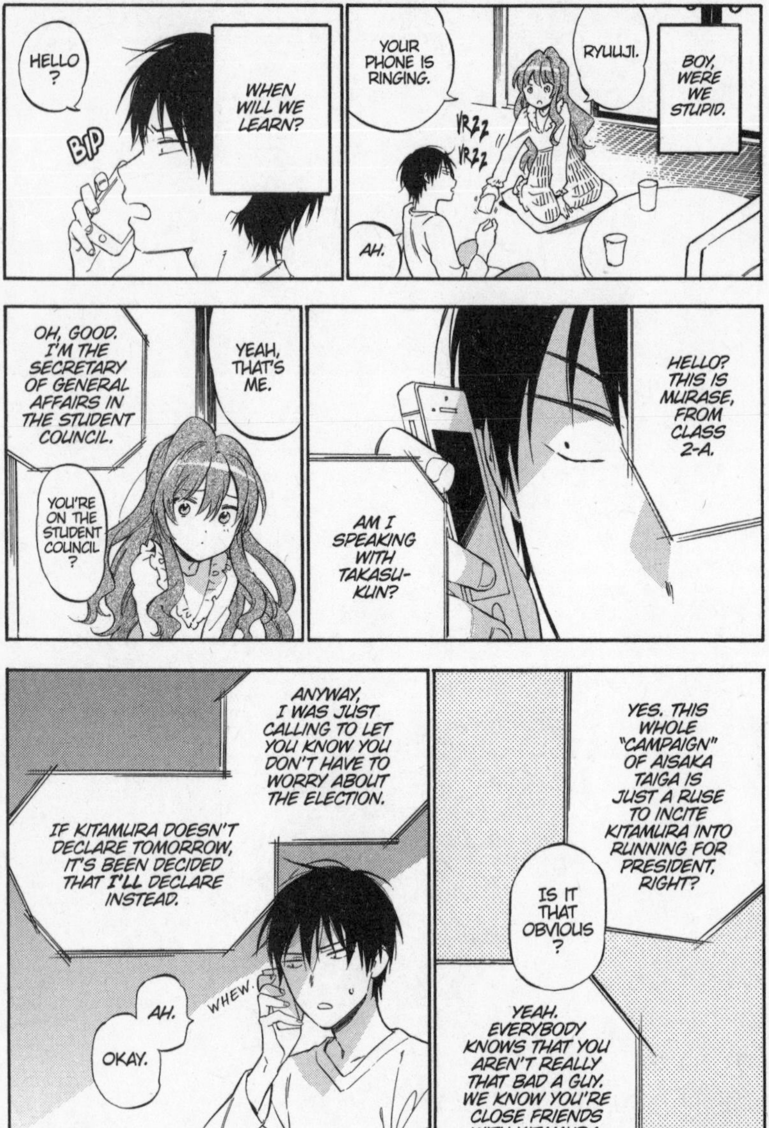
BOY, WERE WE STUPID.
RYUUJI.
YOUR PHONE IS RINGING.
VRZZ
VRZZ
AH.
WHEN WILL WE LEARN?
HELLO?
BIP
HELLO? THIS IS MURASE, FROM CLASS 2-A.
AM I SPEAKING WITH TAKASU-KUN?
YEAH, THAT'S ME.
OH, GOOD. I'M THE SECRETARY OF GENERAL AFFAIRS IN THE STUDENT COUNCIL.
YOU'RE ON THE STUDENT COUNCIL?
YES. THIS WHOLE "CAMPAIGN" OF AISAKA TAIGA IS JUST A RUSE TO INCITE KITAMURA INTO RUNNING FOR PRESIDENT, RIGHT?
IS IT THAT OBVIOUS?
YEAH. EVERYBODY KNOWS THAT YOU AREN'T REALLY THAT BAD A GUY. WE KNOW YOU'RE CLOSE FRIENDS WITH KITAMURA, TOO.
ANYWAY, I WAS JUST CALLING TO LET YOU KNOW YOU DON'T HAVE TO WORRY ABOUT THE ELECTION.
IF KITAMURA DOESN'T DECLARE TOMORROW, IT'S BEEN DECIDED THAT I'LL DECLARE INSTEAD.
WHEW.
AH.
OKAY.

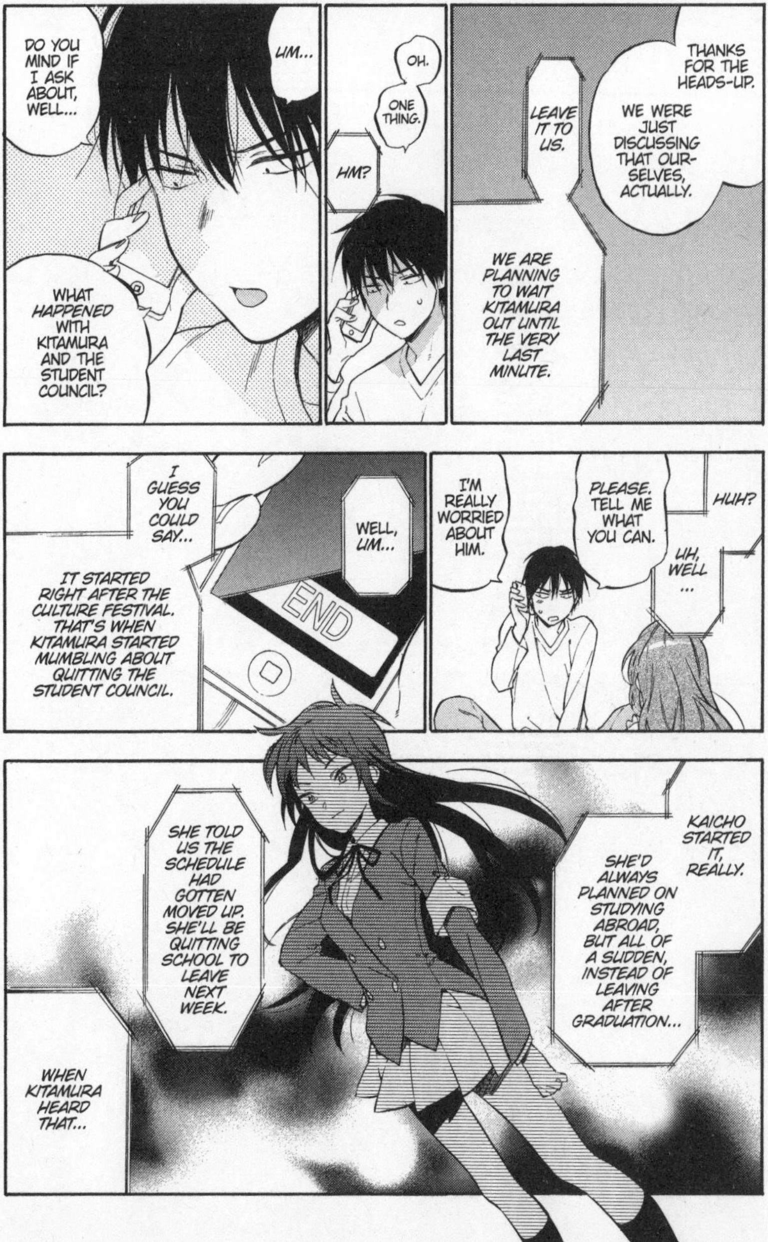
THANKS FOR THE HEADS-UP.
WE WERE JUST DISCUSSING THAT OURSELVES, ACTUALLY.
LEAVE IT TO US.
WE ARE PLANNING TO WAIT KITAMURA OUT UNTIL THE VERY LAST MINUTE.
OH.
ONE THING.
HM?
UM...
DO YOU MIND IF I ASK ABOUT, WELL...
WHAT HAPPENED WITH KITAMURA AND THE STUDENT COUNCIL?
HUH?
UH, WELL ...
PLEASE. TELL ME WHAT YOU CAN.
I'M REALLY WORRIED ABOUT HIM.
WELL, UM...
END
I GUESS YOU COULD SAY...
IT STARTED RIGHT AFTER THE CULTURE FESTIVAL. THAT'S WHEN KITAMURA STARTED MUMBLING ABOUT QUITTING THE STUDENT COUNCIL.
KAICHO STARTED IT, REALLY.
SHE'D ALWAYS PLANNED ON STUDYING ABROAD, BUT ALL OF A SUDDEN, INSTEAD OF LEAVING AFTER GRADUATION...
SHE TOLD US THE SCHEDULE HAD GOTTEN MOVED UP. SHE'LL BE QUITTING SCHOOL TO LEAVE NEXT WEEK.
WHEN KITAMURA HEARD THAT...

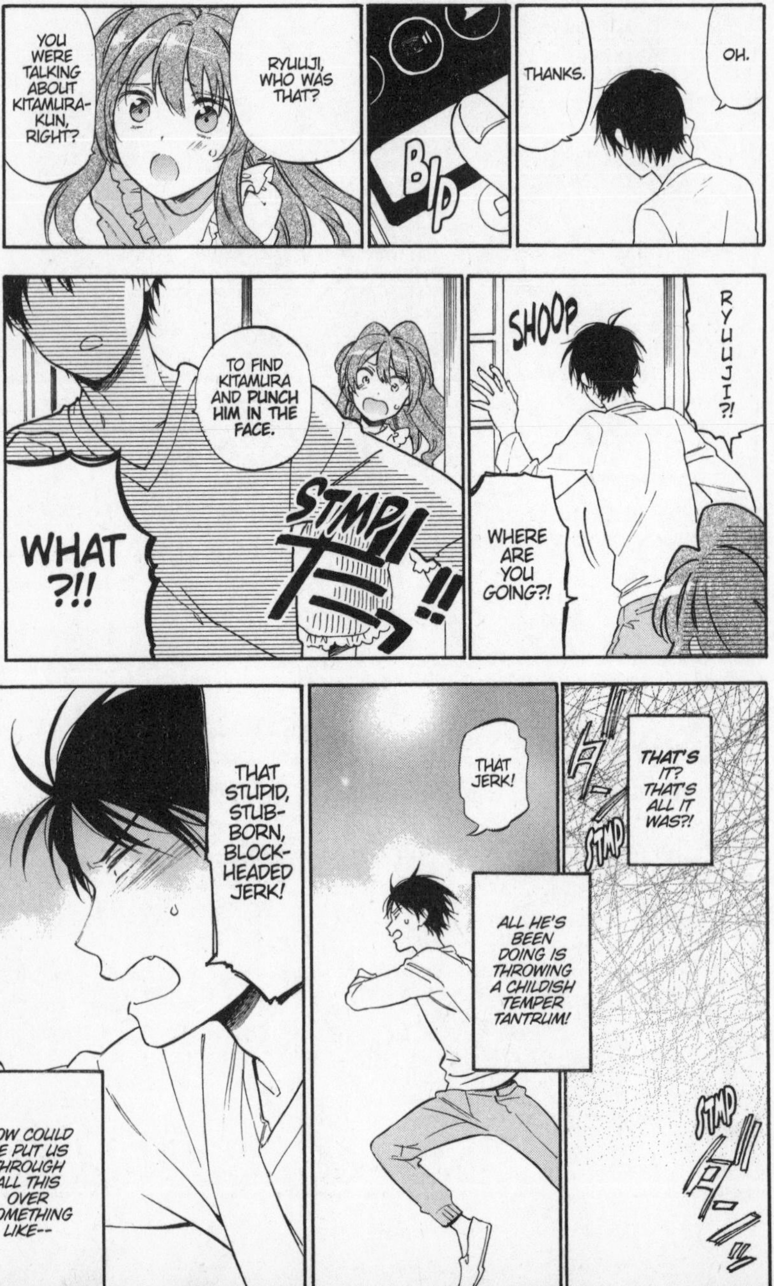
OH.
THANKS.
BIP
RYUUJI, WHO WAS THAT?
YOU WERE TALKING ABOUT KITAMURA-KUN, RIGHT?
RYUUJI?!
SHOOP
WHERE ARE YOU GOING?!
TO FIND KITAMURA AND PUNCH HIM IN THE FACE.
STMP!
WHAT?!!
STMP
THAT'S IT? THAT'S ALL IT WAS?!
STMP
THAT JERK!
ALL HE'S BEEN DOING IS THROWING A CHILDISH TEMPER TANTRUM!
THAT STUPID, STUB-BORN, BLOCK-HEADED JERK!
HOW COULD HE PUT US THROUGH ALL THIS OVER SOMETHING LIKE--

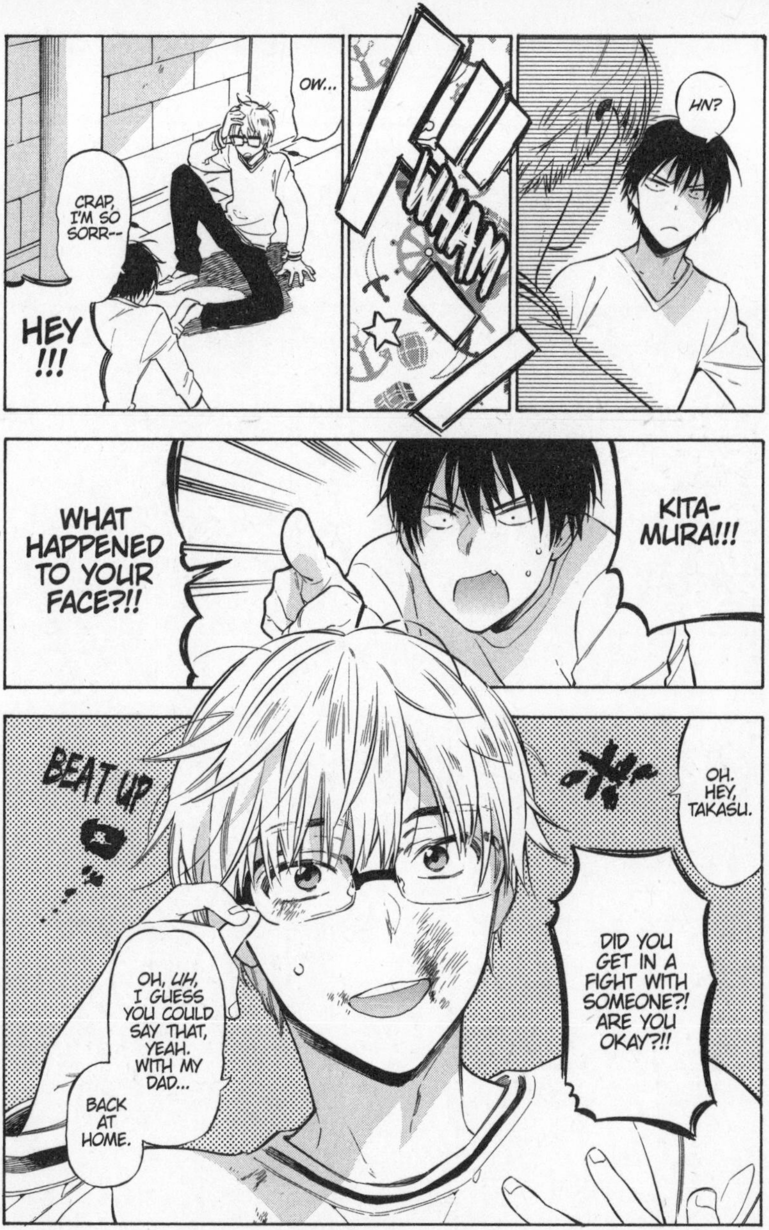
HN?
WHAM
OW...
CRAP, I'M SO SORR--
HEY !!!
KITA-MURA!!!
WHAT HAPPENED TO YOUR FACE?!!
OH. HEY, TAKASU.
BEAT UP
DID YOU GET IN A FIGHT WITH SOMEONE?! ARE YOU OKAY?!!
OH, UH, I GUESS YOU COULD SAY THAT, YEAH. WITH MY DAD...
BACK AT HOME.

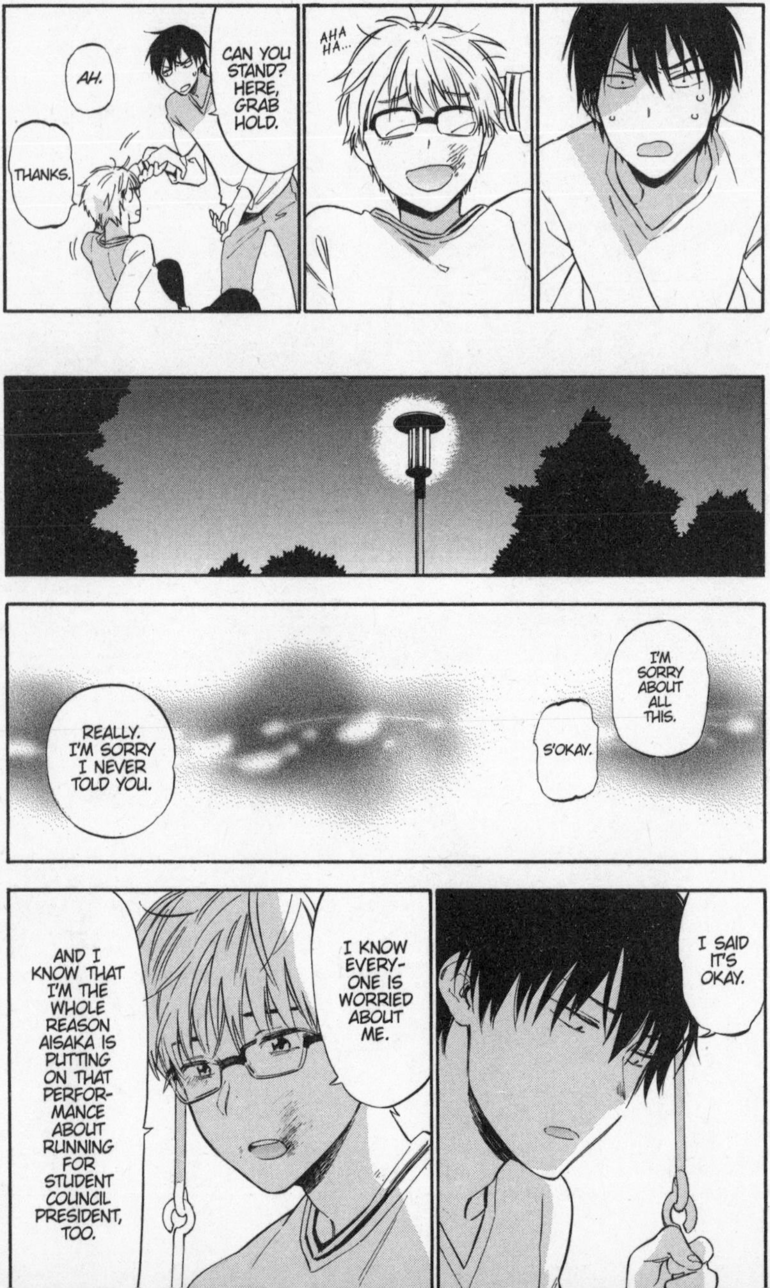
AHA HA...
CAN YOU STAND? HERE, GRAB HOLD.
AH.
THANKS.
I'M SORRY ABOUT ALL THIS.
S'OKAY.
REALLY. I'M SORRY I NEVER TOLD YOU.
I SAID IT'S OKAY.
I KNOW EVERY-ONE IS WORRIED ABOUT ME.
AND I KNOW THAT I'M THE WHOLE REASON AISAKA IS PUTTING ON THAT PERFOR-MANCE ABOUT RUNNING FOR STUDENT COUNCIL PRESIDENT, TOO.

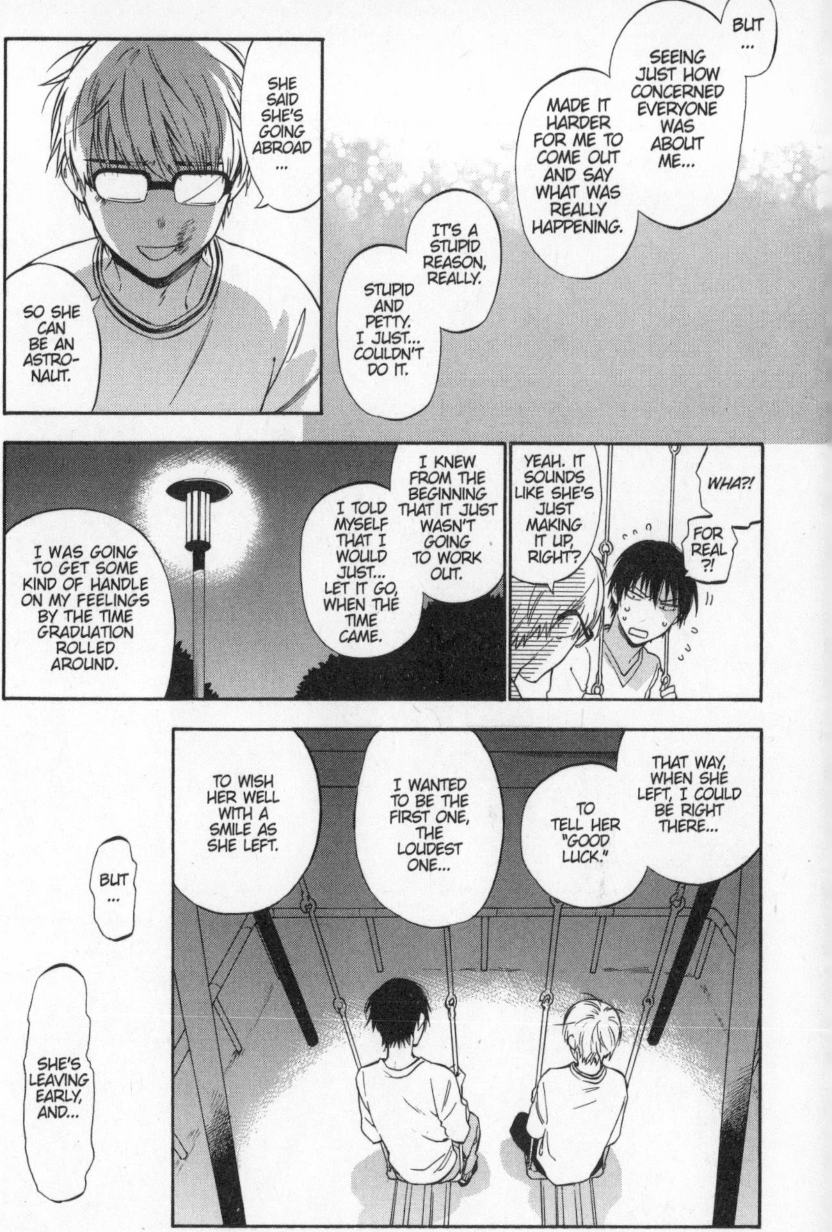
BUT...
SEEING JUST HOW CONCERNED EVERYONE WAS ABOUT ME...
MADE IT HARDER FOR ME TO COME OUT AND SAY WHAT WAS REALLY HAPPENING.
IT'S A STUPID REASON, REALLY.
STUPID AND PETTY. I JUST... COULDN'T DO IT.
SHE SAID SHE'S GOING ABROAD...
SO SHE CAN BE AN ASTRONAUT.
WHA?!
FOR REAL?!
YEAH. IT SOUNDS LIKE SHE'S JUST MAKING IT UP, RIGHT?
I KNEW FROM THE BEGINNING THAT IT JUST WASN'T GOING TO WORK OUT.
I TOLD MYSELF THAT I WOULD JUST... LET IT GO, WHEN THE TIME CAME.
I WAS GOING TO GET SOME KIND OF HANDLE ON MY FEELINGS BY THE TIME GRADUATION ROLLED AROUND.
THAT WAY, WHEN SHE LEFT, I COULD BE RIGHT THERE...
TO TELL HER "GOOD LUCK."
I WANTED TO BE THE FIRST ONE, THE LOUDEST ONE...
TO WISH HER WELL WITH A SMILE AS SHE LEFT.
BUT...
SHE'S LEAVING EARLY, AND...

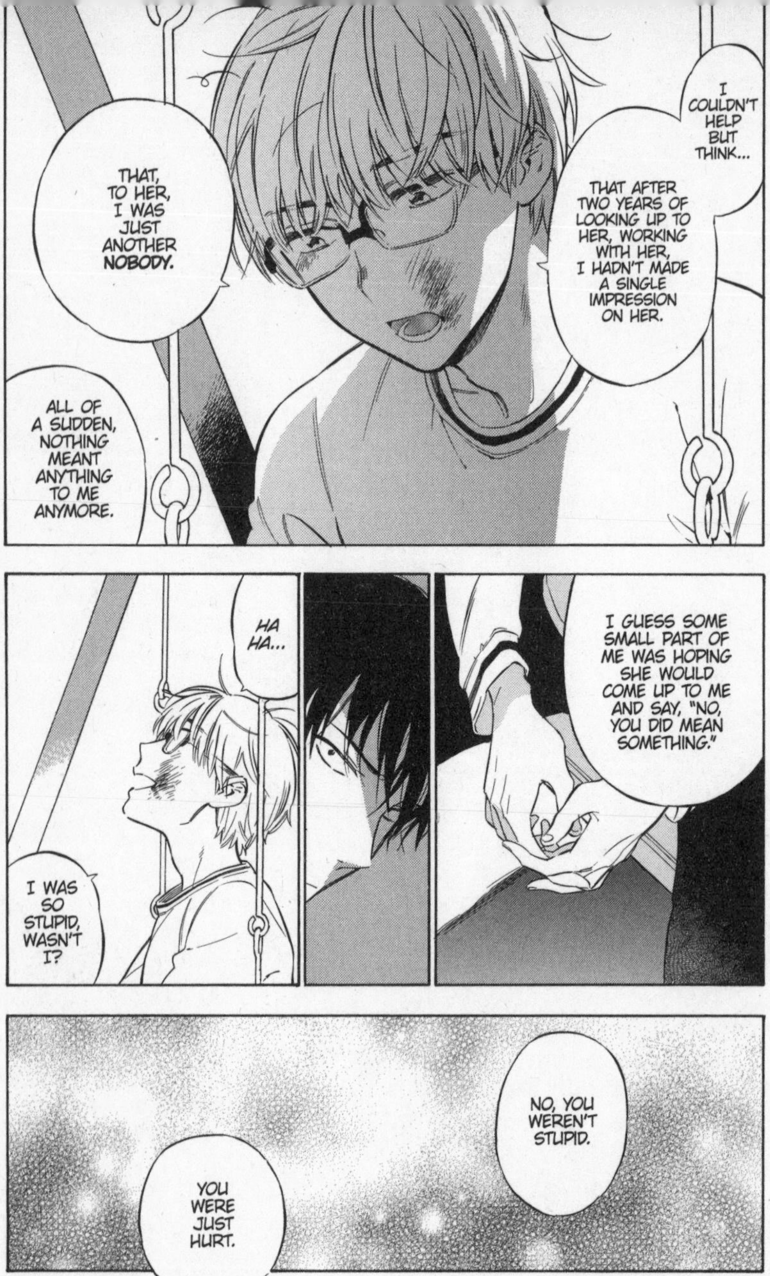
I COULDN'T HELP BUT THINK...
THAT AFTER TWO YEARS OF LOOKING UP TO HER, WORKING WITH HER, I HADN'T MADE A SINGLE IMPRESSION ON HER.
THAT, TO HER, I WAS JUST ANOTHER **NOBODY.**
ALL OF A SUDDEN, NOTHING MEANT ANYTHING TO ME ANYMORE.
I GUESS SOME SMALL PART OF ME WAS HOPING SHE WOULD COME UP TO ME AND SAY, "NO, YOU DID MEAN SOMETHING."
HA HA...
I WAS SO STUPID, WASN'T I?
NO, YOU WEREN'T STUPID.
YOU WERE JUST HURT.

Toradora!

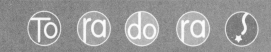

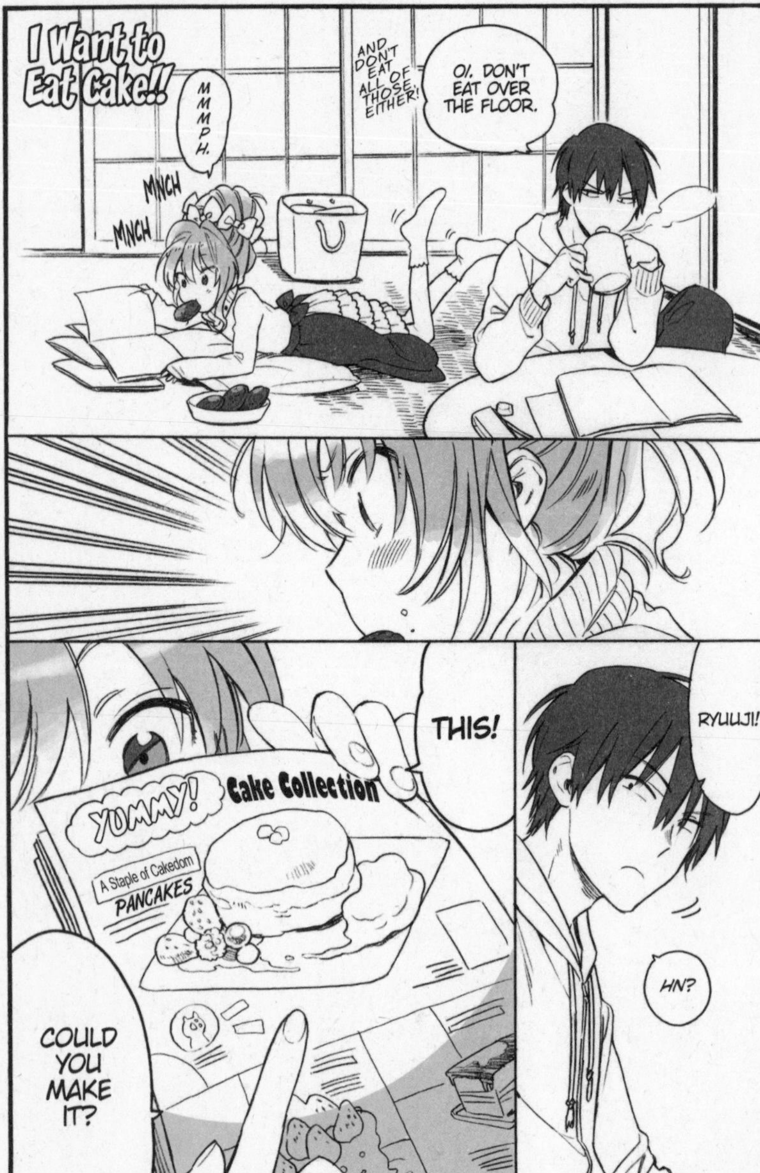
I Want to Eat Cake!!
OI. DON'T EAT OVER THE FLOOR.
AND DON'T EAT ALL OF THOSE, EITHER!
MMMPH.
MNCH
MNCH
RYUUJI!
HN?
THIS!
YUMMY! Cake Collection
A Staple of Cakedom
PANCAKES
COULD YOU MAKE IT?

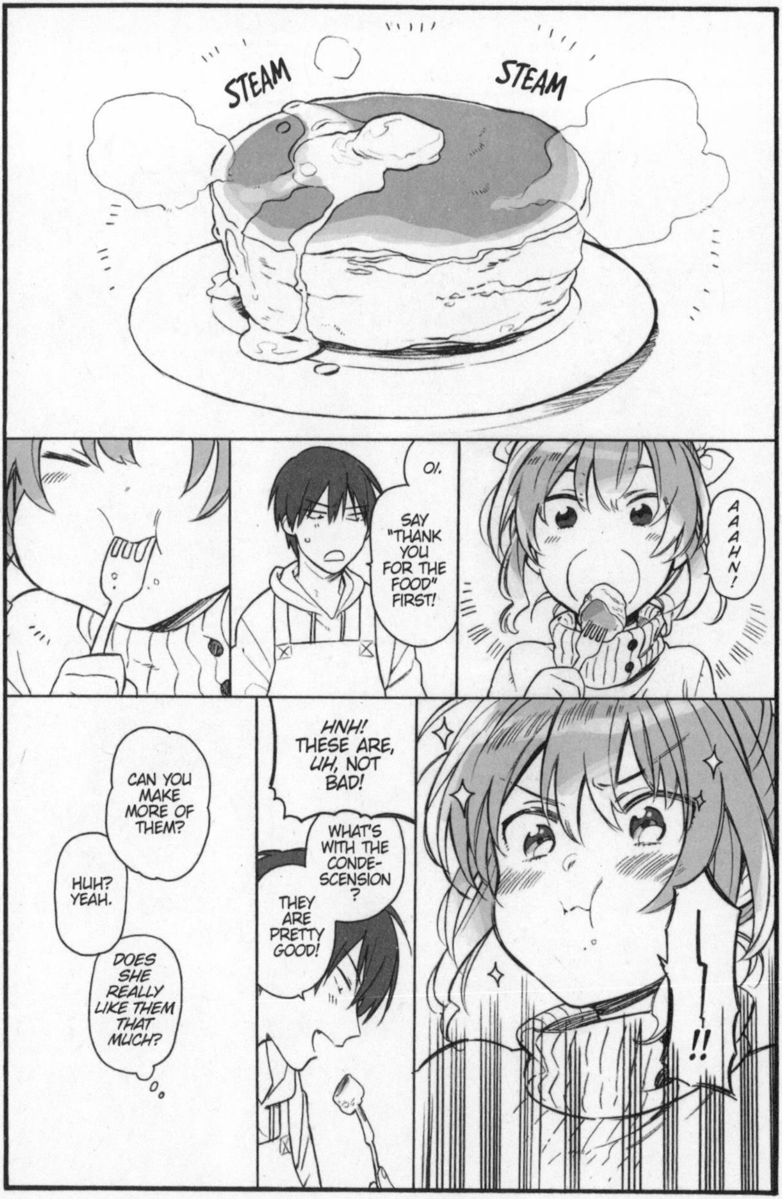
STEAM
STEAM
AAAAHN!
OI.
SAY "THANK YOU FOR THE FOOD" FIRST!
!!
HNH! THESE ARE, UH, NOT BAD!
WHAT'S WITH THE CONDESCENSION?
THEY ARE PRETTY GOOD!
CAN YOU MAKE MORE OF THEM?
HUH? YEAH.
DOES SHE REALLY LIKE THEM THAT MUCH?

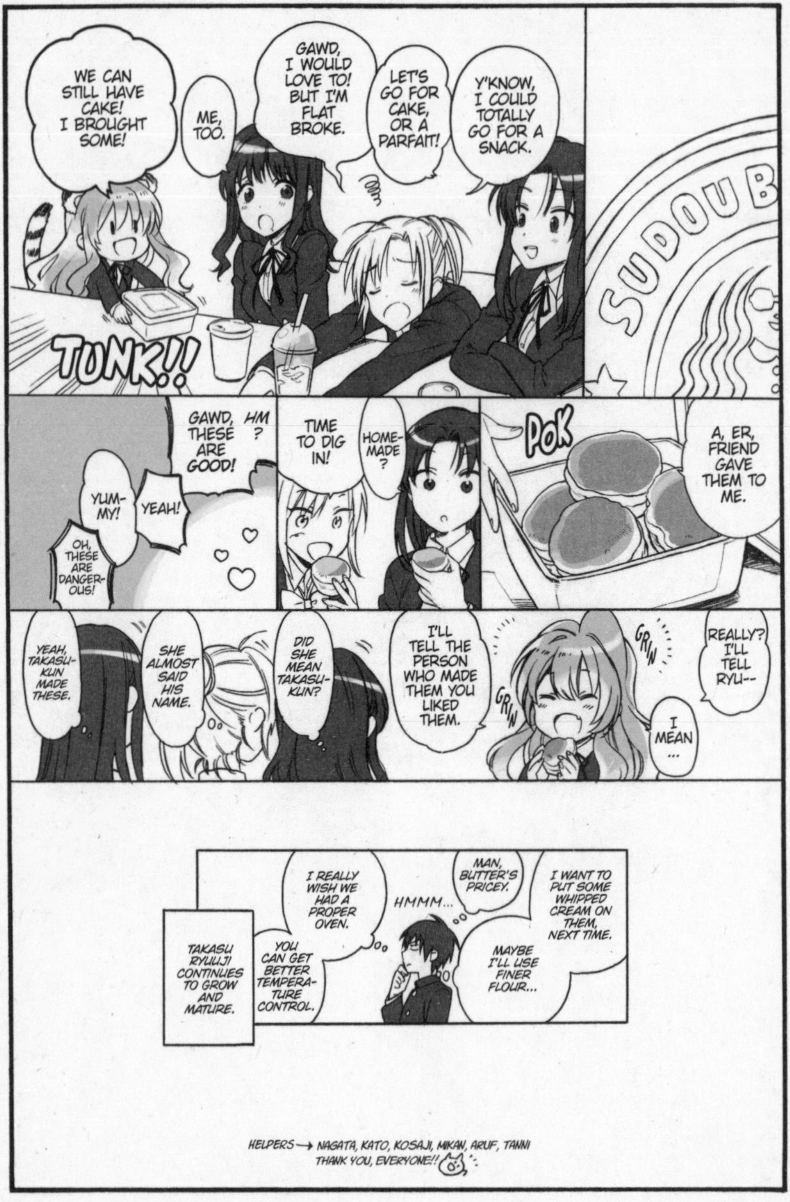
SUDOUB
Y'KNOW, I COULD TOTALLY GO FOR A SNACK.
LET'S GO FOR CAKE, OR A PARFAIT!
GAWD, I WOULD LOVE TO! BUT I'M FLAT BROKE.
ME, TOO.
WE CAN STILL HAVE CAKE! I BROUGHT SOME!
TUNK!!
POK
A, ER, FRIEND GAVE THEM TO ME.
HOME-MADE?
TIME TO DIG IN!
HM?
GAWD, THESE ARE GOOD!
YEAH!
YUMMY!
OH, THESE ARE DANGEROUS!
REALLY? I'LL TELL RYU--
GRIN
GRIN
I MEAN...
I'LL TELL THE PERSON WHO MADE THEM YOU LIKED THEM.
DID SHE MEAN TAKASU-KUN?
SHE ALMOST SAID HIS NAME.
YEAH, TAKASU-KUN MADE THESE.
I WANT TO PUT SOME WHIPPED CREAM ON THEM, NEXT TIME.
MAN, BUTTER'S PRICEY.
MAYBE I'LL USE FINER FLOUR...
HMMM...
I REALLY WISH WE HAD A PROPER OVEN.
YOU CAN GET BETTER TEMPERATURE CONTROL.
TAKASU RYUUJI CONTINUES TO GROW AND MATURE.
HELPERS → NAGATA, KATO, KOSAJI, MIKAN, ARUF, TANNI
THANK YOU, EVERYONE!!

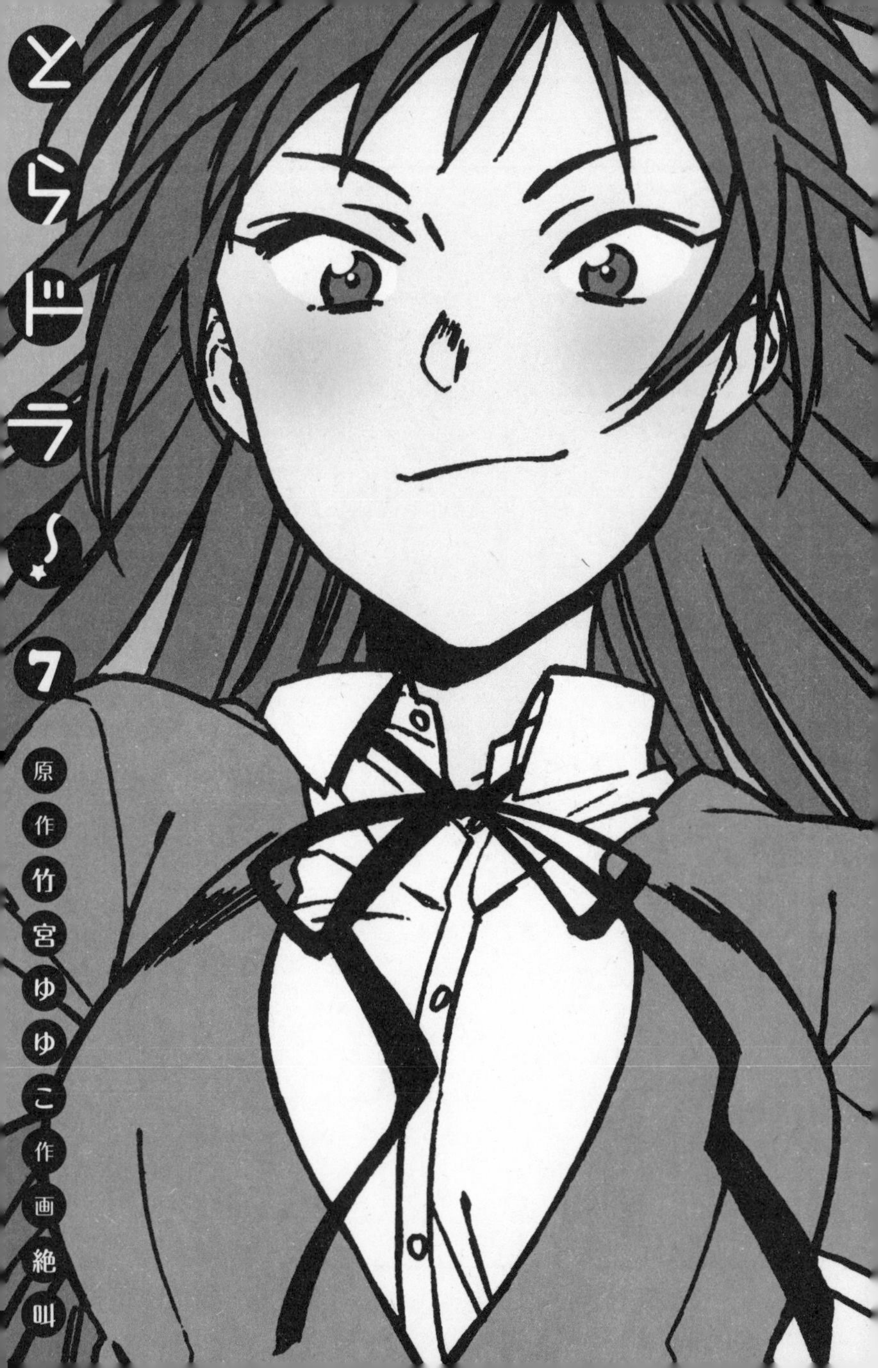
とらドラ～！
7
原作 竹宮ゆゆこ
作画 絶叫

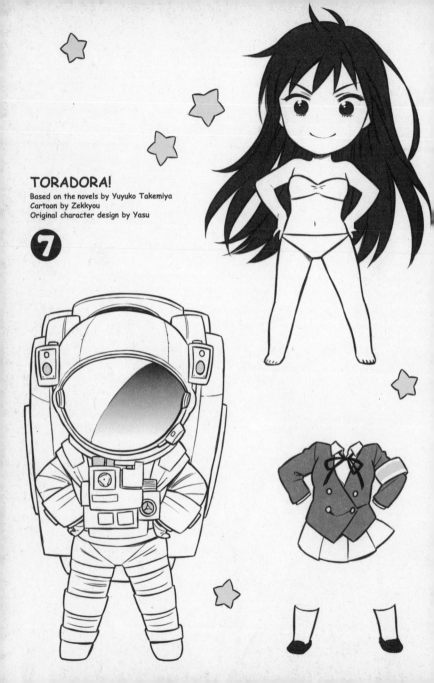

TORADORA!

Based on the novels by Yuyuko Takemiya
Cartoon by Zekkyou
Original character design by Yasu

7

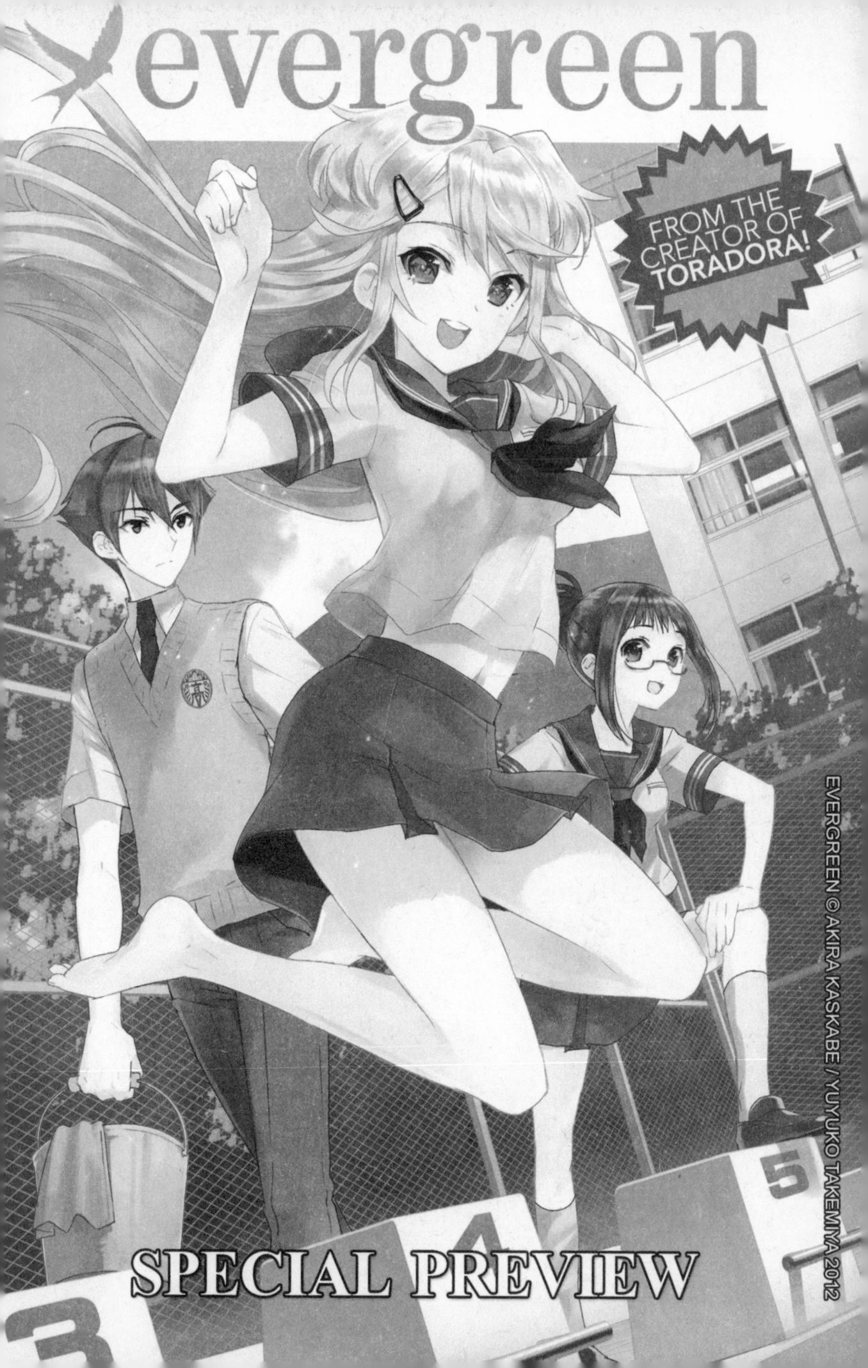
evergreen
FROM THE CREATOR OF TORADORA!
EVERGREEN © AKIRA KASKABE / YUYUKO TAKEMIYA 2012
SPECIAL PREVIEW

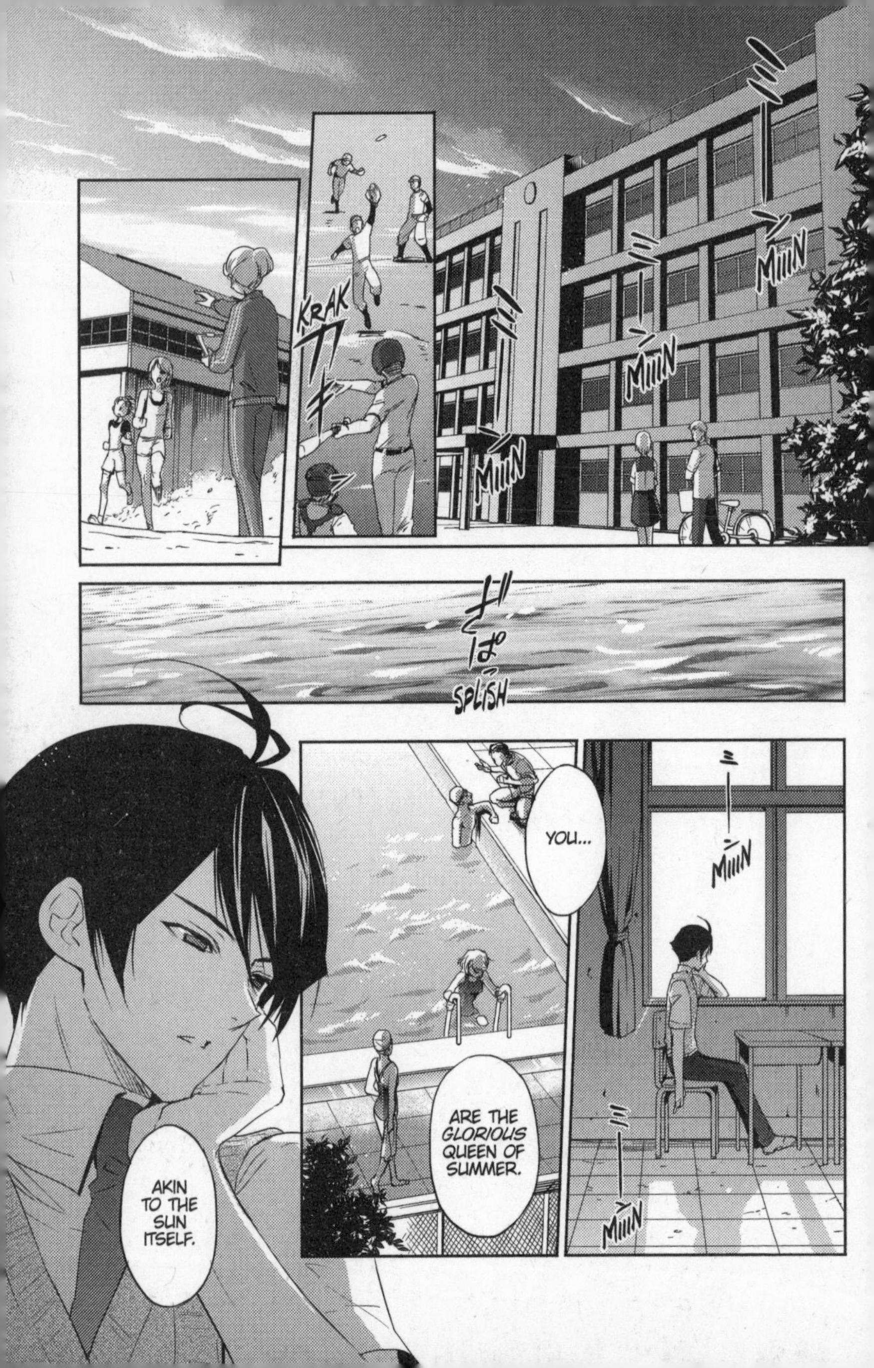
MIIIN
MIIIN
MIIIN
KRAK
SPLISH
MIIIN
MIIIN
YOU...
ARE THE GLORIOUS QUEEN OF SUMMER.
AKIN TO THE SUN ITSELF.

Chapter 1: The Nightmare

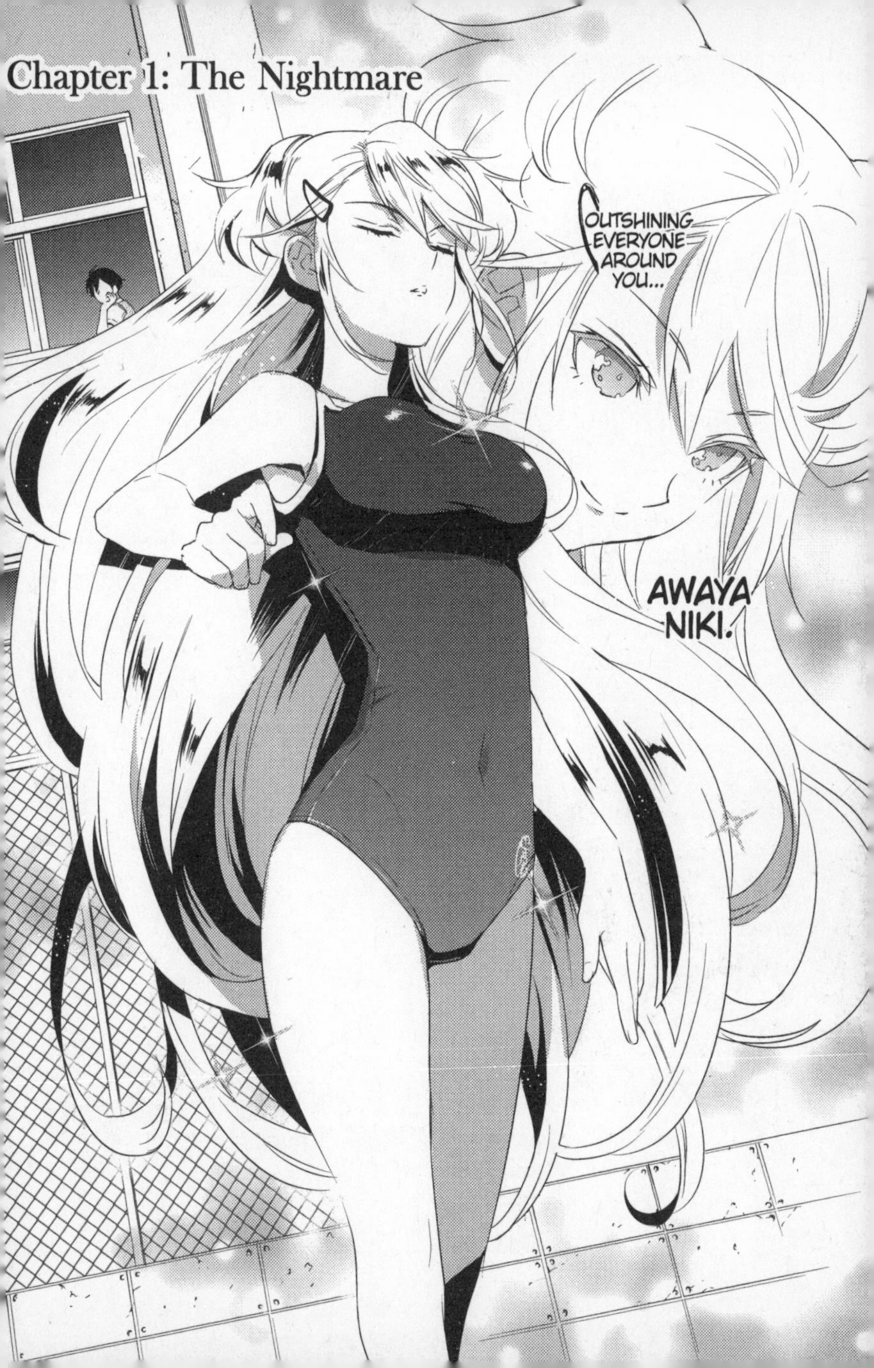
OUTSHINING EVERYONE AROUND YOU...
AWAYA NIKI.

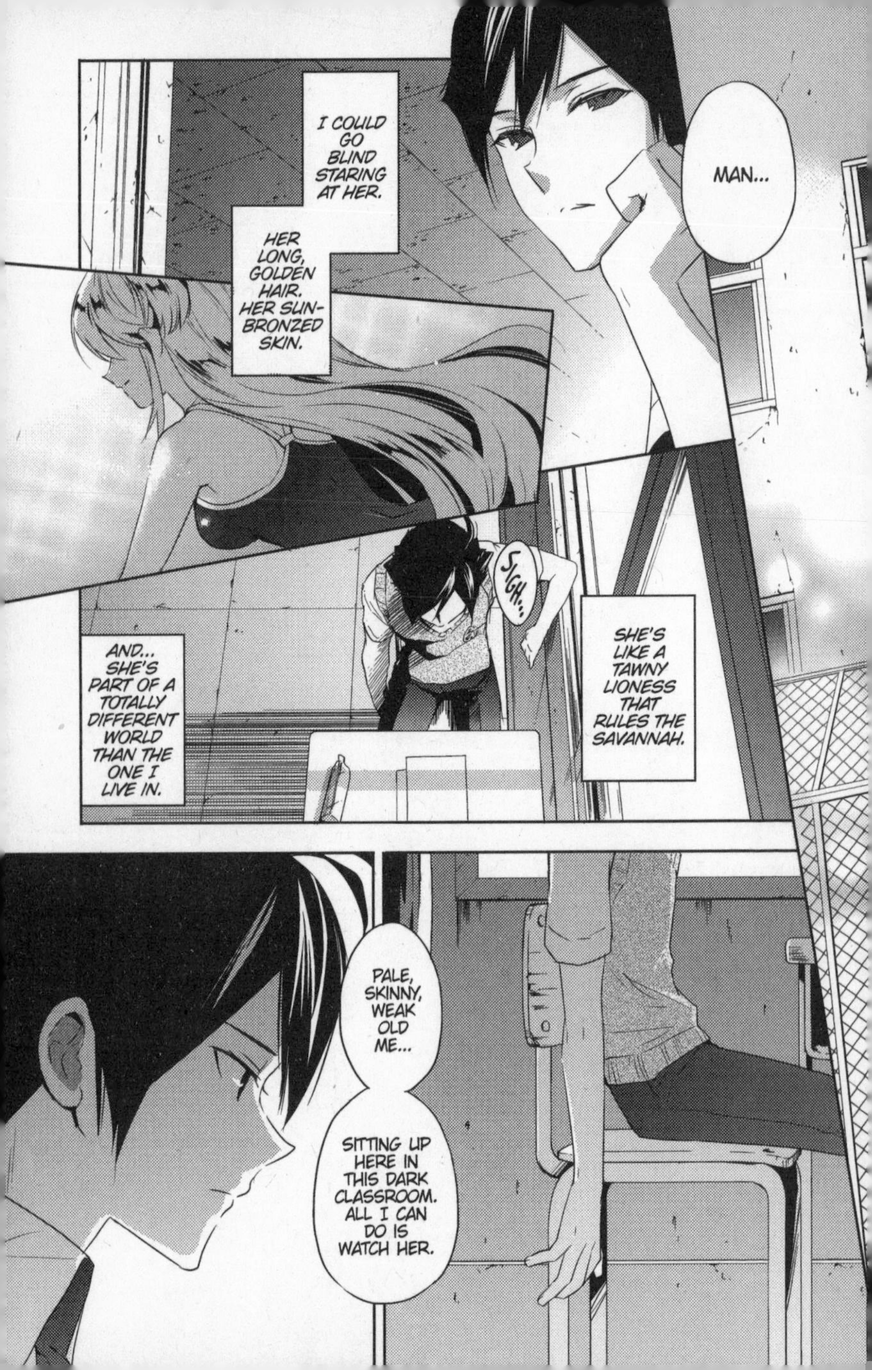
MAN...
I COULD GO BLIND STARING AT HER.
HER LONG, GOLDEN HAIR. HER SUN-BRONZED SKIN.
SHE'S LIKE A TAWNY LIONESS THAT RULES THE SAVANNAH.
SIGH...
AND... SHE'S PART OF A TOTALLY DIFFERENT WORLD THAN THE ONE I LIVE IN.
PALE, SKINNY, WEAK OLD ME...
SITTING UP HERE IN THIS DARK CLASSROOM. ALL I CAN DO IS WATCH HER.

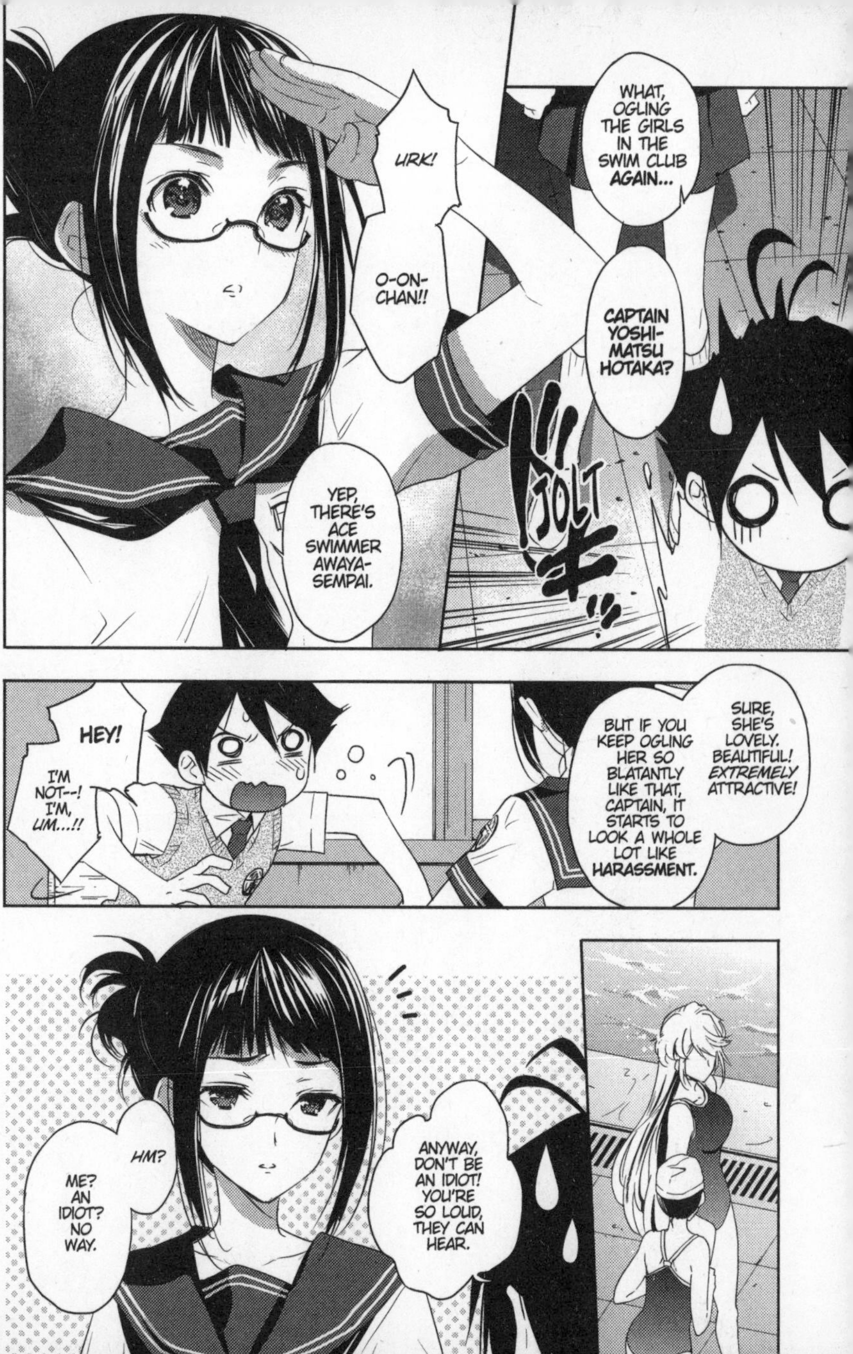
WHAT, OGLING THE GIRLS IN THE SWIM CLUB AGAIN...
CAPTAIN YOSHIMATSU HOTAKA?
JOLT
URK!
O-ON-CHAN!!
YEP, THERE'S ACE SWIMMER AWAYA-SEMPAI.
SURE, SHE'S LOVELY. BEAUTIFUL! EXTREMELY ATTRACTIVE!
BUT IF YOU KEEP OGLING HER SO BLATANTLY LIKE THAT, CAPTAIN, IT STARTS TO LOOK A WHOLE LOT LIKE HARASSMENT.
HEY!
I'M NOT--! I'M, UM...!!
ANYWAY, DON'T BE AN IDIOT! YOU'RE SO LOUD, THEY CAN HEAR.
HM?
ME? AN IDIOT? NO WAY.

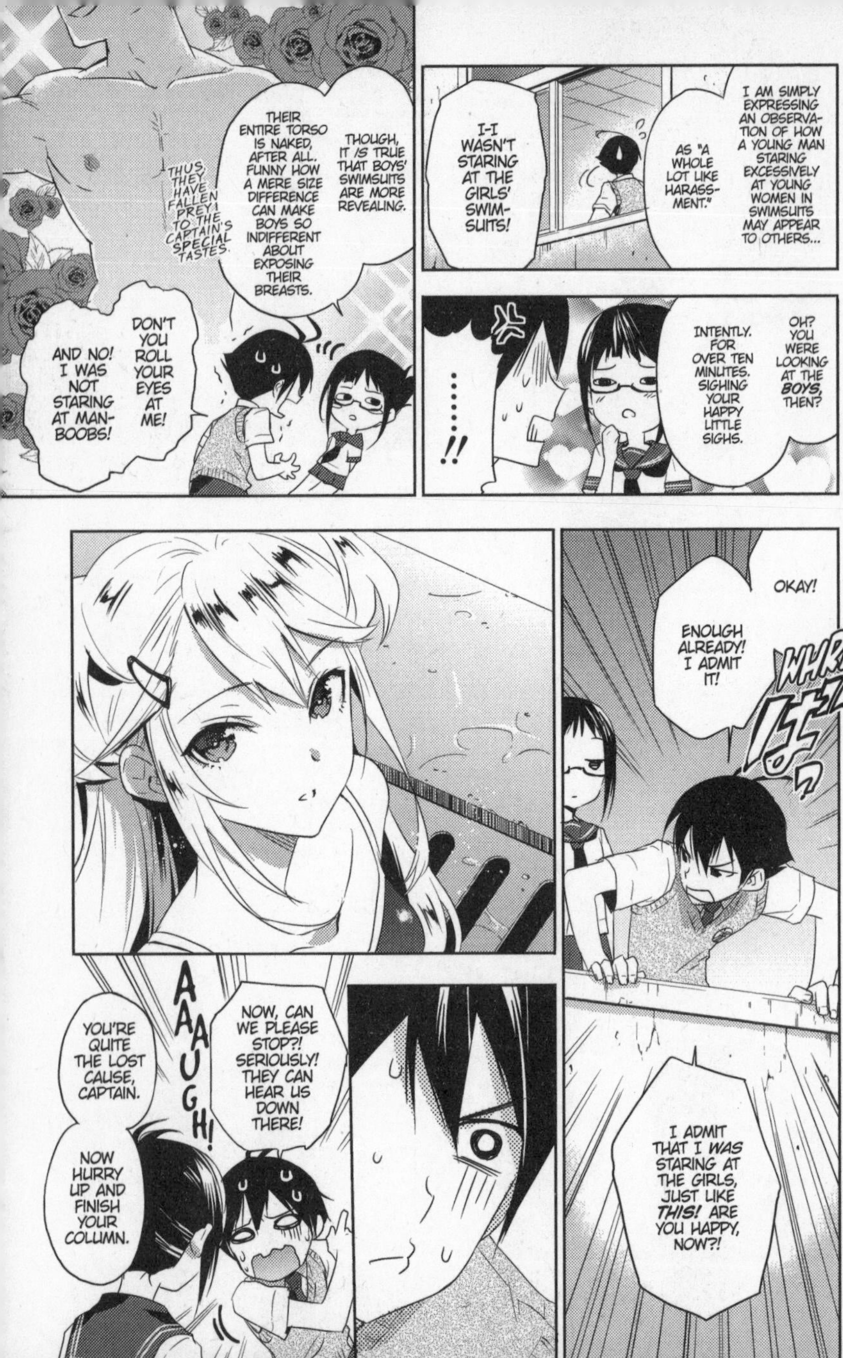
I AM SIMPLY EXPRESSING AN OBSERVATION OF HOW A YOUNG MAN STARING EXCESSIVELY AT YOUNG WOMEN IN SWIMSUITS MAY APPEAR TO OTHERS...
AS "A WHOLE LOT LIKE HARASSMENT."
I-I WASN'T STARING AT THE GIRLS' SWIMSUITS!
OH? YOU WERE LOOKING AT THE *BOYS*, THEN?
INTENTLY. FOR OVER TEN MINUTES. SIGHING YOUR HAPPY LITTLE SIGHS.
......!!
THOUGH, IT *IS* TRUE THAT BOYS' SWIMSUITS ARE MORE REVEALING.
THEIR ENTIRE TORSO IS NAKED, AFTER ALL. FUNNY HOW A MERE SIZE DIFFERENCE CAN MAKE BOYS SO INDIFFERENT ABOUT EXPOSING THEIR BREASTS.
THUS THEY HAVE FALLEN PREY TO THE CAPTAIN'S SPECIAL TASTES.
DON'T YOU ROLL YOUR EYES AT ME!
AND NO! I WAS NOT STARING AT MAN-BOOBS!
OKAY!
ENOUGH ALREADY! I ADMIT IT!
WHRL
ばっ
I ADMIT THAT I *WAS* STARING AT THE GIRLS, JUST LIKE *THIS!* ARE YOU HAPPY, NOW?!
AAAUGH!
NOW, CAN WE PLEASE STOP?! SERIOUSLY! THEY CAN HEAR US DOWN THERE!
YOU'RE QUITE THE LOST CAUSE, CAPTAIN.
NOW HURRY UP AND FINISH YOUR COLUMN.

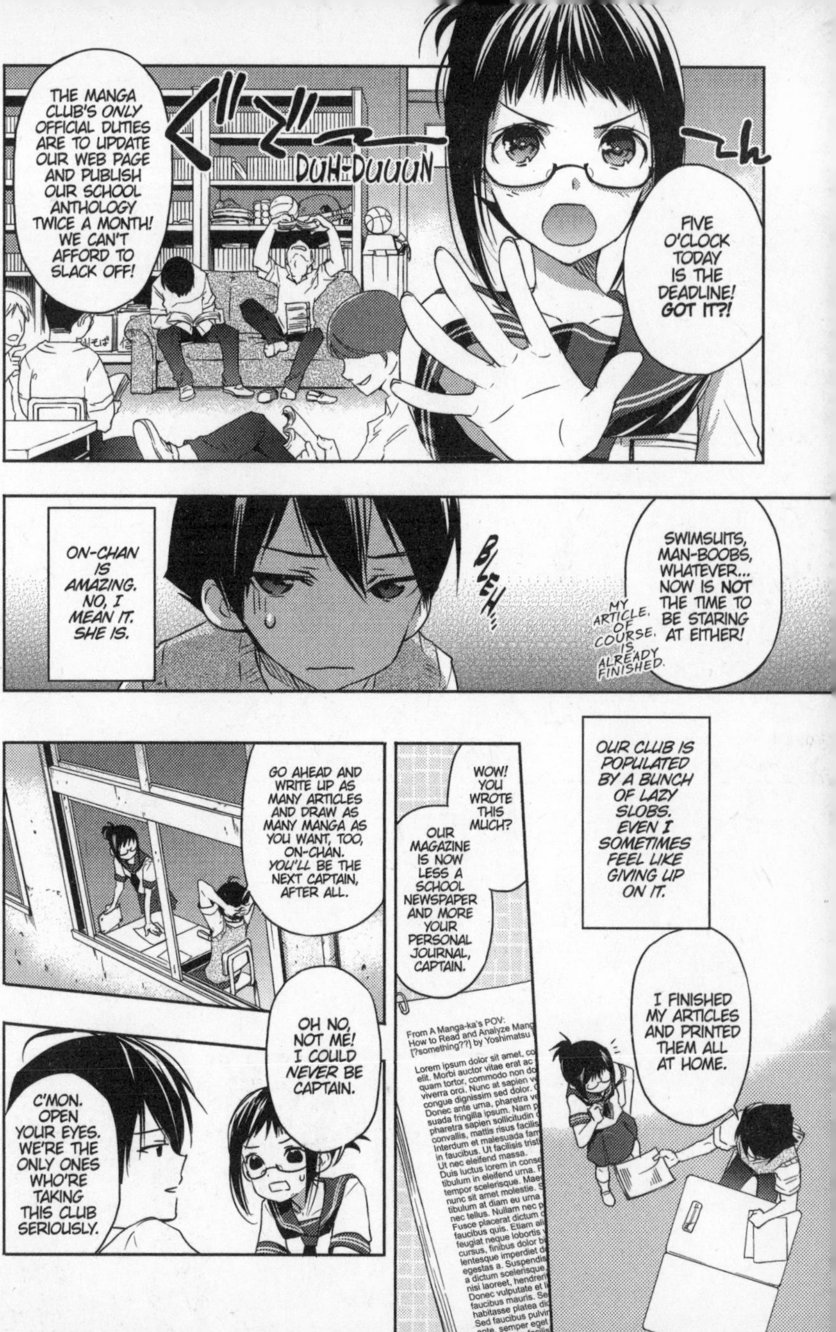
ぐ゛ぞ゛ーーーん
DUH-DUUUN
THE MANGA CLUB'S *ONLY* OFFICIAL DUTIES ARE TO UPDATE OUR WEB PAGE AND PUBLISH OUR SCHOOL ANTHOLOGY TWICE A MONTH! WE CAN'T AFFORD TO SLACK OFF!
FIVE O'CLOCK TODAY IS THE DEADLINE! GOT IT?!
SWIMSUITS, MAN-BOOBS, WHATEVER... NOW IS NOT THE TIME TO BE STARING AT EITHER!
MY ARTICLE, OF COURSE, IS ALREADY FINISHED.
BLEH...
ON-CHAN IS AMAZING. NO, I MEAN IT. SHE IS.
OUR CLUB IS POPULATED BY A BUNCH OF LAZY SLOBS. EVEN I SOMETIMES FEEL LIKE GIVING UP ON IT.
I FINISHED MY ARTICLES AND PRINTED THEM ALL AT HOME.
WOW! YOU WROTE THIS MUCH?
OUR MAGAZINE IS NOW LESS A SCHOOL NEWSPAPER AND MORE YOUR PERSONAL JOURNAL, CAPTAIN.
From A Manga-ka's POV:
How to Read and Analyze Mang
[?something??] by Yoshimatsu
GO AHEAD AND WRITE UP AS MANY ARTICLES AND DRAW AS MANY MANGA AS YOU WANT, TOO, ON-CHAN. *YOU'LL* BE THE NEXT CAPTAIN, AFTER ALL.
OH NO, NOT ME! I COULD *NEVER* BE CAPTAIN.
C'MON. OPEN YOUR EYES. WE'RE THE ONLY ONES WHO'RE TAKING THIS CLUB SERIOUSLY.

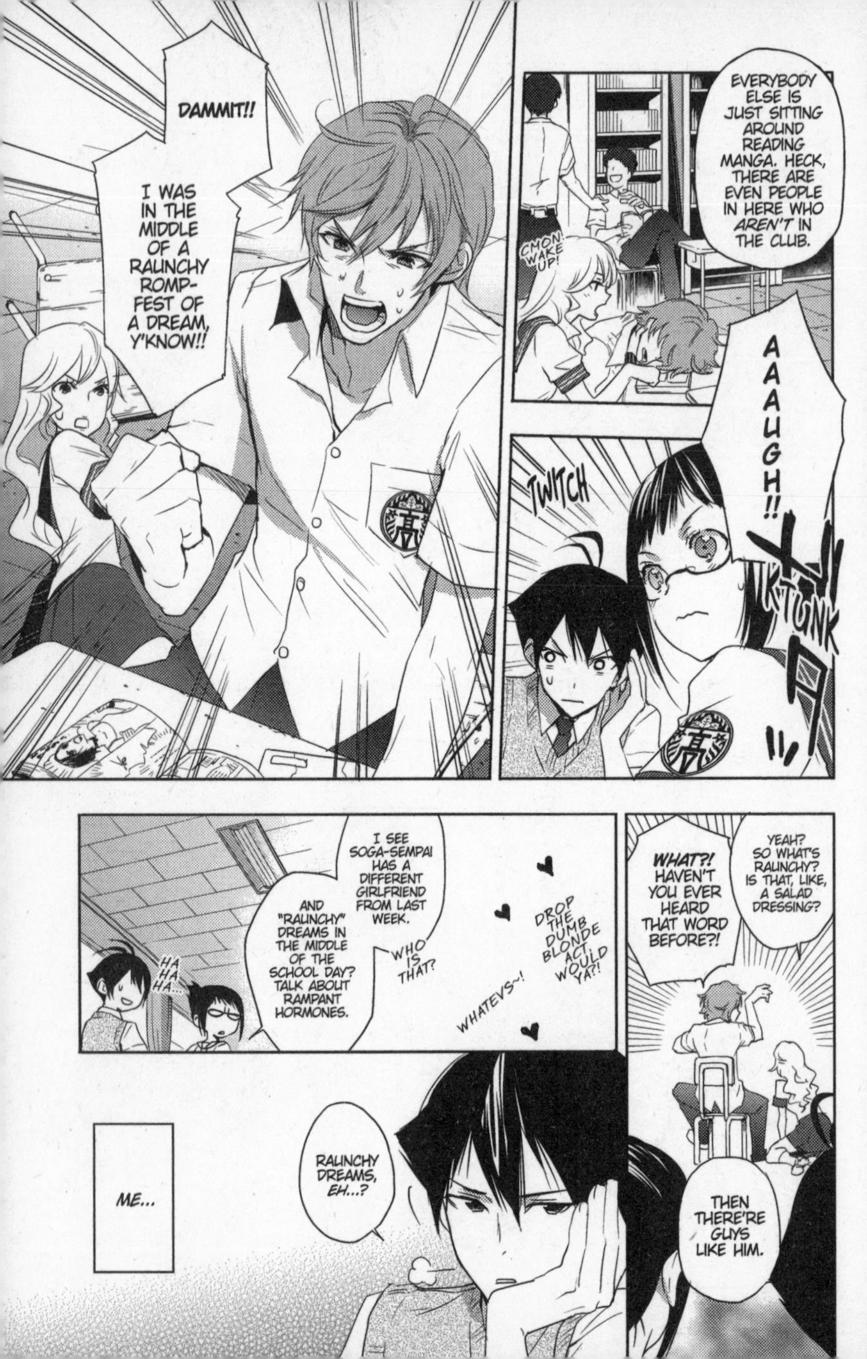
EVERYBODY ELSE IS JUST SITTING AROUND READING MANGA. HECK, THERE ARE EVEN PEOPLE IN HERE WHO *AREN'T* IN THE CLUB.
C'MON, WAKE UP!
AAAAUGH!!
TWITCH
KTUNK
DAMMIT!!
I WAS IN THE MIDDLE OF A RAUNCHY ROMP-FEST OF A DREAM, Y'KNOW!!
YEAH? SO WHAT'S RAUNCHY? IS THAT, LIKE, A SALAD DRESSING?
WHAT?! HAVEN'T YOU EVER HEARD THAT WORD BEFORE?!
I SEE SOGA-SEMPAI HAS A DIFFERENT GIRLFRIEND FROM LAST WEEK.
DROP THE DUMB BLONDE ACT, WOULD YA?!
WHO IS THAT?
AND "RAUNCHY" DREAMS IN THE MIDDLE OF THE SCHOOL DAY? TALK ABOUT RAMPANT HORMONES.
WHATEVS~!
HA HA HA...
THEN THERE'RE GUYS LIKE HIM.
RAUNCHY DREAMS, *EH*...?
ME...

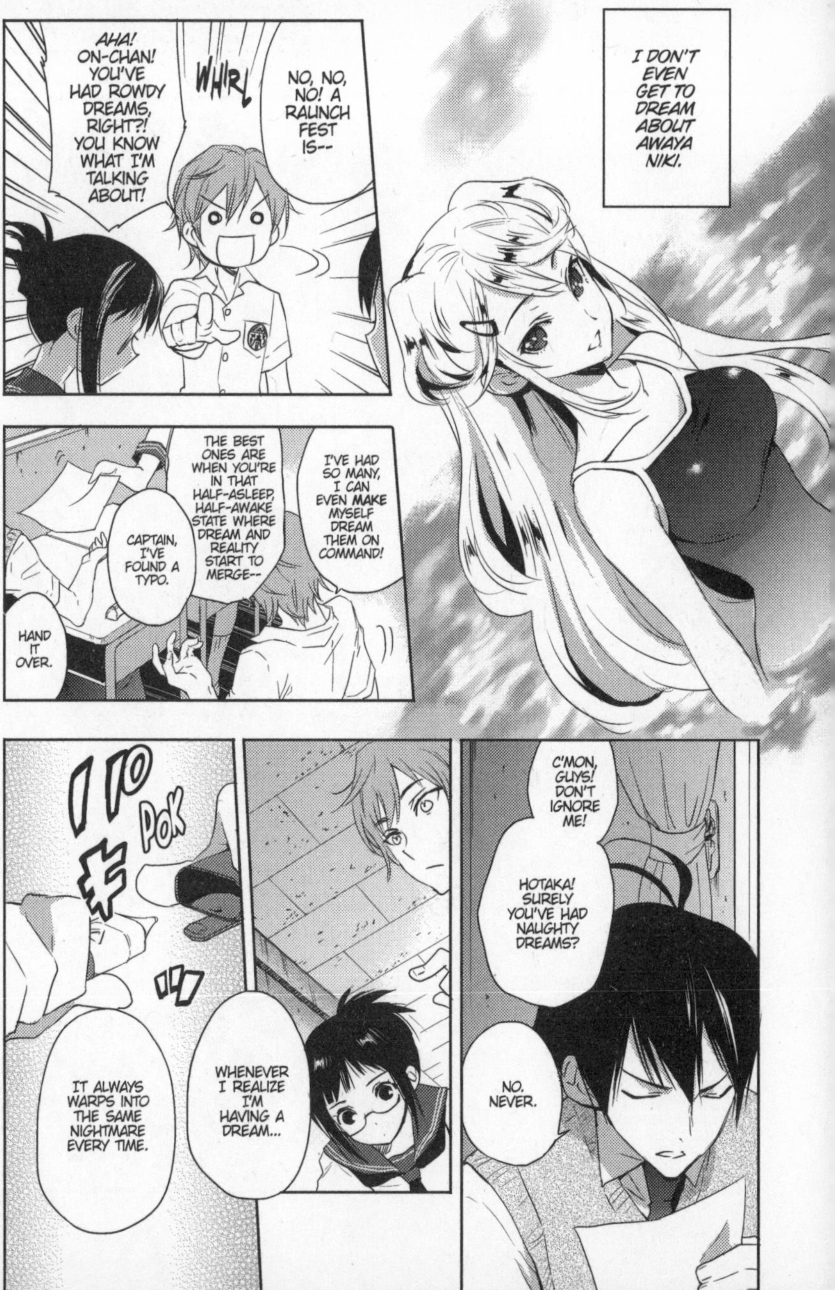
I DON'T EVEN GET TO DREAM ABOUT AWAYA NIKI.
NO, NO, NO! A RAUNCH FEST IS--
WHIRL
AHA! ON-CHAN! YOU'VE HAD ROWDY DREAMS, RIGHT?! YOU KNOW WHAT I'M TALKING ABOUT!
I'VE HAD SO MANY, I CAN EVEN MAKE MYSELF DREAM THEM ON COMMAND!
THE BEST ONES ARE WHEN YOU'RE IN THAT HALF-ASLEEP, HALF-AWAKE STATE WHERE DREAM AND REALITY START TO MERGE--
CAPTAIN, I'VE FOUND A TYPO.
HAND IT OVER.
C'MON, GUYS! DON'T IGNORE ME!
HOTAKA! SURELY YOU'VE HAD NAUGHTY DREAMS?
NO. NEVER.
WHENEVER I REALIZE I'M HAVING A DREAM...
POK
IT ALWAYS WARPS INTO THE SAME NIGHTMARE EVERY TIME.

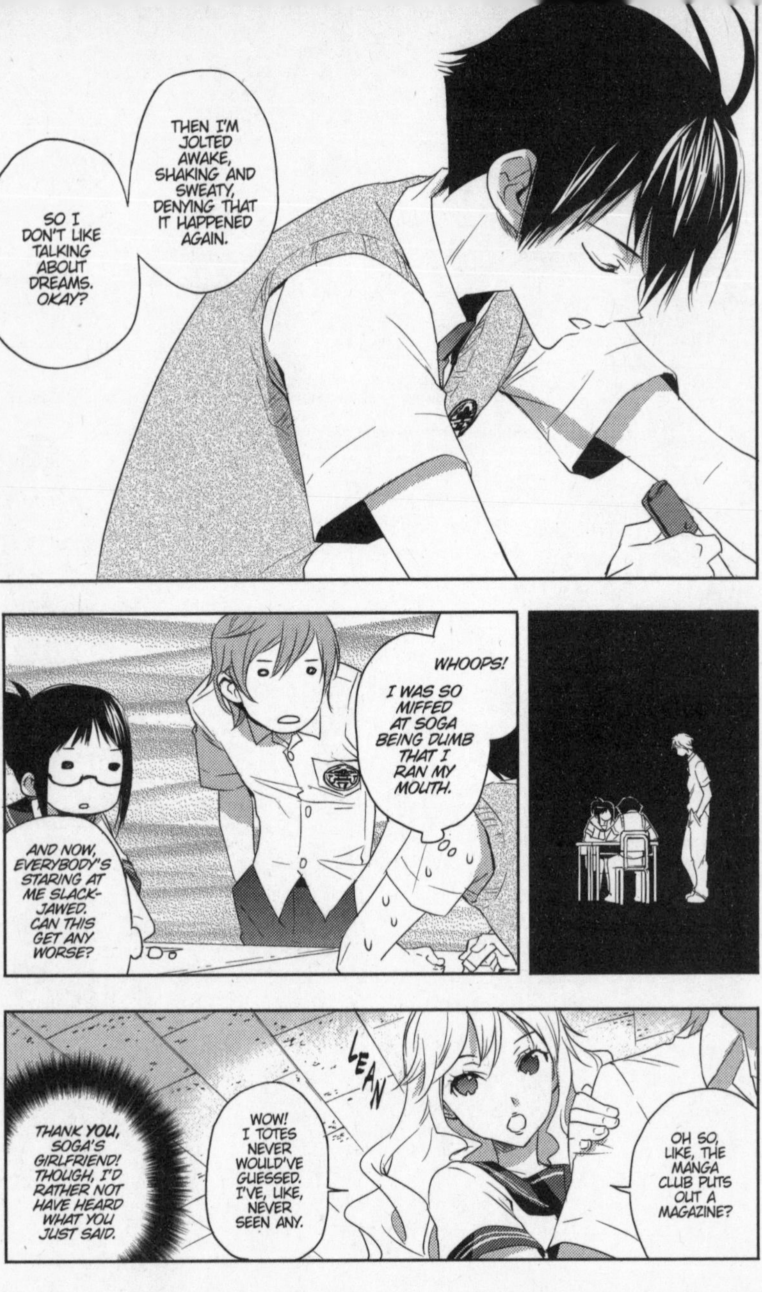
THEN I'M JOLTED AWAKE, SHAKING AND SWEATY, DENYING THAT IT HAPPENED AGAIN.
SO I DON'T LIKE TALKING ABOUT DREAMS. OKAY?
WHOOPS! I WAS SO MIFFED AT SOGA BEING DUMB THAT I RAN MY MOUTH.
AND NOW, EVERYBODY'S STARING AT ME SLACK-JAWED. CAN THIS GET ANY WORSE?
OH SO, LIKE, THE MANGA CLUB PUTS OUT A MAGAZINE?
LEAN
WOW! I TOTES NEVER WOULD'VE GUESSED. I'VE, LIKE, NEVER SEEN ANY.
THANK YOU, SOGA'S GIRLFRIEND! THOUGH, I'D RATHER NOT HAVE HEARD WHAT YOU JUST SAID.

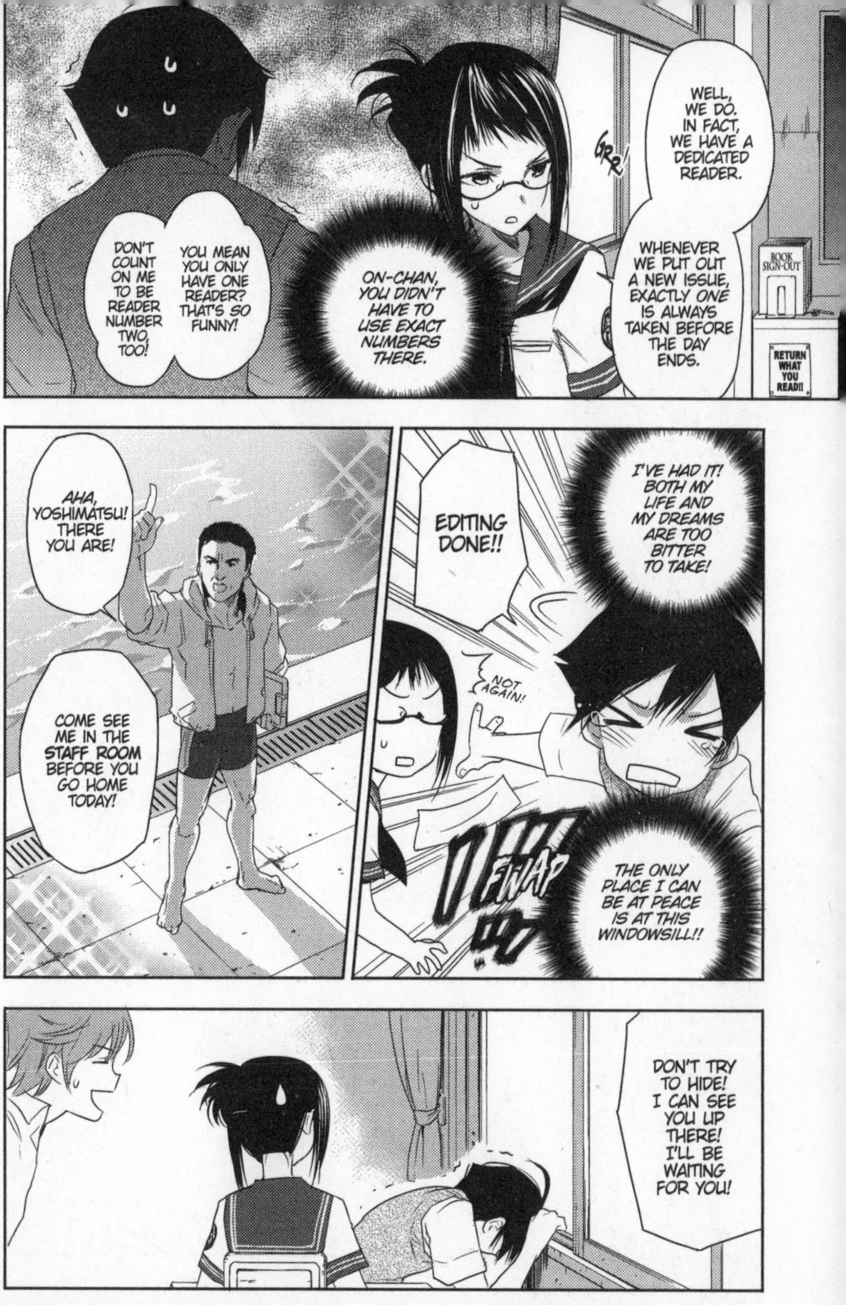
WELL, WE DO. IN FACT, WE HAVE A DEDICATED READER.
GRR!
WHENEVER WE PUT OUT A NEW ISSUE, EXACTLY ONE IS ALWAYS TAKEN BEFORE THE DAY ENDS.
BOOK SIGN-OUT
RETURN WHAT YOU READ!!
ON-CHAN, YOU DIDN'T HAVE TO USE EXACT NUMBERS THERE.
YOU MEAN YOU ONLY HAVE ONE READER? THAT'S SO FUNNY!
DON'T COUNT ON ME TO BE READER NUMBER TWO, TOO!
I'VE HAD IT! BOTH MY LIFE AND MY DREAMS ARE TOO BITTER TO TAKE!
EDITING DONE!!
NOT AGAIN!
FWAP
THE ONLY PLACE I CAN BE AT PEACE IS AT THIS WINDOWSILL!!
AHA, YOSHIMATSU! THERE YOU ARE!
COME SEE ME IN THE STAFF ROOM BEFORE YOU GO HOME TODAY!
DON'T TRY TO HIDE! I CAN SEE YOU UP THERE! I'LL BE WAITING FOR YOU!

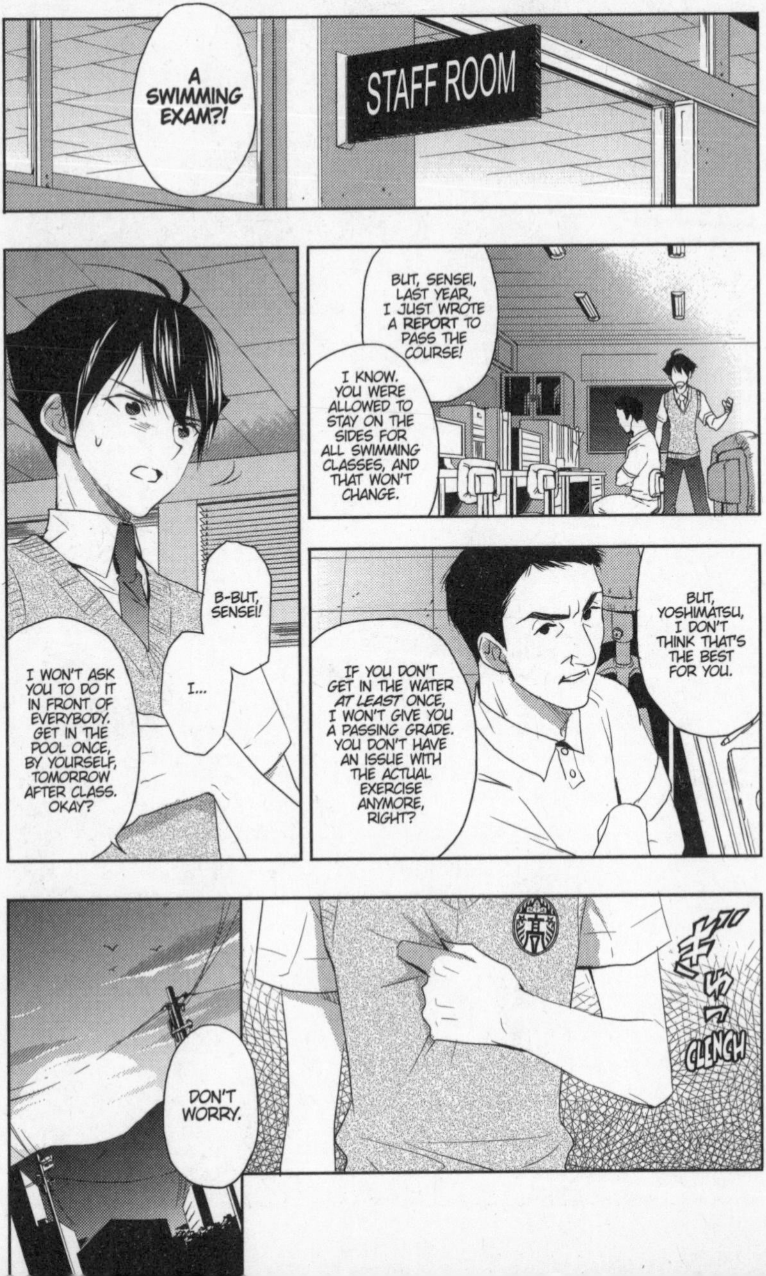
STAFF ROOM
A SWIMMING EXAM?!
BUT, SENSEI, LAST YEAR, I JUST WROTE A REPORT TO PASS THE COURSE!
I KNOW. YOU WERE ALLOWED TO STAY ON THE SIDES FOR ALL SWIMMING CLASSES, AND THAT WON'T CHANGE.
BUT, YOSHIMATSU, I DON'T THINK THAT'S THE BEST FOR YOU.
IF YOU DON'T GET IN THE WATER *AT LEAST* ONCE, I WON'T GIVE YOU A PASSING GRADE. YOU DON'T HAVE AN ISSUE WITH THE ACTUAL EXERCISE ANYMORE, RIGHT?
B-BUT, SENSEI!
I...
I WON'T ASK YOU TO DO IT IN FRONT OF EVERYBODY. GET IN THE POOL ONCE, BY YOURSELF, TOMORROW AFTER CLASS. OKAY?
ぎゅっ
CLENCH
DON'T WORRY.

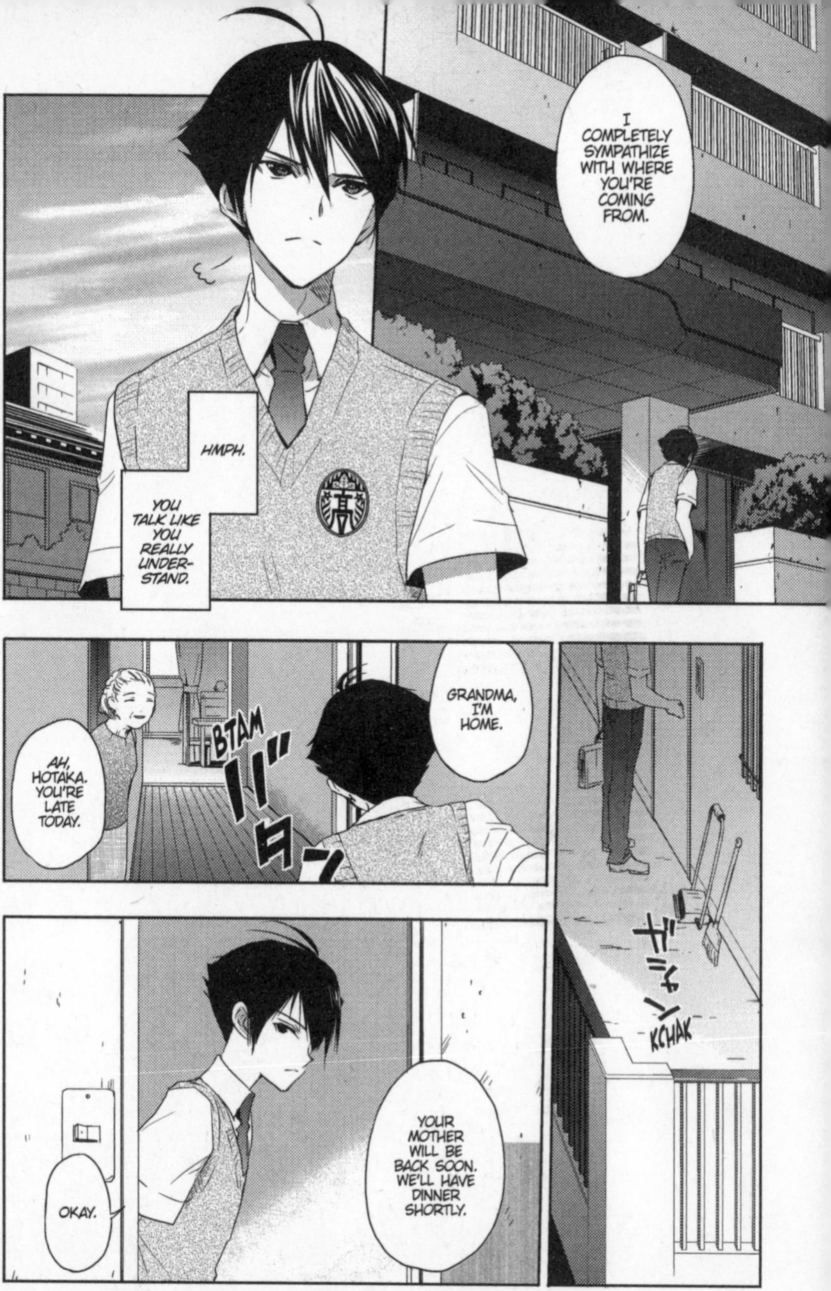
I COMPLETELY SYMPATHIZE WITH WHERE YOU'RE COMING FROM.
HMPH.
YOU TALK LIKE YOU REALLY UNDER-STAND.
ガチャン
KCHAK
GRANDMA, I'M HOME.
バタン
BTAM
AH, HOTAKA. YOU'RE LATE TODAY.
YOUR MOTHER WILL BE BACK SOON. WE'LL HAVE DINNER SHORTLY.
OKAY.

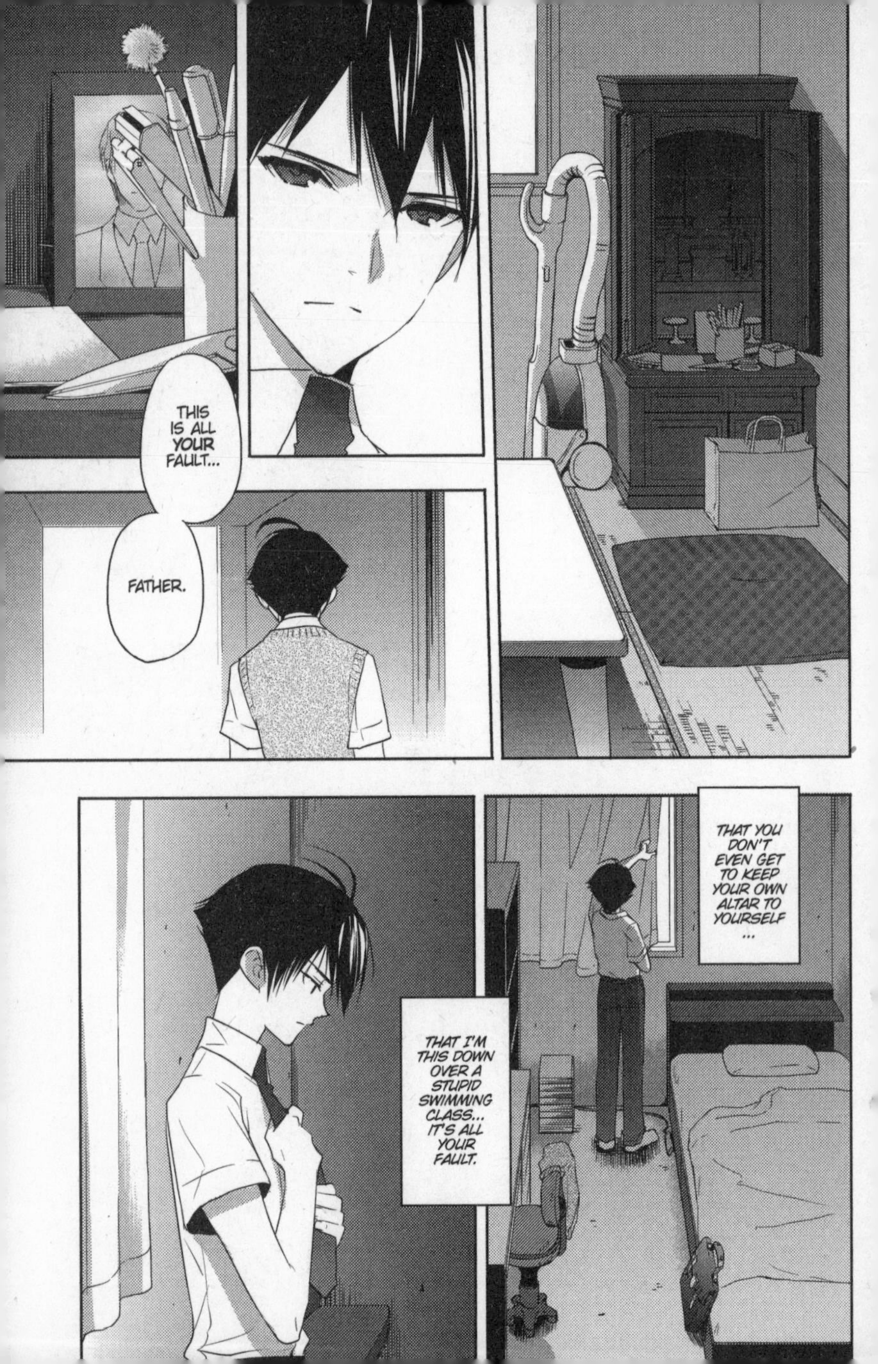
THIS IS ALL YOUR FAULT...
FATHER.
THAT YOU DON'T EVEN GET TO KEEP YOUR OWN ALTAR TO YOURSELF ...
THAT I'M THIS DOWN OVER A STUPID SWIMMING CLASS... IT'S ALL YOUR FAULT.

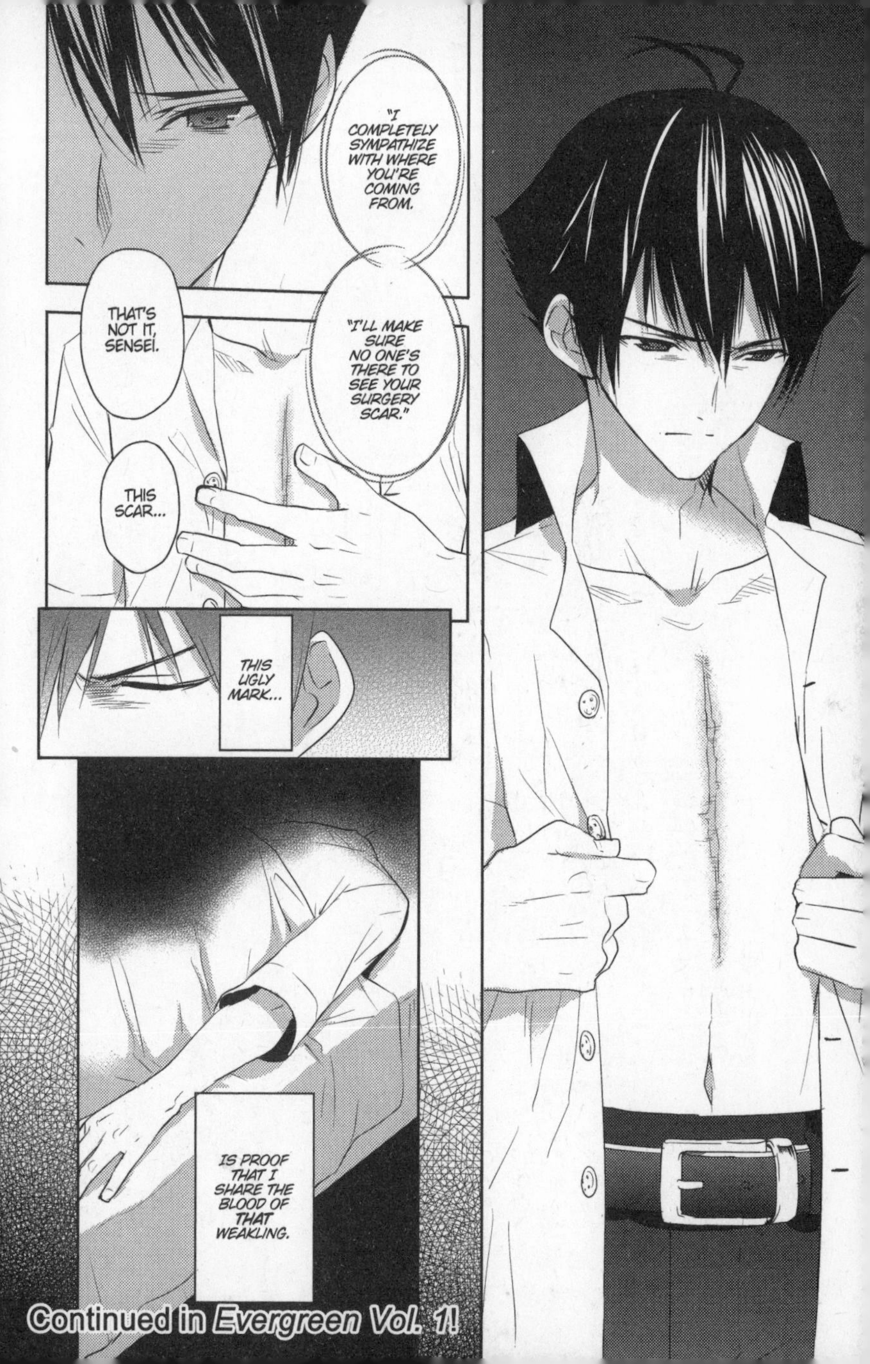
"I COMPLETELY SYMPATHIZE WITH WHERE YOU'RE COMING FROM.
"I'LL MAKE SURE NO ONE'S THERE TO SEE YOUR SURGERY SCAR."
THAT'S NOT IT, SENSEI.
THIS SCAR...
THIS UGLY MARK...
IS PROOF THAT I SHARE THE BLOOD OF THAT WEAKLING.
Continued in *Evergreen* Vol. 1!